HIGH COURT CASE SUMMARIES

FEDERAL INCOME TAXATION

Keyed to Klein, Bankman, Shaviro and Stark's Casebook on Federal Income Taxation, 15th Edition

WEST®

A Thomson Reuters business

Mat #41045319

© West, a Thomson business, 2005, 2007
© 2010 Thomson Reuters
 610 Opperman Drive
 St. Paul, MN 55123
 1–800–313–9378
Printed in the United States of America

ISBN: 978–0–314–26601–9

Table of Contents

	Page
CHAPTER TWO. Some Characteristics of Income	**1**
Benaglia v. Commissioner	5
Turner v. Commissioner	7
Commissioner v. Glenshaw Glass Co.	9
Commissioner v. Duberstein	11
United States v. Harris	15
Taft v. Bowers	17
Inaja Land Co. v. Commissioner	19
Clark v. Commissioner	21
Burnet v. Sanford & Brooks	23
North American Oil Consolidated v. Burnet	25
United States v. Lewis	29
United States v. Kirby Lumber Co.	31
Zarin v. Commissioner	33
Diedrich v. Commissioner	35
Crane v. Commissioner	37
Commissioner v. Tufts	39
Gilbert v. Commissioner	41
CHAPTER THREE. Problems of Timing	**43**
Eisner v. Macomber	47
Helvering v. Bruun	49
Woodsam Associates, Inc. v. Commissioner	51
Cottage Savings Association v. Commissioner	53
Burnet v. Logan	55
Amend v. Commissioner	57
Pulsifer v. Commissioner	59
Minor v. United States	61
Cramer v. Commissioner	63
United States v. Davis	65
Farid-Es-Sultaneh v. Commissioner	67
Diez–Arguelles v. Commissioner	69
Georgia School–Book Depository v. Commissioner	71
American Automobile Association v. United States	73
Westpac Pacific Food v. Commissioner	75
CHAPTER FOUR. Personal Deductions, Exemptions and Credits	**77**
Dyer v. Commissioner	79
Chamales v. Commissioner	81
Blackman v. Commissioner	83
Taylor v. Commissioner	85
Henderson v. Commissioner	87
Ochs v. Commissioner	89
Ottawa Silica Co. v. United States	91
Bob Jones University v. United States	93
King v. Commissioner	97
CHAPTER FIVE. Allowances for Mixed Business and Personal Outlays	**99**
Nickerson v. Commissioner	103
Popov v. Commissioner	105
Moller v. United States	107
Whitten v. Commissioner	109
Henderson v. Commissioner	111

Page

Rudolph v. United States 113
Moss v. Commissioner 115
Danville Plywood Corporation v. United States 117
Churchill Downs, Inc. v. Commissioner 119
Smith v. Commissioner 121
Commissioner v. Flowers 123
Hantzis v. Commissioner 125
Pevsner v. Commissioner 129
United States v. Gilmore 131
Carroll v. Commissioner 133

CHAPTER SIX.   Deductions for the Costs of Earning Income **135**
Encyclopaedia Britannica v. Commissioner 139
Midland Empire Packing Co. v. Commissioner 143
Norwest Corporation and Subsidiaries v. Commissioner 145
Starr's Estate v. Commissioner 149
Welch v. Helvering 151
Gilliam v. Commissioner 153
Stephens v. Commissioner 157
Knetsch v. United States 161
Estate of Franklin v. Commissioner 165
Winn–Dixie Stores, Inc. v. Commissioner 169
Klaassen v. Commissioner 171
Prosman v. Commissioner 173

CHAPTER SEVEN.   The Splitting of Income **175**
Lucas v. Earl 177
Poe v. Seaborn 179
Armantrout v. Commissioner 181
Blair v. Commissioner 183
Helvering v. Horst 185
Helvering v. Eubank 187
Heim v. Fitzpatrick 189
Brooke v. United States 191
Foglesong v. Commissioner 193
United States v. Basye 195

CHAPTER EIGHT.   Capital Gains and Losses **197**
Bielfeldt v. Commissioner 201
Biedenharn Realty Co. v. United States 203
Corn Products Refining Co. v. Commissioner 205
Arkansas Best Corp. v. Commissioner 207
Hort v. Commissioner 209
Womack v. Commissioner 211
McAllister v. Commissioner 213
Commissioner v. P.G. Lake, Inc. 215
Commissioner v. Brown 217
Baker v. Commissioner 221
Commissioner v. Ferrer 223
Miller v. Commissioner 225
Gregory v. Helvering 227
Williams v. McGowan 229
Merchants National Bank v. Commissioner 231
Arrowsmith v. Commissioner 233

Alphabetical Table of Cases

Amend v. Commissioner, 13 T.C. 178 (Tax Ct.1949), 57

American Auto. Ass'n v. United States, 367 U.S. 687, 81 S.Ct. 1727, 6 L.Ed.2d 1109 (1961), 73

Arkansas Best Corp. v. Commissioner, 485 U.S. 212, 108 S.Ct. 971, 99 L.Ed.2d 183 (1988), 207

Armantrout v. Commissioner, 67 T.C. 996 (U.S.Tax Ct.1977), 181

Arrowsmith v. Commissioner, 344 U.S. 6, 73 S.Ct. 71, 97 L.Ed. 6 (1952), 233

Baker v. Commissioner, 118 T.C. 452 (U.S.Tax Ct.2002), 221

Basye, United States v., 410 U.S. 441, 93 S.Ct. 1080, 35 L.Ed.2d 412 (1973), 195

Benaglia v. Commissioner, 36 B.T.A. 838 (B.T.A.1937), 5

Biedenharn Realty Co., Inc. v. United States, 526 F.2d 409 (5th Cir.1976), 203

Bielfeldt v. Commissioner, 231 F.3d 1035 (7th Cir.2000), 201

Blackman v. Commissioner, 88 T.C. No. 38, 88 T.C. 677 (U.S.Tax Ct.1987), 83

Blair v. Commissioner, 300 U.S. 5, 57 S.Ct. 330, 81 L.Ed. 465 (1937), 183

Bob Jones University v. United States, 461 U.S. 574, 103 S.Ct. 2017, 76 L.Ed.2d 157 (1983), 93

Brooke v. United States, 468 F.2d 1155 (9th Cir.1972), 191

Brown, Commissioner v., 380 U.S. 563, 85 S.Ct. 1162, 14 L.Ed.2d 75 (1965), 217

Bruun, Helvering v., 309 U.S. 461, 60 S.Ct. 631, 84 L.Ed. 864 (1940), 49

Burnet v. Logan, 283 U.S. 404, 51 S.Ct. 550, 75 L.Ed. 1143 (1931), 55

Burnet v. Sanford & Brooks Co., 282 U.S. 359, 51 S.Ct. 150, 75 L.Ed. 383 (1931), 23

Carroll v. Commissioner, 418 F.2d 91 (7th Cir.1969), 133

Chamales v. Commissioner, T.C. Memo. 2000–33 (U.S.Tax Ct.2000), 81

Churchill Downs v. Commissioner, 307 F.3d 423 (6th Cir.2002), 119

Clark v. Commissioner, 40 B.T.A. 333 (B.T.A.1939), 21

Commissioner v. _____ (see opposing party)

Corn Products Refining Co. v. Commissioner, 350 U.S. 46, 76 S.Ct. 20, 100 L.Ed. 29 (1955), 205

Cottage Sav. Ass'n v. Commissioner, 499 U.S. 554, 111 S.Ct. 1503, 113 L.Ed.2d 589 (1991), 53

Cramer v. Commissioner, 64 F.3d 1406 (9th Cir.1995), 63

Crane v. Commissioner, 331 U.S. 1, 67 S.Ct. 1047, 91 L.Ed. 1301 (1947), 37

Danville Plywood Corp. v. United States, 899 F.2d 3 (Fed.Cir.1990), 117

Davis, United States v., 370 U.S. 65, 82 S.Ct. 1190, 8 L.Ed.2d 335 (1962), 65

Diedrich v. Commissioner, 457 U.S. 191, 102 S.Ct. 2414, 72 L.Ed.2d 777 (1982), 35

Diez–Arguelles v. Commissioner, 48 T.C.M. 496 (U.S.Tax Ct.1984), 69

Duberstein, Commissioner v., 363 U.S. 278, 80 S.Ct. 1190, 4 L.Ed.2d 1218 (1960), 11

Dyer v. Commissioner, 20 T.C.M. 705 (Tax Ct.1961), 79

Eisner v. Macomber, 252 U.S. 189, 40 S.Ct. 189, 64 L.Ed. 521 (1920), 47

Encyclopaedia Britannica, Inc. v. Commissioner, 685 F.2d 212 (7th Cir.1982), 139

Eubank, Helvering v., 311 U.S. 122, 61 S.Ct. 149, 85 L.Ed. 81 (1940), 187

Farid–Es–Sultaneh v. Commissioner, 160 F.2d 812 (2nd Cir.1947), 67

Ferrer, Commissioner v., 304 F.2d 125 (2nd Cir.1962), 223

Flowers, Commissioner v., 326 U.S. 465, 66 S.Ct. 250, 90 L.Ed. 203 (1946), 123

Foglesong v. Commissioner, 621 F.2d 865 (7th Cir.1980), 193

Franklin's Estate v. Commissioner, 544 F.2d 1045 (9th Cir.1976), 165

Georgia School–Book Depository, Inc. v. Commissioner, 1 T.C. 463 (Tax Ct.1943), 71

Gilbert v. Commissioner, 552 F.2d 478 (2nd Cir.1977), 41

Gilliam v. Commissioner, 51 T.C.M. 515 (U.S.Tax Ct.1986), 153

Gilmore, United States v., 372 U.S. 39, 83 S.Ct. 623, 9 L.Ed.2d 570 (1963), 131

Glenshaw Glass Co., Commissioner v., 348 U.S. 426, 75 S.Ct. 473, 99 L.Ed. 483 (1955), 9

Gregory v. Helvering, 293 U.S. 465, 55 S.Ct. 266, 79 L.Ed. 596 (1935), 227

Hantzis v. Commissioner, 638 F.2d 248 (1st Cir.1981), 125

Harris, United States v., 942 F.2d 1125 (7th Cir.1991), 15

Heim v. Fitzpatrick, 262 F.2d 887 (2nd Cir.1959), 189

Helvering v. _____ (see opposing party)

Henderson v. Commissioner, T.C. Memo. 2000–321 (U.S.Tax Ct.2000), 87

Henderson v. Commissioner, 46 T.C.M. 566 (U.S.Tax Ct.1983), 111

Horst, Helvering v., 311 U.S. 112, 61 S.Ct. 144, 85 L.Ed. 75 (1940), 185

Hort v. Commissioner, 313 U.S. 28, 61 S.Ct. 757, 85 L.Ed. 1168 (1941), 209

Inaja Land Co., Ltd. v. Commissioner, 9 T.C. 727 (Tax Ct.1947), 19

King v. Commissioner, 121 T.C. No. 12 (U.S.Tax Ct.2003), 97

Kirby Lumber Co., United States v., 284 U.S. 1, 52 S.Ct. 4, 76 L.Ed. 131 (1931), 31

Klaassen v. Commissioner, 182 F.3d 932 (10th Cir.1999), 171

Knetsch v. United States, 364 U.S. 361, 81 S.Ct. 132, 5 L.Ed.2d 128 (1960), 161

Lewis, United States v., 340 U.S. 590, 71 S.Ct. 522, 95 L.Ed. 560 (1951), 29

Lucas v. Earl, 281 U.S. 111, 50 S.Ct. 241, 74 L.Ed. 731 (1929), 177

McAllister v. Commissioner, 157 F.2d 235 (2nd Cir.1946), 213

Merchants Nat. Bank of Mobile v. Commissioner, 199 F.2d 657 (5th Cir.1952), 231

Midland Empire Packing Co. v. Commissioner, 14 T.C. 635 (Tax Ct.1950), 143

Miller v. Commissioner, 299 F.2d 706 (2nd Cir.1962), 225

Minor v. United States, 772 F.2d 1472 (9th Cir.1985), 61

Moller v. United States, 721 F.2d 810 (Fed.Cir.1983), 107

Moss v. Commissioner, 758 F.2d 211 (7th Cir.1985), 115

Nickerson v. Commissioner, 700 F.2d 402 (7th Cir.1983), 103

North Am. Oil Consolidated v. Burnet, 286 U.S. 417, 52 S.Ct. 613, 76 L.Ed. 1197 (1932), 25

Norwest Corp. and Subsidiaries v. Commissioner, 108 T.C. 265 (U.S.Tax Ct.1997), 145

Ochs v. Commissioner, 195 F.2d 692 (2nd Cir.1952), 89

Ottawa Silica Co. v. United States, 699 F.2d 1124 (Fed.Cir. 1983), 91

Pevsner v. Commissioner, 628 F.2d 467 (5th Cir.1980), 129
P. G. Lake, Inc., Commissioner v., 356 U.S. 260, 78 S.Ct. 691, 2 L.Ed.2d 743 (1958), 215
Poe v. Seaborn, 282 U.S. 101, 51 S.Ct. 58, 75 L.Ed. 239 (1930), 179
Popov v. Commissioner, 246 F.3d 1190 (9th Cir.2001), 105
Prosman v. Commissioner, 77 T.C.M. 1580 (U.S.Tax Ct.1999), 173
Pulsifer v. Commissioner, 64 T.C. 245 (U.S.Tax Ct.1975), 59

Rudolph v. United States, 370 U.S. 269, 82 S.Ct. 1277, 8 L.Ed.2d 484 (1962), 113

Smith v. Commissioner, 40 B.T.A. 1038 (B.T.A.1939), 121
Starr's Estate v. Commissioner, 274 F.2d 294 (9th Cir.1959), 149
Stephens v. Commissioner, 905 F.2d 667 (2nd Cir.1990), 157

Taft v. Bowers, 278 U.S. 470, 49 S.Ct. 199, 73 L.Ed. 460 (1929), 17
Taylor v. Commissioner, 54 T.C.M. 129 (U.S.Tax Ct.1987), 85

Tufts, Commissioner v., 461 U.S. 300, 103 S.Ct. 1826, 75 L.Ed.2d 863 (1983), 39
Turner v. Commissioner, 13 T.C.M. 462 (Tax Ct.1954), 7

United States v. _____ (see opposing party)

Welch v. Helvering, 290 U.S. 111, 54 S.Ct. 8, 78 L.Ed. 212 (1933), 151
Westpac Pacific Food v. Commissioner, 451 F.3d 970 (9th Cir.2006), 75
Whitten v. Commissioner, T.C. Memo. 1995–508 (U.S.Tax Ct.1995), 109
Williams v. McGowan, 152 F.2d 570 (2nd Cir.1945), 229
Winn–Dixie Stores, Inc. v. Commissioner, 254 F.3d 1313 (11th Cir.2001), 169
Womack v. Commissioner, 510 F.3d 1295 (11th Cir.2007), 211
Woodsam Associates, Inc. v. Commissioner, 198 F.2d 357 (2nd Cir.1952), 51

Zarin v. Commissioner, 916 F.2d 110 (3rd Cir.1990), 33

CHAPTER TWO

Some Characteristics of Income

Benaglia v. Commissioner

Instant Facts: Hotel manager who lived in hotel room on hotel property did not include rental value of the room on his taxes.

Black Letter Rule: The value of lodging and meals provided to an employee by an employer for the convenience of the employer does not constitute taxable income to the employee.

Turner v. Commissioner

Instant Facts: Taxpayer, who won two round-trip first-class tickets to Buenos Aires but negotiated four round-trip tourist-class tickets to Rio de Janeiro instead, challenged tax due based on value of first-class tickets.

Black Letter Rule: Taxpayers who win prizes must report it as income, although valuing the property received may be difficult.

Commissioner v. Glenshaw Glass Co.

Instant Facts: Two companies sought to avoid the payment of taxes on punitive damages awarded in unrelated litigation.

Black Letter Rule: Punitive damage awards are taxable as gross income.

Commissioner v. Duberstein

Instant Facts: The Commissioner asked the United States Supreme Court to consider two cases which had reached different outcomes in different circuits. In Duberstein, the taxpayer had received a car from a business associate after providing useful information, and in Stanton, the taxpayer had received a $20,000 gratuity from his employer upon his resignation.

Black Letter Rule: A transfer is a gift, excludable from income under section 102(a) [General income does not include the value of property acquired by gift, bequest, devise or inheritance.] if it proceeds from a detached and disinterested generosity motivated by affection, respect, charity or similar feeling. Whether a transfer meets this standard is a matter of fact to be determined by the district court.

United States v. Harris

Instant Facts: Mistresses of wealthy widower were criminally convicted for not reporting money received from widower as income.

Black Letter Rule: A recipient's good faith belief that money received was a gift, rather than income, precludes a finding of "willfulness" for purposes of criminal liability for willful tax evasion.

Taft v. Bowers

Instant Facts: A donee of stock sought to recover income taxes paid on the amount the stock appreciated while in the hands of the donor.

Black Letter Rule: The Constitution does not prevent Congress from treating as taxable income to the recipient of a gift the increase in the value of the gift while it is owned by the donor.

Inaja Land Co. v. Commissioner

Instant Facts: Taxpayer contended that money received in settlement over easement rights and damage to land was subject to recovery-of-capital exclusion and not taxable.

Black Letter Rule: Where it would be impracticable and impossible to apportion a definite basis to an easement, no portion of settlement money received for conveyance of an easement should be considered as income, but the full amount must be treated as a return of capital and applied in reduction of the cost basis.

Clark v. Commissioner

Instant Facts: Clark (P) received money from his tax counsel to compensate for loss suffered due to erroneous tax advice and IRS asserted money received was income.

Black Letter Rule: Payment received by a taxpayer from his tax counsel for compensation for damages or loss caused by the tax counsel's error is not considered income.

Burnet v. Sanford & Brooks

Instant Facts: Sanford & Brooks (P) failed to report income, and claimed that taxes should not be imposed with respect to a transaction, from which it received no profit.

Black Letter Rule: The gain or profit, which is the subject of income tax, must be ascertained based on fixed accounting periods, rather than net profit ascertained based on particular transactions of the taxpayer when they are brought to a conclusion.

North American Oil Consolidated v. Burnet

Instant Facts: Net profits earned by North American Oil Consolidated (NorthAm) (D) in 1916 while under a (partial) receivership were held not to be income to NorthAm (D) until 1917 when the receivership was vacated and the net profits paid over to the company.

Black Letter Rule: A taxpayer with a claim of right over an amount earned must include that amount in income in the year the claim of right accrues, which is not necessarily the year the amount is earned.

United States v. Lewis

Instant Facts: A taxpayer who paid income tax on $11,000 of an employee bonus sought to have his taxes refunded to him when he was forced to give the $11,000 back to his employer.

Black Letter Rule: If a taxpayer receives income under a claim of right without any restriction as to how he may dispose of it, he has received income on which he must pay taxes, even though it may still be claimed that he is not entitled to retain the money, and even though he may still be adjudged liable to restore its equivalent.

U.S. v. Kirby Lumber Co.

Instant Facts: After a company had purchased, for less than par value, bonds which it had issued at par value, the government sought to tax the difference as gross income.

Black Letter Rule: If a corporation purchases and retires any bonds at a price less than the issuing price or face value, the excess of the issuing price or face value over the purchase price is a gain or income for the taxable year.

Zarin v. Commissioner

Instant Facts: A taxpayer owed to a casino nearly $3.5 million, a debt that was unenforceable under state law, but which he settled for $500,000; the government sought to tax the difference as income from the discharge of indebtedness.

Black Letter Rule: An unenforceable obligation is not "indebtedness" within the meaning of the Code.

Diedrich v. Commissioner

Instant Facts: Donor parents, who gave shares of stock to donee children on condition that children pay gift tax, realized taxable income to the extent the tax paid exceeded the donors' adjusted basis.

Black Letter Rule: A donor who makes a gift of property on condition that the donee pay the resulting gift tax receives taxable income to the extent that the gift tax paid by the donee exceeds the donor's adjusted basis in the property transferred.

Crane v. Commissioner

Instant Facts: Mrs. Crane (P) sold her property subject to a nonrecourse mortgage for $2,500, and realized a gain on the sale in the amount of the mortgage plus the additional consideration.

Black Letter Rule: A taxpayer who acquires depreciable property subject to an unassumed mortgage and later sells it still so encumbered and for additional consideration realizes a taxable gain on the sale in the amount of the mortgage plus any equity.

Commissioner v. Tufts

Instant Facts: A partnership reported a loss on the sale of property encumbered by a nonrecourse mortgage equal to the excess of the balance on the mortgage over the fair market value of the property, an amount of $55,740.

Black Letter Rule: When a party transfers property encumbered by a nonrecourse mortgage with an unpaid balance that exceeds the fair market value of the property, the transferor has realized, for tax liability purposes, an amount equal to the unpaid mortgage balance.

Gilbert v. Commissioner

Instant Facts: Gilbert (P) plead guilty to embezzling funds, and he appealed tax court's decision that he realized income from the unauthorized withdrawal of corporate funds.

Black Letter Rule: Where a taxpayer withdraws funds from a corporation which he fully intends to repay, and which he expects with reasonable certainty he will be able to repay, where he believes that his withdrawals will be approved by the corporation, and where he makes a prompt assignment of assets sufficient to secure the amount owed, he does not realize income on the withdrawals.

Benaglia v. Commissioner

(Food and Lodging Taxpayer) v. *(IRS)*

36 B.T.A. 838, acq. 1940–1 C.B. 1 (1937)

COMMON LAW "CONVENIENCE OF EMPLOYER" RULE HOLDS THAT VALUE OF MEALS AND LODGING TO THE EMPLOYEE IS NOT TAXABLE INCOME

■ **INSTANT FACTS** Hotel manager who lived in hotel room on hotel property did not include rental value of the room on his taxes.

■ **BLACK LETTER RULE** The value of lodging and meals provided to an employee by an employer for the convenience of the employer does not constitute taxable income to the employee.

■ **PROCEDURAL BASIS**

Petition to federal court from determination of Internal Revenue Commissioner concerning taxes owed.

■ **FACTS**

Mr. and Mrs. Benaglia (P) filed joint income tax returns for two years without adding as gross income the fair market value of rooms and meals furnished by their employer. Mr. Benaglia (P) is employed by a corporation owning two hotels and a golf club in Honolulu, Hawaii. His job required that he constantly be on duty in order to properly perform his duties. For the convenience of his employer, Mr. and Mrs. Benaglia (P) occupied a suite of rooms in one of the hotels that Mr. Benaglia (P) managed and they received their meals from the hotel as well. [Sounds like a great job!] Benaglia's (P) salary was fixed, without reference to the meals and lodging. Neither the Benaglias (P) nor the employer ever regarded the meals and lodging as part of his compensation. The internal Review Commissioner (D) issued a deficiency notice to the Benaglias (P) adding as gross income a certain amount judged to be the fair market value of the rooms and meals. The Benaglias (P) petitioned the court for review of the determination.

■ **ISSUE**

Is the value of lodging and meals provided to an employee by an employer for the convenience of the employer taxable income to the employee?

■ **DECISION AND RATIONALE**

(Stemhagen, J.) No. The value of lodging and meals provided to an employee by an employer for the convenience of the employer does not constitute taxable income to the employee. From the evidence there is no doubt that the Benaglia's (P) residence at the hotel was not compensation for services or for the personal convenience, comfort or pleasure of Mr. Benaglia (P). Rather, it was solely because he could not otherwise perform the services required of him, such as being on call at a moment's notice. Benaglia (P) testified that one living outside the hotel could not perform the functions of a manager of a resort such as this. The Commissioner (D) however asserts that the rooms and meals were not supplied merely as a convenience to the hotels of the employer. The Commissioner (D) relies upon Article 52 Regulations 77, which provides: "When living quarters ... are furnished to the employees for the convenience of the employer, the ratable value need not be added to the cash compensation of the employees, but where a person receives as compensation for services rendered a salary and in addition thereto living quarters, the value to such person of the quarters furnished constitutes income subject to tax." As previous cases have held, the character of the living quarters for tax purposes is controlled by whether the occupation of the premises was imposed upon the employee for the convenience of the employer. Benaglia (P) would not consider undertaking the job and the hotel would not consider employing a manager unless he lived on the premises. When it came time to change Benaglia's (P) compensation, no mention was ever made of the lodging and meals. Both he and the hotel took it for granted. Therefore, the value of the meals and lodging is not income to the employee. The determination of the Commissioner is reversed. Judgment entered.

■ DISSENT

(Arnold, J.) I disagree with the conclusion of fact that the rooms and meals were entirely for the convenience of the employer and that the cash salary was fixed without reference thereto and was never regarded as part of Benaglia's (P) income. When Benaglia (P) originally accepted employment he sent a letter to the employer confirming the yearly salary, *together with living quarters and meals*, etc. This letter, in my opinion, constitutes the basic contract of employment and clearly shows that the living quarters and meals were understood and intended to be compensation in addition to the cash salary. In addition, Benaglia (P) was manager of both hotels and the golf club, yet he occupied the premises of only one hotel. It would seem that if his occupancy were solely for the benefit of the employer, his occupancy at the other hotel would be just as essential as far as management was concerned. Moreover, Mr. and Mrs. Benaglia (P) were absent for a total of 5 months in one year, and 3 ½ months in another year. Yet, during his absences, the hotels continued in operations. I would hold that the reasonable value of the lodging and meals is taxable income.

Analysis:

When one receives something other than money for services rendered, the fair market value of the thing taken in payment is generally included as taxable income. This case involves an exception to the general rule and reflects the common law rule whereby the value of meals and lodging provided to employees is excluded from their gross income if they are provided for the convenience of the employer on the employer's business premises. A number of years following the decision in this case, § 119 of the Internal Revenue Code was enacted. Section 119 follows *Benaglia* quite closely but provides various detailed rules in order to assure uniformity in the meals and lodging exclusionary rule.

■ CASE VOCABULARY

COURT OF CLAIMS: Also known as the United States Court of Federal Claims, constituting a specialized federal court with nationwide jurisdiction over claims against the United States founded on the Constitution, a federal statute, a federal regulation, a contract with the United States, or any other non-tort claim.

DEFICIENCY NOTICE: Referring to a notice of a tax deficiency sent by the IRS to a taxpayer.

FINDINGS OF FACT: Court weighs the evidence and makes a determination as to the facts.

Turner v. Commissioner

(Ticket–Winning Taxpayers) v. *(IRS)*

13 T.C.M. 462 (1954)

DIFFICULTY EXISTS IN DETERMINING THE VALUE OF TAXABLE PRIZES

■ **INSTANT FACTS** Taxpayer, who won two round-trip first-class tickets to Buenos Aires but negotiated four round-trip tourist-class tickets to Rio de Janeiro instead, challenged tax due based on value of first-class tickets.

■ **BLACK LETTER RULE** Taxpayers who win prizes must report it as income, although valuing the property received may be difficult.

■ **PROCEDURAL BASIS**

Petition to federal court from determination of Internal Revenue Commissioner concerning taxes owed.

■ **FACTS**

Reginald Turner (P) won two round-trip first-class steamship tickets for a cruise between New York City and Buenos Aires. The tickets were not transferable and were good only for only one year. Turner (P) negotiated with the steamship company for four round-trip tourist-class tickets to Rio de Janeiro in place of his winning tickets. Turner (P), his wife, and their two sons, used the tickets to travel to Rio de Janeiro. The two Buenos Aires tickets had a retail value of $2,220. The Turners (P) reported income on their tax return from the award of the two tickets in the sum of $520. [Where did this figure come from?] The Commissioner (D) increased the income from this source to $2,220, the retail price of the tickets. The Turners (P) petitioned the tax court for review of the Commissioner's (D) determination.

■ **ISSUE**

Must taxpayers who win prizes report it as income?

■ **DECISION AND RATIONALE**

(Name of judge not provided) Yes. Taxpayers who win prizes must report it as income, although valuing the property received may be difficult. Persons who buy round-trip first-class tickets between New York and Buenos Aires would pay $2,220 for them. The Turners (P), however, were not such persons. The winning of the tickets did not provide them with something which they needed in the ordinary course of their lives and for which they would have made expenditure in any event. The tickets merely gave them an opportunity to enjoy a luxury beyond their means. The value to the Turners (P) was not equal to their retail cost. However, they did obtain some benefits from the winning tickets by taking a cruise with their two sons for free board, with some savings in living expenses, and obtaining the pleasure of the trip. It seems proper that a substantial amount should be included in their income on account of the winning of the tickets. The problem of arriving at a proper fair figure is difficult. The evidence to assist is meager. The Court must arrive at some figure. It has arrived at the figure of $1,400. [And where did this figure come from?]

Analysis:

In this case, there is no explanation for how the court arrived at the figure of $1,400 as the value of the winning tickets. The IRS Commissioner (D) contended that the $2,220 retail value of the two tickets should be used for reportable income. The Turners (P) argued for the sum of $520. One possible suggestion for arriving at $1,400 is averaging the two sides' numbers ($520 + $2,220 = $2,740 ÷ 2 = $1,370, rounded up to the nearest $100 = $1,400). The court clearly rejected the Commissioner's (D) position that the retail value of the two winning tickets was appropriate. It noted that the value to the Turners (P) was not equal to the retail value. Nevertheless, they did receive benefits from the tickets for which a tax was due. As the court noted, the difficulty is arriving at a proper fair figure.

Commissioner v. Glenshaw Glass Co.

(*Internal Revenue Commissioner*) v. (*Taxpayer*)

348 U.S. 426, 75 S.Ct. 473 (1955)

GROSS INCOME IS AN ACCESSION TO WEALTH, CLEARLY REALIZED, AND OVER WHICH THE TAXPAYER HAS COMPLETE DOMINION

■ **INSTANT FACTS** Two companies sought to avoid the payment of taxes on punitive damages awarded in unrelated litigation.

■ **BLACK LETTER RULE** Punitive damage awards are taxable as gross income.

■ PROCEDURAL BASIS

Certiorari to the United State Supreme Court, from the Court of Appeals decision to affirm the Tax Court's separate rulings that punitive damages are not taxable.

■ FACTS

Glenshaw Glass Co. (Glenshaw) (P) and William Goldman Theatres, Inc. (Goldman) (P) were involved in unrelated antitrust litigation. As part of a settlement, Glenshaw (P) received $800,000, of which $324,529.94 represented punitive damages. Glenshaw did not report the latter amount as income. In its antitrust suit, Goldman was awarded treble damages amounting to $375,000. As did Glenshaw (P), Goldman (P) failed to report the punitive amount—$250,000—as taxable income. The Internal Revenue Commissioner sought to recover the deficiencies, but both the Tax Court and the Court of Appeals found for the taxpayers.

■ ISSUE

Are punitive damages gross income under the Internal Revenue Code?

■ DECISION AND RATIONALE

(Warren, C.J.) Yes. Punitive damages are includable as gross income. In pertinent part, the Internal Revenue Code defines gross income as "gains or profits and income derived from any source whatever." We have previously held that this language was intended to exert Congress' full taxing power. Consequently, this Court has given the phrase liberal construction in order to recognize Congress' intent to tax all gains unless specifically exempted. Here we have instances of undeniable accessions to wealth, clearly realized, and over which the taxpayers have complete dominion. The fact that payments were extracted from wrongdoers does not detract from their character as taxable income. Moreover, it would be anomalous to permit compensatory damages to be taxed, while holding that punitive damages are not taxable. We find no evidence of an intent on the part of Congress to exempt these payments. We also reject the argument that re-enactment of the statute without change since the Board Tax of Appeal held punitive damages nontaxable indicated congressional satisfaction with that holding. We have no indication that the Board's decision was before Congress. Furthermore, immediately after that holding, the Commissioner published his nonacquiescence, maintaining the position that punitive damages are taxable. Thus, it cannot be said that Congress intended to codify the holding of Board of Tax Appeals.

Analysis:

In holding that punitive damages are gross income, the Supreme Court affirms the presumption that all gains are taxable, unless they are specifically exempted. In this case, the presumption is used to reject the argument that Congressional re-enactment of the statute, without any reference to overturning case law, would impliedly exclude punitive damages from gross income. But the significance of this case lies not with the Court's holding that punitive damages are taxable; rather, this case is oft-cited for the definition of gross income that it provides, a definition which has become a standard for analyzing what is gross income. According to the Court, gross income is an "accession to wealth, clearly realized, and over which the taxpayer has complete dominion." The test is purposefully broad in order to fulfill what the Court deems to be Congress's intent—to exert the full measure of its constitutional taxing power.

Commissioner v. Duberstein

(IRS) v. *(Taxpayer)*
363 U.S. 278, 80 S.Ct. 1190 (1960)

SUPREME COURT REFUSES TO ESTABLISH A NEW TEST OF WHAT CONSTITUTES A GIFT FOR TAX PURPOSES

■ **INSTANT FACTS** The Commissioner asked the United States Supreme Court to consider two cases which had reached different outcomes in different circuits. In Duberstein, the taxpayer had received a car from a business associate after providing useful information, and in Stanton, the taxpayer had received a $20,000 gratuity from his employer upon his resignation.

■ **BLACK LETTER RULE** A transfer is a gift, excludable from income under section 102(a) [General income does not include the value of property acquired by gift, bequest, devise or inheritance.] if it proceeds from a detached and disinterested generosity motivated by affection, respect, charity or similar feeling. Whether a transfer meets this standard is a matter of fact to be determined by the district court.

■ **PROCEDURAL BASIS**

Appeal to the United States Supreme Court of two separate and apparently contradictory opinions issued by the Second and Sixth Circuits.

■ **FACTS**

Commissioner v. Duberstein: Duberstein (D) was president of Duberstein Iron & Metal. He did business in that capacity with Berman, who was president of Mohawk Metal Corp. Berman asked Duberstein (D) for the names of potential customers. Duberstein (D) provided this information. Most of their transactions were carried out over the phone, though Duberstein (D) did state that he knew Berman personally. Berman found Duberstein's (D) information so useful that he wished to give him a gift. Berman called Duberstein (D) to inform him that he was giving him a brand new Cadillac. [This was back in 1951, when Cadillacs were still cool.] Duberstein (D) stated that that was not necessary, but Berman insisted. Duberstein (D) had not requested such a gift, and already had two cars of his own. Berman deducted the cost of the car as a business expense. Duberstein (D) acknowledged that he did not believe that Berman would have given him the car if he had not provided Berman with the helpful information. Duberstein (D) did not report the car as income, arguing it was a gift. The Commissioner (P) asserted a deficiency, arguing the car was not a gift, but rather remuneration for services rendered, and won in district court. The Court of Appeals for the Sixth Circuit reversed and found that the car was a gift. The Commissioner (P) then sought cert before the United States Supreme Court. *Stanton v. United States*: By 1942, Stanton (P) had worked for Trinity Church for ten years. He was comptroller of the Church Corporation and president of Trinity Operating Company, the company that managed the church's extensive real estate holdings. He resigned on November 30, 1942 to form his own business. At that time his annual salary was $22,500. The Trinity Operating Company board of directors voted to grant him a gratuity of $20,000 to be paid in ten monthly installments of $2,000. The board explained this action as arising from their great personal fondness for Stanton (P) and in recognition of his having done a good job in a very difficult time. However, there was also some indication of possible friction between Stanton (P) and the board. The board had decided to fire the company's treasurer and Stanton (P) had attempted to intervene on his behalf. The board fired the treasurer anyway and resented Stanton's (P) interference. The treasurer was given a six-month settlement, which was similar to what

Stanton received, but without the word gratuity. Stanton's (P) secretary was also given a gratuity when she resigned at the same time as Stanton (P). Stanton (P) did not include the gratuity in his income. The Commissioner (D) asserted a delinquency. Stanton (P) paid the delinquency and then sued for a refund. Stanton (P) won in district court, where a bare finding was made that the gratuity was a gift. This was overturned by the Court of Appeals for the Second Circuit. Stanton (P) petitioned for cert before the Supreme Court. The Commissioner (D) acquiesced in order to get a resolution to the apparent disparity between the Sixth and Second Circuits. It was the Commissioner's assertion in these two cases that the Supreme Court should adopt a new test to define a gift for these purposes. The Commissioner suggested several elements to this test. First, payments from an employer to an employee, even when wholly voluntary, ought to be taxable. Second, the concept of a gift is inconsistent with anything the donor exempts as a business expense. Third, that a gift must have a "personal" element. And finally, that a corporation can't properly make a gift of its assets.

■ ISSUE

Is a gift for purposes of *Section 102(a) Int.Rev.Code* properly defined as a transfer that proceeds from a detached and disinterested generosity motivated by affection, respect, admiration, charity or other similar feeling?

■ DECISION AND RATIONALE

(Brennan, J.) Yes. We do not believe that a new test is necessary. The principles governing the determination of what is a gift in this circumstance are necessarily general. The specifics have been sufficiently spelled out by prior opinions of this Court. In these prior opinions several requirements have been established. First a gift can not be a transfer that is required under any moral or legal obligation. It can not be a transfer that is based on the anticipation of future economic benefit. It can not be a transfer made in exchange for services rendered, even if the donor receives no economic benefit. For a transfer to be a gift it must proceed from a detached and disinterested generosity. A gift should result from feelings of affection, respect, admiration, charity or similar emotions. Thus, the most important test of whether a transfer is a gift is the underlying intention of the donor. The test proposed by the Commissioner would extend the limitations on the meaning of gift far beyond what is justified by the statute or the case law. It is true that it is likely that most transfers from employer to employee are not gifts. The fact that the donor deducts a gift as a business expense is relevant to determining the donor's intentions, as is the personal contact between the parties, and the status of the donor as a corporation. But these are factual questions to be considered in the context of the entire transaction. We do not want to create a situation where a court which is supposed to be deciding if a transfer was a gift instead becomes a trial of the appropriateness of the donor's business deductions, or a matter of fiduciary or corporate law. The tax tribunals are busy enough without having to decide whether a corporation should legally have made a transfer that could be considered a gift. Whether a transfer is a gift is closely tied to the specific circumstances. It is a non-technical decision with which the trier of fact is likely to have personal experience. Therefore primary weight must be given to the conclusions of the trier of fact. Those who feel that this is too messy or leads to too much litigation must apply to Congress for greater specificity within the statute. Because this is a question of fact appellate review will be quite limited. If the trier of facts in the case is a jury the judgment must stand unless it is found that reasonable men could not differ on the issue. And if the trier of fact is a judge then the appellate court must find the judgment "clearly erroneous". Based on this we find that the Court of Appeals for the Sixth Circuit was incorrect in reversing the original finding in *Duberstein*, and that the car was not a gift as it was transferred in recognition of services rendered and in the hope that future services would follow. In *Stanton* we are in disagreement. We do not feel that the judgment of the Court of Appeals for the Second Circuit can stand. However, the findings of the District Court were so sparse that they gave no insight as to the court's concepts of the determining facts and legal standard. Thus we vacate the judgment of the Court of Appeals and the case is remanded to the District Court for further findings not inconsistent with this opinion.

■ CONCURRENCE AND DISSENT

(Frankfurter, J.) The only addition made by this case to previous decisions on this subject is the direction that it is the trier of fact's job to search among the competing motives found in each case to discover the intent that was at the root of the transfer. If they are to do this we should not create new phrases which lower courts will inevitably spend a great deal of energy interpreting. I am particularly concerned about the direction by the Court that lower courts should rely upon their "experience with human affairs" or their understanding of "the mainsprings of human conduct." The experience and understanding of human conduct vary greatly from one person to another. Thus relying on these will lead to a great diversity in the administration of the tax laws. And I believe that the tax law should be as uniform as possible in a country such as ours. I agree with the judgment in *Duberstein*. But I would have upheld the Appellate Court in *Stanton.*

Analysis:

The term "gift" is not defined in § 102(a). This section simply states that gross income does not include the value of property acquired by gift, bequest, devise, or inheritance. Under common law, a gift is any voluntary transfer of property to another, made freely without obligation or consideration. Earlier cases determined that this definition was not sufficient to make something a gift that should be excluded from income, though it is a starting point. The gift must have been made with a detached and disinterested generosity arising out of affection, respect, charity, or like impulses. This is a good definition of what a gift is, but it does leave the courts with the problem of determining the intent of the donor. Deciding a person's intent is a subjective determination and leads to disparate judgments. The test proposed here by the Commissioner would have cleared up the disparities, but the Supreme Court is refusing to legislate from the bench, and referring the problem to Congress if it needs to be fixed.

■ CASE VOCABULARY

"CLEARLY ERRONEOUS": The standard applied when an Appellate Court reviews the findings of a judge. A finding can be clearly erroneous even if supported by some evidence when the Appellate Court after reviewing all of the evidence has a definite and firm conviction that a mistake has been made.

GRATUITOUS: Freely given without consideration.

SHIBBOLETH: A saying particular to a group of people, something that definitively identifies a group.

TRANSFER: To convey or pass over possession or control from one to another. Gifts, a sale, a transfer of title, are all examples of possible ways a transfer can take place.

United States v. Harris

(*United States*) v. (*Mistresses*)

942 F.2d 1125 (7th Cir.1991)

COURT HOLDS MISTRESSES WERE WRONGFULLY CONVICTED FOR NOT REPORTING MONEY RECEIVED FROM WEALTHY WIDOWER AS INCOME

■ **INSTANT FACTS** Mistresses of wealthy widower were criminally convicted for not reporting money received from widower as income.

■ **BLACK LETTER RULE** A recipient's good faith belief that money received was a gift, rather than income, precludes a finding of "willfulness" for purposes of criminal liability for willful tax evasion.

■ **PROCEDURAL BASIS**

Appeal from criminal convictions for willfully evading income tax.

■ **FACTS**

Mr. Kritzik, a wealthy widower, partial to the company of young women and now deceased [perhaps there is a correlation], gave Harris (D1) and her twin sister Conley (D2) each more than half a million dollars over several years. Harris (D1) and Conley (D2) were criminally prosecuted in separate trials for willfully evading their income tax obligations on the money. The United States (P) was required to prove beyond a reasonable doubt that the money received was income rather than a gift. After being convicted, Harris (D1) and Conley (D2) appealed.

■ **ISSUE**

Does a recipient's good faith belief that money received was a gift, rather than income, preclude a finding of "willfulness" for purposes of criminal liability for willful tax evasion?

■ **DECISION AND RATIONALE**

(Eschbach, J.) Yes. A recipient's good faith belief that money received was a gift, rather than income, precludes a finding of "willfulness" for purposes of criminal liability for willful tax evasion. With respect to Conley's (D2) case, we hold that the Government's (P) evidence was insufficient to show either that the money Conley (D2) received was income or that she acted in knowing disregard of her obligations. Regarding the critical consideration of the donor's intent as laid down in *Commissioner v. Duberstein* [a transfer is a gift, excludable from income, if it proceeds from a detached and disinterested generosity motivated by affection, respect, charity or similar feeling], the only direct evidence that the Government (P) presented was Mr. Kritzik's gift tax returns. These returns however identified gifts to Conley (D2) substantially less than the total amount of money transferred to her. The gift tax returns merely raise the question of whether the other payments were taxable income, or whether he just underreported his gifts; they do not resolve the question. This failure to show Mr. Kritzik's intent is fatal to the Government's (P) case. Evidence concerning a bank card Conley (D2) signed listing Mr. Kritzik in a space marked "employer" is open to conflicting interpretations since she contends that she listed him merely as a reference. The form of payment—Conley (D2) picked up her regular check at Mr. Kritzik's office ever week to ten days—could easily be that of a dependent picking up regular support checks. [What do you think the office staff thought she was?] With respect to Harris' (D1) case, the district court excluded three letters that Mr. Kritzik wrote on the ground of hearsay, and the possibility that the prejudice from them exceeded their probative value. We hold that the exclusion of these letters was error and Harris' (D1) conviction must therefore be reversed. The first letter from Mr. Kritzik to Harris (D1) told her that he loved and trusted her, and that so far as the things he gave her, he received greater pleasure in giving than she would get in receiving. He also said that he loved giving things to her and to see her happy and enjoying them. The second letter also to Harris (D1) referred to his love for her and that he would do all that he could to make her happy, and would arrange for her financial security. The third letter, six years later, written to his insurance company referred to the value of certain jewelry that he had given to Harris (D1) as a gift. He forwarded a copy of the letter to Harris (D1). These letters were not hearsay for the purpose of showing what Harris (D1) believed, because her belief does not depend on the actual truth of the matters asserted in the letters. Even if Mr. Kritzik were lying, the letters could have caused Harris (D1) to believe in good faith that the things he gave her were intended as gifts. This good faith belief would preclude a finding of willfulness on the part of Harris (D1). We further conclude that the current law on the tax treatment of payments to mistresses provided Harris (D1) no fair warning that her conduct was criminal. [In other words, the law is not clear on the subject of mistresses.] For this reason, we remand with instructions that the indictment against Harris (D1) be dismissed. Although we do not say it does, even if prior case law establishes that a person is entitled to treat cash and property received from a lover as gifts as long as the relationship consists of something more than specific payments for specific sessions of sex, the Government (P) does not allege that Harris (D1) received specific payments for specific sessions of sex. We are unaware of a single case finding tax liability for payments that a mistress received from her lover, absent proof of specific payments for specific sex acts. Even if such proof is present, the cases have not applied penalties for civil fraud, much less criminal sanctions. Therefore, we reverse both Harris's (D1) conviction and Conley's (D2) conviction and remand with instructions to dismiss the indictments against them.

■ CONCURRENCE

(Flaum, J.) I part company with the majority only when it distills from our gift/income jurisprudence a rule that would tax only the most base type of cash-for-sex exchange and categorically exempt from tax liability all other transfers of money and property to so-called mistresses or companions.

Analysis:

The court did not make a definitive ruling here concerning transfers to mistresses; instead, it noted that other cases had required proof of specific payments for specific sex acts, and there was no such proof in this case. The court relied on the leading case of *Commissioner v. Duberstein* to determine Mr. Kritzik's intent. The excluded letters in the Harris (D1) case not only showed that he intended to give the money as gifts, but they showed Harris's (D1) belief that the money was not income, thereby precluding a finding of "willfulness." The concurring justice agreed that the Government (P) had not proven its case, but took issue with a holding that would categorically exempt from tax liability all transfers of money and property to so-called mistresses or companions.

■ CASE VOCABULARY

INDICTMENT: Document whereby Grand Jury recommends charging one with a crime.

Taft v. Bowers

(Taxpayer) v. *(Collector of Internal Revenue)*

278 U.S. 470, 49 S.Ct. 199 (1929)

THE BASIS IN PROPERTY ACQUIRED BY GIFT IS THE SAME AS ITS BASIS IN THE HANDS OF A DONOR

■ **INSTANT FACTS** A donee of stock sought to recover income taxes paid on the amount the stock appreciated while in the hands of the donor.

■ **BLACK LETTER RULE** The Constitution does not prevent Congress from treating as taxable income to the recipient of a gift the increase in the value of the gift while it is owned by the donor.

■ **PROCEDURAL BASIS**

Appeal to the United State Supreme Court, challenging the decision of the Court of Appeal to reverse the district court's finding that the government could not tax the appreciation in stock received by gift while the stock was owned by the donor.

■ **FACTS**

During the calendar years 1921 and 1922 the father of Elizabeth C. Taft (P) gave her shares of Nash Motors Company stock, then more valuable than when acquired by him. She sold them in 1923 for more than their market value when the gift was made. The United States demanded an income tax imposed upon the difference between the cost to Taft's (P) father and price received after sale by the Taft (P). Taft (P) paid the tax exacted and sued to recover the portion imposed on the advance in value while her father owned the stock. Taft (P) argued that only the appreciation during her ownership could be regarded as income, and any appreciation occurring before her ownership of the stock is not income within the meaning of the Sixteenth Amendment. The District Court agreed, and the Court of Appeals reversed.

■ **ISSUE**

Does the Sixteenth Amendment prohibit Congress from exacting a tax upon the appreciation in the value of property received by a donee occurring prior to the gift?

■ **DECISION AND RATIONALE**

(McReynolds, J.) No. The Constitution does not prevent Congress from treating as taxable income to the recipient of a gift the increase in the value of the gift while it is owned by the donor. The mandate of § 1015 of the Internal Revenue Code is clear. The statute provides that "if property was acquired by gift . . ., the basis shall be the same as it would be in the hands of the donor or the last preceding owner by whom it was not acquired by gift, except that if such basis is greater than the fair market value of the property at the time of the gift, then for the purpose of determining loss, the basis shall be such fair market value." Congress' intent was to require Ms. Taft (P) to pay the tax. The only question is whether Congress had the power to do so. The Sixteenth Amendment provides: "The Congress shall have power to lay and collect taxes on incomes from whatever source derived, without apportionment among the several States, and without regard to any census or enumeration." The Amendment does not define income, but it is settled that Congress cannot define as income something which prior to the Amendment's enactment was not regarded as income. This Court has defined income as "the gain derived from capital, from labor, or from both combined, provided it include profit gained through a sale or conversion of capital assets." If Taft's (P) father had sold the stock at market value he would have realized income taxable under the Sixteenth Amendment. We do not think that he could deprive the government of its share simply by making a gift. The stock represented only a single investment of capital—that made by Taft's (P) father. When through sale the increase in capital was separated from the investment, it became taxable income under the Sixteenth Amendment. The statute has deprived Taft (P) of no right, nor has it subjected her to any hardship. To accept Taft's (P) view would defeat Congress' intent to take part of all gain derived from capital investments. To prevent that result, Congress had the power to require donees to accept the position of the donor in respect to the property received. Affirmed.

Analysis:

Section 1015 creates a carryover basis for donees. Under § 1012, basis is usually determined by referring to the cost of acquiring the property. But a cost basis cannot be used where property is acquired by gift because the donee's basis would be zero. A zero basis to the donee would mean that he would be taxed on the entire amount realized upon disposition of the property, a result that is contrary to the exclusion of gifts from gross income as provided in § 1012. The Court's holding here is consistent with both § 1012 and § 1015. As the Court here holds, any appreciation that occurs in the hands of the donor does not affect the basis in the property; the basis itself, however, is not taxable.

Inaja Land Co. v. Commissioner

(*Easement Holding Taxpayer*) v. (*Commissioner*)

9 T.C. 727, acq. 1948–1 C.B. 2 (1947)

CAPITAL RECOVERIES IN EXCESS OF COST CONSTITUTE TAXABLE INCOME

■ **INSTANT FACTS** Taxpayer contended that money received in settlement over easement rights and damage to land was subject to recovery-of-capital exclusion and not taxable.

■ **BLACK LETTER RULE** Where it would be impracticable and impossible to apportion a definite basis to an easement, no portion of settlement money received for conveyance of an easement should be considered as income, but the full amount must be treated as a return of capital and applied in reduction of the cost basis.

■ **PROCEDURAL BASIS**

Decision by tax court concerning issue of whether income taxes were due.

■ **FACTS**

For the sum of $61,000, Inaja Land Co. (Inaja) (P) bought many acres of land on the banks of a river in California, together with certain water rights, for use primarily as a private fishing club. Thereafter, the City of Los Angeles built a tunnel nearby and began to divert "foreign waters" into the river upstream from Inaja's (P) property. The foreign waters contained concrete dust, sediment, and foreign matter, which affected the fishing [the fish probably split or died, rather than swim in polluted water], and also caused flooding and erosion. A settlement was reached between Inaja (P) and the City under which the City paid Inaja (P) $50,000 to release and forever discharge it from any liability. In settling its claim, Inaja (P) incurred attorney's fees and costs of $1,000. The IRS Commissioner (D) asserted that the net amount of $49,000 was taxable income. Inaja (P) contends that the money was paid to it for the easement granted to the City and the consequent damage to its property rights; that the loss of past or future profits was not considered; that the character of the easement made it impracticable to apportion a basis to the property affected; and that since the sum received is less than the basis of the entire property, taxation should be postponed until final disposition of the property.

■ **ISSUE**

Is settlement money received for conveyance of an easement taxable income?

■ **DECISION AND RATIONALE**

(Leech, J.) No. We hold that where it would be impracticable and impossible to apportion a definite basis to an easement, no portion of settlement money received for conveyance of an easement should be considered as income, but the full amount must be treated as a return of capital and applied in reduction of the cost basis. Based upon the record, we have determined that no part of the recovery was paid for loss of profits, but was paid for the conveyance of a right of way and easements, and for damages to Inaja's (P) land and its property rights. Capital recoveries in excess of cost do constitute taxable income. Inaja (P) has made no attempt to allocate a basis to that part of the property covered by the easements. It is conceded that all of Inaja's (P) lands were not affected by the easements conveyed. Inaja (P) asserts that it would be impracticable and impossible to apportion a definite basis to the easements. As a previous court has stated, a taxpayer should not be charged with gain on pure conjecture unsupported by any foundation of ascertainable fact. Apportionment with reasonable accuracy of the amount received not being possible, and this amount being less than Inaja's (P) cost basis for the property, it cannot be determined that Inaja (P) has, in fact, realized gain in any amount. Thus, no portion of the payment should be considered as income, but the full amount must be treated as a return of capital and applied in reduction of Inaja's (P) cost basis. [This means it will eventually affect Inaja (P).]

Analysis:

This case looks at whether or not the amounts received by way of settlement concerning easement rights are taxable income or subject to the recovery-of-capital exclusion. Inaja (P) argued that it would be impracticable and impossible to apportion a definite basis to the easement since it could not be described by metes and bounds; that the flow of the water had changed and will change the course of the river; that the extent of the flood was and is not predictable; and that the City had not released the full measure of water to which it is entitled. The court agreed with Inaja (P) that a definite basis could not be apportioned to the easement and held that it was impossible to determine whether a gain had been realized.

■ **CASE VOCABULARY**

EASEMENT: The right of one to use the land of another for a certain purpose.

RIPARIAN OWNER: An owner of property on the bank of a river.

Clark v. Commissioner

(Taxpayer) v. *(IRS)*
40 B.T.A. 333, acq. 1957–1 C.B. 4 (1939)

REIMBURSEMENT FROM A TAX ADVISER TO COMPENSATE TAXPAYER FOR HAVING ERRONEOUS-LY PAID MORE THAN THE MINIMUM AMOUNT OF TAX ACTUALLY DUE IS NOT TAXABLE INCOME

■ **INSTANT FACTS** Clark (P) received money from his tax counsel to compensate for loss suffered due to erroneous tax advice and IRS asserted money received was income.

■ **BLACK LETTER RULE** Payment received by a taxpayer from his tax counsel for compensation for damages or loss caused by the tax counsel's error is not considered income.

■ **PROCEDURAL BASIS**

Tax court proceeding to determine issue of deficiency in income tax.

■ **FACTS**

Clark (P) and his wife could have filed a joint return or separate returns. Clark's (P) tax counsel advised him to file a joint return and he prepared it for Clark (P) and his wife. Thereafter, the IRS audited Clark (P) and claimed that additional tax was due. Clark (P) paid the tax. His tax counsel admitted that if he had not erred in computing the tax liability shown on the joint return he would have advised Clark (P) and his wife to file separate returns. Accordingly, tax counsel paid Clark (P) over $19,000, which was the difference between what would have been paid if separate returns had been filed and the amount which was actually paid on the joint return. [In other words, Clark (P) paid over $19,000 too much due to the lawyer's error.] The Commissioner (D) determined that this sum paid to Clark (P) was income, on the theory that it constituted taxes paid by a third party and consequently Clark (P) was in receipt of income to that extent. [If the IRS prevailed, Clark (P) would still be damaged since he would have to pay taxes on the supposed "income" received as reimbursement for overpaid taxes. That's not fair!] Clark (P) asserted that the payment was compensation for damages or loss caused by the error of tax counsel, and therefore no income was realized from its receipt.

■ **ISSUE**

Is payment received by a taxpayer from his tax counsel for compensation for damages or loss caused by the tax counsel's error considered income?

■ **DECISION AND RATIONALE**

(Leech, J.) No. Payment received by a taxpayer from his tax counsel for compensation for damages or loss caused by the tax counsel's error is not considered income. The sum paid to Clark (P) was compensation for his loss. Payments in settlement for 1) breach of promise to marry, 2) damages for injury to reputation, 3) injuries by libel and slander, and 4) damages for personal injury all are not income since such are recoupment of losses, not income derived from capital, from labor or from both combined. Thus, the amount received by Clark (P) by way of recompense is not includable in his gross income. The money received was compensation for a loss that impaired Clark's (P) capital. Moreover, so long as Clark (P) neither could nor did take a deduction in a prior year of this loss in such a way to offset income for the prior year, the amount received by him in the taxable year, by way of recompense, is not then includable in his gross income. Decision entered for Clark (P). [Lessen learned—seek reimbursement from your tax counsel when wrong advice results in overpayment of taxes.]

Analysis:

The underlying ground for the holding in this case, that the money received was not income derived from capital, from labor, or from both combined, is no longer good law. Nevertheless, the precise holding of the case is still good law. The IRS has held that the nontaxable holding from *Clark* does not apply to reimbursement from a tax adviser unless it compensates one for having paid more than the minimum amount of tax that was actually due. Here, Clark (P) paid over $19,000 more than he should have if there had been no error. Thus, the money received was not income. The court may have considered the matter as a "transaction" in which Clark (P) overpaid the tax and then was reimbursed for the overpayment. By concluding that the transaction yielded no overall gain, there should thus be no overall income tax consequences.

■ CASE VOCABULARY

QUA: As

Burnet v. Sanford & Brooks

(IRS) v. *(Taxpayer)*
282 U.S. 359, 51 S.Ct. 150 (1931)

■ **INSTANT FACTS** Sanford & Brooks (P) failed to report income, and claimed that taxes should not be imposed with respect to a transaction, from which it received no profit.

■ **BLACK LETTER RULE** The gain or profit, which is the subject of income tax, must be ascertained based on fixed accounting periods, rather than net profit ascertained based on particular transactions of the taxpayer when they are brought to a conclusion.

■ **PROCEDURAL BASIS**

Petition to United States Supreme Court from reversal by court of appeals of lower court's ruling concerning tax deficiency assessment.

■ **FACTS**

From 1913 to 1915, Sanford & Brooks Co. (Sanford) (P) carried out a contract for another company for dredging a river. Sanford (P), in making its income tax returns for the years 1913 to 1916, added to gross income for each year the payments made under the contract that year, and deducted its expenses paid that year in performing the contract. The total expenses exceeded the payments received by $176,271.88. The tax returns for 1913, 1915, and 1916 showed net losses. That for 1914 showed net income. In 1915, work under the contract was abandoned, and in 1916 suit was brought to recover for a breach of warranty of the character of the material to be dredged. Judgment under the contract was awarded, and Sanford (P) received in that year the sum of $192,577.59, which included the $176,271.88 by which its expenses under the contract had exceeded receipts from it, and accrued interest amounting to $16,305.71. Because Sanford (P) failed to include these amounts as gross income in its tax returns for 1920, the IRS (D) made the deficiency assessment, based on the addition of both items to gross income for that year. The Court of Appeals ruled that only the item of interest was properly included as income, and that the item of $176,271.88 was a return of losses suffered by Sanford (P) in earlier years and hence was wrongly assessed as income. Sanford (P) contends that as the Sixteenth Amendment and the Revenue Act of 1918 (which was in force in 1920) plainly contemplate a tax only on net income or profits, any application of the statute which operates to impose a tax with respect to the present transaction, from which it received no profit, cannot be upheld.

■ **ISSUE**

Can the gain or profit, which is the subject of income tax, be ascertained on net profit ascertained on the basis of particular transactions of the taxpayer when they are brought to a conclusion?

■ **DECISION AND RATIONALE**

(Stone, J.) No. We hold that the gain or profit, which is the subject of income tax, must be ascertained based on fixed accounting periods, rather than net profit ascertained based on particular transactions of the taxpayer when they are brought to a conclusion. All the revenue acts which have been enacted since the adoption of the Sixteenth Amendment have uniformly assessed the tax on the basis of annual returns showing the net result of all the taxpayer's transactions during a fixed accounting period, either calendar year or fiscal year. Under the Revenue Act of 1918, Sanford (P) was subject to tax upon its annual net income, arrived at by deducting from gross income for each taxable year all the ordinary and necessary expenses paid during that year in carrying on any trade or business, interest and taxes paid, and losses sustained, during the year. Gross income includes income derived from business or the transaction of any business carried on for gain or profit, or gains or profits and income derived from any source whatever. The amount of all such items is required to be included in the gross income for the taxable year in which received by the taxpayer, unless they may be properly accounted for on the accrual basis. It cannot be doubted that the recovery made by Sanford (P) in 1920 was gross income for that year. The money received was derived from a contract entered into in the course of Sanford's (P) business operations for profit. While it equaled, and in a loose sense was a return of, expenditures made in performing the contract, still, as the Board of Tax Appeals found, the expenditures were made in defraying the expenses incurred in the prosecution of the work under the contract, for the purpose of earning profits. They were not capital investments, the cost of which, if converted, must first be restored from the proceeds before there is a capital gain taxable as income. A taxpayer may be in receipt of net income in one year and not in another. The net result of the two years, if combined in a single taxable period, might still be a loss; but it has never been supposed that that fact would relieve him from a tax on the first, or that it affords any reason for postponing the assessment of the tax until the end of a lifetime, or for some other indefinite period, to ascertain more precisely whether the final outcome of the period, or of a given transaction, will be a gain or a loss. The original assessment was proper.

Analysis:

This case stands for the proposition that the tax system uses annual accounting, rather than transactional accounting. The facts of the case demonstrate that the annual accounting method can sometimes produce harsh results. The tax system does not provide for negative taxes, which would result in the government issuing payment refunds based on reportable losses. Under the present system, a loss results in zero tax, no matter how great the loss may be.

North American Oil Consolidated v. Burnet

(*Company Under Receivership*) v. (*IRS*)

286 U.S. 417, 52 S.Ct. 613 (1932)

THE CLAIM OF RIGHT DOCTRINE REQUIRES INCLUSION OF INCOME IN THE YEAR THE CLAIM ACCRUES AND NOT NECESSARILY THE YEAR INCOME IS EARNED

■ **INSTANT FACTS** Net profits earned by North American Oil Consolidated (NorthAm) (D) in 1916 while under a (partial) receivership were held not to be income to NorthAm (D) until 1917 when the receivership was vacated and the net profits paid over to the company.

■ **BLACK LETTER RULE** A taxpayer with a claim of right over an amount earned must include that amount in income in the year the claim of right accrues, which is not necessarily the year the amount is earned.

■ **PROCEDURAL BASIS**

On writ of certiorari to the U.S.S.C. affirming the Circuit Court of Appeals decision in favor of the IRS.

■ **FACTS**

Prior to 1916 the Government instituted suit against NorthAm (D) attempting to oust it from possession of a particular section of oil land to which the United States held legal title, and NorthAm (D) operated. The Government also claimed beneficial ownership of the land. On February 2, 1916, a receiver was appointed to operate the property, or supervise its operations, and to hold the net income from the land. In 1916, the land earned a net profit of $171,979.22 and the receiver was paid such amount as was earned. After entry by the District Court in 1917 of the final decree dismissing the bill, the receiver paid to NorthAm (D) the net profit from the prior year. The Government appealed to the Circuit Court of Appeals which affirmed the decision to dismiss the Government's action. An appeal to the U.S.S.C. was dismissed by stipulation. The net profit from 1916 was entered into NorthAm's (D) books as income for 1916, but was not accounted for in that year's return. In 1918, an amended return for 1916 was filed which accounted for the 1916 net profit. The Commissioner (P) audited NorthAm's (D) 1917 return and determined a deficiency based upon other items. NorthAm (D) appealed to the Board of Tax Appeals (Board). In 1927 [ten years later!] the Commissioner (P) asserted that the deficiency should also include a tax on the amount paid by the receiver to NorthAm (D) in 1917. The Board held that the profits were taxable to the receiver as income of 1916. The Board did not make a finding whether NorthAm's (D) accounts were kept on a cash receipts and disbursements basis or on the accrual basis. Upon appeal, the Circuit Court of Appeals held that the profits were taxable to NorthAm (D) as income of 1917, regardless of its method of accounting. It is conceded that the net profits earned during the receivership (1916) constituted income. NorthAm (D) contends that, 1) the net profits should have been reported by the receiver for taxation in 1916; 2) that if not returnable by him, they should have been returned by the company for 1916, because they constitute income accrued in that year; 3) that if not taxable as income for NorthAm (D) in 1916, they were taxable to it as income in 1922, since the litigation was not finally terminated in its favor until 1922.

■ **ISSUE**

Is income which is earned, but to which a taxpayer does not have a claim of right, includable in income in the year earned?

■ DECISION AND RATIONALE

(Brandeis, J.) No. First, the 1916 net profits impounded by the receiver were not taxable to him because he was the receiver of only part of the properties operated by the company. Only in situations where receivers are in control of an entire property or business does the Internal Revenue Act of 1916 as adopted by the Revenue Act of 1918 [I.R.C. § 6012(b)(3)] and as interpreted under the Treasury Regulations require that the receiver make returns in the same manner as if it was the corporation over which it had custody and control. In all other cases, the corporations themselves have to report their income. The language of this section contemplates a complete, not a partial, substitution of the receiver for the company. There is no provision which allows for the consolidation of the receiver's return into the corporate return, nor which allows two separate returns for the same year, each covering only a part of the corporate return. Second, the net profits were not taxable to NorthAm (D) as income of 1916 (the year the profits were earned). NorthAm (D) was not required in 1916 to report as income an amount which it might never receive. There was no constructive receipt of the net profits by NorthAm (D) in 1916, because at no time during the year was there a right in the company to demand that the receiver pay over the money. Throughout the year it was uncertain who would be entitled to the net profits. It was not until 1917, when the District Court entered a final decree vacating the receivership and dismissing the bill, that NorthAm (D) became entitled to receive the money. Whether NorthAm (D) was a cash method or accrual taxpayer, it was not taxable in 1916 on income which it had not yet received and which it might never receive. Third, the net profits from 1916 were not taxable in 1922, the year the litigation was terminated. The net profits became taxable to NorthAm (D) in 1917, when it first became entitled to them and when it actually received them. If a taxpayer receives earnings under a claim of right and without restriction as to its disposition, he has received income which he is required to return, even though it may still be claimed that he is not entitled to retain the money, and even though he may still be held to repay the same amount. [The last sentence is the basic explanation of the "claim of right" doctrine. The idea here is that if a taxpayer has a claim of right in income he has constructively received it regardless of his status as a cash or an accrual taxpayer, and regardless of his possible desire to not claim an amount as income.] If the Government had prevailed in 1922, and NorthAm (D) was obligated to return the net profits, it would have been entitled to a deduction from its profits of 1922, not from those of any earlier year. The Circuit Court of Appeals which held that the profits were taxable to NorthAm (D) as income of 1917, regardless of its method of accounting, is affirmed.

Analysis:

Note that there are two different lawsuits referenced here. The first suit was brought (and lost) by the Government against NorthAm (D) regarding legal and beneficial title to a piece of oil land. The suit at issue here is the tax case against NorthAm (D). The Commissioner (P) argued for inclusion in 1917 of the net profits from 1916. The Commissioner's (P) argument is probably motivated by the fact that he had already determined a deficiency for 1917, and if NorthAm's (D) income was increased for that year, then the amount of the deficiency would likely increase, which means more money for the IRS. The Court held that the amount must be included in NorthAm's (D) 1917 return. This decision indicates the Board of Tax Appeal was incorrect when it found that the net profits were taxable to the receiver, and that NorthAm (D) was incorrect when it included the net profits in its 1916 return.

■ CASE VOCABULARY

BENEFICIAL OWNERSHIP: The equitable ownership of property having all the usual rights associated with ownership, but not the legal title to the property.

BILL: What is now generally referred to as the complaint in a civil action; a bill used to be filed for equitable claims, and complaints for legal claims.

CLAIM OF RIGHT: The unrestricted right to claim income, even though there may be other or later claims regarding the amount received.

DECREE: The final determination of a court of equity, now generally referred to as the judgment of a court.

LEGAL TITLE: The legally enforceable right to hold the title to property (e.g., as a fiduciary), while the equitable or beneficial right to the property is held by another.

STIPULATION: An agreement between opposing parties (particularly in litigation) whereby certain facts, conditions, or issues are accepted to be true or proven.

VACATING: To cancel or void a judgment or entry in the record [think of it as completely erasing the words of a judgment or record]; to leave or empty-out something (to vacate the premises).

United States v. Lewis

(*IRS*) v. (*Taxpayer*)
340 U.S. 590, 71 S.Ct. 522 (1951)

THE "CLAIM OF RIGHT" INTERPRETATION OF THE TAX LAWS IS DEEPLY ROOTED IN THE FEDERAL TAX SYSTEM AND WILL NOT BE SET ASIDE SIMPLY BECAUSE IT DISADVANTAGES SOME TAXPAYERS

■ **INSTANT FACTS** A taxpayer who paid income tax on $11,000 of an employee bonus sought to have his taxes refunded to him when he was forced to give the $11,000 back to his employer.

■ **BLACK LETTER RULE** If a taxpayer receives income under a claim of right without any restriction as to how he may dispose of it, he has received income on which he must pay taxes, even though it may still be claimed that he is not entitled to retain the money, and even though he may still be adjudged liable to restore its equivalent.

■ **PROCEDURAL BASIS**

Certification to the United States Supreme Court of a Court of Claims judgment ordering the IRS to refund the tax mistakenly paid by a taxpayer on $11,000.

■ **FACTS**

In his 1944 income tax return, Lewis (P) reported $22,000 which he had received that year as a bonus. In 1946, however, following protracted litigation, Lewis (P) was required to pay back $11,000 of that sum. Until that point, he had claimed and made use of the full amount of the original bonus in the good faith belief that it belonged to him. When he was required to return half of the bonus, Lewis (P) brought suit in the Court of Claims seeking a refund of the overpayment of the 1944 tax. The IRS (D) responded that the tax should not be recomputed, but instead Lewis (P) should claim an $11,000 loss on his 1946 return. The Court of Claims found for Lewis (P), and the IRS (D) appealed.

■ **ISSUE**

When a taxpayer receives income under a mistake of fact which he is later required to pay back after having already reported that income on his taxes, can he have his taxes for the year in which he paid the taxes recomputed and thereafter receive a refund from the IRS?

■ **DECISION AND RATIONALE**

(Black, J.) No. We granted certiorari to this case because the holding of the Court of Claims conflicts with many decisions of the courts of appeals, as well as with the principles that we announced in *North American Oil v. Burnet*. In *North American Oil*, we stated: "If a taxpayer receives earnings under a claim of right and without restriction as to its disposition, he has received income which he is required to return, even though it may still be claimed that he is not entitled to retain the money, and even though he may still be adjudged liable to restore its equivalent." Nothing in this language permits an exception to that rule merely because a taxpayer is "mistaken" as to the validity of his claim to the income. Income taxes must be paid on income received or accrued during an annual accounting period. Further, the claim of right interpretation of the tax laws has long been used to give finality to that period, and is now deeply rooted in the federal tax system. We see no reason to depart from that well-settled interpretation merely because it results in an advantage or disadvantage to a taxpayer. Reversed.

■ DISSENT

(Douglas, J.) Many inequities are inherent in the income tax system, and we only multiply them needlessly by making distinctions which have no place in the practical administration of the law. If the refund were allowed, the integrity of the taxable year would not be violated. The tax would be paid when due; but the Government would not be permitted to maintain the unconscionable position that it can keep the tax after it is shown that payment was made on money which was not income to the taxpayer.

Analysis:

Under the claim of right doctrine, any income received during a taxable year that a taxpayer has a claim to, and unrestricted use of, must be reported to the government in that taxable year, even if the taxpayer may later become obligated to return part or all of the income received. The claim of right doctrine supports the integrity of the tax year system. *Lewis* also addresses what happens when a taxpayer receives and claims money as income in a certain year (meaning taxes are paid on that money), but sometime later is forced to repay all or part of it. In *Lewis*, the court held that the only way in which relief may be obtained is by permitting the taxpayer to deduct the amount of repayment in the year in which it is repaid. *Lewis*, however, is an early 1950's case, and since that time things have changed. For instance, Internal Revenue Code (IRC) § 1341 now permits the use of a second approach when money previously taxed as income must be repaid. Under IRC § 1341(a)(5), a taxpayer, instead of merely taking a deduction, is permitted to reduce her tax due for the year of repayment by the amount of tax for the prior year that is attributable to the specific amount repaid.

■ CASE VOCABULARY

CLAIM OF RIGHT DOCTRINE: A rule of tax law that requires a taxpayer to report on his income tax return any income that is constructively received, regardless of whether or not he holds an unrestricted claim to it.

United States v. Kirby Lumber Co.

(Government) v. *(Taxpayer)*
284 U.S. 1, 52 S.Ct. 4 (1931)

TAXABLE INCOME IS REALIZED WHEN A LEGAL OBLIGATION IS SETTLED FOR LESS THAN THE TOTAL AMOUNT OF THE OBLIGATION

■ **INSTANT FACTS** After a company had purchased, for less than par value, bonds which it had issued at par value, the government sought to tax the difference as gross income.

■ **BLACK LETTER RULE** If a corporation purchases and retires any bonds at a price less than the issuing price or face value, the excess of the issuing price or face value over the purchase price is a gain or income for the taxable year.

■ **PROCEDURAL BASIS**

Not provided.

■ **FACTS**

The Kirby Lumber Company (P) issued its own bonds for $12,126,800, for which it received their par value. Later that year it purchased some of those bonds in the open market for less than par value, the difference in price being $137,521.30. The government (D) sought to tax this difference as income to Kirby (P).

■ **ISSUE**

Does a company realize income if it purchases and retires bonds at less than face value?

■ **DECISION AND RATIONALE**

(Holmes, J.) Yes. If a corporation purchases and retires any bonds at a price less than the issuing price or face value, the excess of the issuing price or face value over the purchase price is a gain or income for the taxable year. Section 61 of the Internal Revenue Code provides that gross income "means all income from whatever source derived." If these words are taken in their popular meaning, Kirby (P) had realized an accession to income. Reversed.

Analysis:

A discharge of indebtedness is gross income within the meaning of the Code. When Kirby (P) issued bonds, it essentially took out a loan. The company received and used funds, but realized no income because there was a legal obligation to repay the bondholders. When Kirby (P) purchased the bonds for less than face value, they essentially paid off a loan for less than the loan amount. Thus, Kirby realized income on the difference. This case was decided under the catch-all provision of § 61(a), but sub-section (a)(12) now codifies the rule and expressly provides that gross income includes the discharge of indebtedness. There are, however, several exceptions to the inclusion of *Kirby*-type income: (1) when the discharge occurs in bankruptcy; (2) when the discharge occurs while the taxpayer is insolvent, but only to the extent of the insolvency; (3) when the discharge is of a qualified farm debt;

(4) when the debt relates to business property; (5) when the debt arises out of a purchase directly from the creditor, i.e., purchase-money debts; and (6) when the discharge is a "gift" under § 102.

■ **CASE VOCABULARY**

CORPORATE BONDS: Written instruments, usually negotiable, that evidence a company's promise to pay a fixed amount at a future time, usually with intermittent interest payments.

Zarin v. Commissioner

(*Taxpayer*) v. (*Internal Revenue Commissioner*)

916 F.2d 110 (3d Cir. 1990)

THE SETTLEMENT FOR LESS THAN FACE VALUE OF A DEBT DISPUTED IN GOOD FAITH IS NOT GROSS INCOME TO THE OBLIGOR

■ **INSTANT FACTS** A taxpayer owed to a casino nearly $3.5 million, a debt that was unenforceable under state law, but which he settled for $500,000; the government sought to tax the difference as income from the discharge of indebtedness.

■ **BLACK LETTER RULE** An unenforceable obligation is not "indebtedness" within the meaning of the Code.

■ **PROCEDURAL BASIS**

Appeal to the Third Circuit, reversing the decision of the Tax Court, which held that the taxpayer recognized income from the discharge of indebtedness resulting from his gambling activities.

■ **FACTS**

David Zarin (P) incurred a gambling debt of $3,435,000 owed to Resorts International Hotel (Resorts). Resorts facilitated Zarin's (P) gambling activities by offering him a credit line in June 1978. As a result of its investigation, the State of New Jersey issued an order making further extensions of credit to Zarin (P) illegal. Nevertheless, Resorts continued to grant Zarin (P) credit through two procedures later found to be illegal. Zarin (P) began to lose, and became heavily indebted to Resorts. Although Zarin (P) indicated he would pay the obligations, Resorts filed an action in state court. Zarin (P) denied liability on the ground that the debt was unenforceable under New Jersey gaming regulations. The parties settled out of court for $500,000. The Commissioner determined deficiencies in Zarin's federal income taxes, arguing that Zarin recognized $2,935,000 of income from the discharge of indebtedness on the ground that Zarin owed $3,435,000 but paid only $500,000. The Tax Court agreed, and held for the Commissioner.

■ **ISSUE**

Does a taxpayer recognize income from the discharge of indebtedness when he settles an unenforceable debt for less than the contested amount?

■ **DECISION AND RATIONALE**

(Cowen, Cir. J.) No. Gross income does not include the settlement of an unenforceable obligation for less than the total amount of the obligation. The Commissioner's (D) position is flawed for two reasons. Section 61(a)(12) expressly includes in the definition of gross income any "income from the discharge of indebtedness." Section 108(d)(1) defines the term indebtedness. That section provides that indebtedness means any indebtedness "(A) for which the taxpayer is liable, or (B) subject to which the taxpayer holds property." Neither of these definitions is applicable here. Under New Jersey law, it is clear that the debt owed to Resorts was unenforceable. Therefore, it was not a debt for which Zarin (P) was liable. Furthermore, Zarin did not have a debt subject to which he held property. The debt arose out of his acquisition of gambling chips. These chips were not property because Zarin (P) could do nothing more with the chips than gamble and purchase services at the casino. They had no other economic benefit. Instead, the chips are best characterized as an accounting mechanism. New Jersey law supports this view, for it provides that gambling chips are merely the evidence of indebtedness. Thus, the chips were not property within the meaning of Section 108(d)(1). The second reason why the Commissioner's position is flawed is that we believe the transaction should be viewed as a disputed debt or contested liability, rather than as a canceled debt,. Under the contested liability doctrine, if a taxpayer, in good faith, disputes the amount of a debt, a subsequent settlement of the dispute is treated as the actual amount of the debt for tax purposes. The excess of the original debt over the settled amount is ignored for tax purposes. We adopt this view. We also reject the Commissioner's argument that the contested liability doctrine does not apply here. Its is true that the contested liability doctrine applies only when the debt is for an amount which cannot be determined, i.e., an unliquidated debt. We believe, however, that Zarin's (P) debt was unliquidated. The settlement itself shows that the parties attached a value to the debt that was lower than face value. In other words, the parties agreed that Zarin's (P) acquisition of the chips was worth less than $3.4 million, but failed to agree on the exact amount. The transaction between Zarin (P) and resorts can best be characterized as a disputed debt. Zarin (P) owed an unenforceable debt of $3,435,000 to Resorts. After disputing this obligation, the parties settled for $500,000. That settlement fixed the amount of the loss and the amount of the debt for tax purposes. Since Zarin (P) paid the $500,000, he has no adverse tax consequences. Reversed.

■ DISSENT

(Stapleton, Cir. J.) I respectfully dissent. The *only* reason Zarin (P) did not have to report the $3.4 million credit advancement as gross income was that he had an offsetting obligation to pay. When Resorts released Zarin (P) of his obligation he recognized gross income under *United States v. Kirby Lumber Co.* [Supreme Court holds that the discharge of indebtedness is gross income]. This case should turn on the treatment the debt is given by the parties. For present purposes, it will suffice to say that where something that would otherwise be includable in gross income is received on credit in a purchase money transaction, there should be no recognition of gross income where the debtor continued to recognize an obligation to repay. But once the debtor no longer recognizes the obligation, he has recognized gross income.

Analysis:

The discharge of a legally unenforceable debt is not gross income. But there are many questions posed by the court's holding here. The court relies on state law to determine federal tax consequences, and in doing so it ignores the economic reality of the situation, as the dissent points out. The court holds that under the definition provided in § 108, Zarin's (P) debt is not "indebtedness" within the meaning of the code, but the problem with relying on § 108 is that the definition provided therein expressly applies only to that section. Furthermore, even if the § 108 definition were applicable, that would mean that Zarin (P) would have no tax liability, regardless of the settlement. The court also bases its decision on the contested liability doctrine, but the doctrine is only applicable when the amount of the liability cannot be ascertained. The court strains to apply the doctrine, holding that the settlement was proof that the parties attached a different value to the debt, thus the actual value could not be determined.

Diedrich v. Commissioner

(Donor Taxpayer) v. *(IRS)*

457 U.S. 191, 102 S.Ct. 2414 (1982)

GROSS INCOME INCLUDES INCOME FROM WHATEVER SOURCE DERIVED, INCLUDING GIFT TAXES PAID BY A DONEE THAT EXCEED THE ADJUSTED BASIS OF THE PROPERTY

■ **INSTANT FACTS** Donor parents, who gave shares of stock to donee children on condition that children pay gift tax, realized taxable income to the extent the tax paid exceeded the donors' adjusted basis.

■ **BLACK LETTER RULE** A donor who makes a gift of property on condition that the donee pay the resulting gift tax receives taxable income to the extent that the gift tax paid by the donee exceeds the donor's adjusted basis in the property transferred.

■ **PROCEDURAL BASIS**

Certiorari granted by United States Supreme Court to resolve conflict in circuit court of appeals concerning issue of what constitutes taxable income.

■ **FACTS**

Mr. and Mrs. Diedrich (P) made gifts of shares of stock to their three children, subject to a condition that the children, as donees, pay the resulting federal and state gift taxes. The donors' basis in the transferred stock was $51,073; and, the gift tax paid by the donee children was $62,992. The Court of Appeals held that the Diedrichs (P) realized income, because their children paid gift taxes on their behalf. [So much for trying to avoid taxes.] The Diedrichs (P) petitioned the United States Supreme Court for review.

■ **ISSUE**

Does a donor who makes a gift of property on condition that the donee pay the resulting gift tax receive taxable income to the extent that the gift tax paid by the donee exceeds the donor's adjusted basis in the property transferred?

■ **DECISION AND RATIONALE**

(Burger, J.) Yes. A donor who makes a gift of property on condition that the donee pay the resulting gift tax receives taxable income to the extent that the gift tax paid by the donee exceeds the donor's adjusted basis in the property transferred. Congress had defined "gross income" as income from whatever source derived, including income from discharge of indebtedness. It is settled that realization of gain need not be in cash derived from a sale of an asset. Gain may occur as a result of exchange of property, payment of the taxpayer's indebtedness, relief from a liability, or other profit realized from the completion of a transaction. When a gift is made, the gift of tax liability falls on the donor. When a donor makes a gift to a donee, a debt to the United States for the amount of the gift tax is incurred by the donor. Those taxes are as much the legal obligation of the donor as the donor's income taxes. Similarly, when a donee agrees to discharge indebtedness in consideration of the gift, the person relieved of the tax liability realizes an economic benefit. In short, the donor realizes an immediate economic benefit by the donee's assumption of the donor's legal obligation to pay the gift tax. The Commissioner (D) has treated these conditional gifts as a discharge of indebtedness through a part gift and part sale of the gift property transferred. The transfer is treated as if the donor sells the property to the donee for less than the fair market value. The sale price is the amount necessary to discharge the gift tax indebtedness; the balance of the value-transferred property is treated as a gift. The gain thus derived by the donor is the amount of the gift tax liability less the donor's adjusted basis in the entire property. Accordingly, income is realized to the extent that the gift tax exceeds the donor's adjusted basis in property.

Analysis:

This case demonstrates that even though a donor attempts to have the donee pay the gift taxes resulting from a gift, the donor realizes an economic benefit, which is treated as a discharge of indebtedness. The income realized is taxable. The Court viewed the matter as part gift and part sale in arriving at its decision. The Court also noted that Congress has structured gift transactions to encourage transfer of property by limiting the tax consequences of a transfer. *See, e.g.,* 26 U.S.C. § 102 (gifts excluded from donee's gross income). However, the Court felt that if Congress wanted to provide a similar exclusion for the conditional gift, thereby encouraging "net gifts," it should do so by way of legislation. The Court thus stood by the mandate of the current law that gross income includes income from whatever source derived.

■ **CASE VOCABULARY**

ADJUSTED BASIS: Refers to certain adjustments, either increases by capital improvements or decreases by depreciation deductions, in the amount of the original basis resulting in an "adjusted basis."

Crane v. Commissioner

(Taxpayer) v. *(IRS)*

331 U.S. 1, 67 S.Ct. 1047 (1947)

TAXPAYER WHO SELLS PROPERTY ENCUMBERED BY A NONRECOURSE MORTGAGE MUST IN-CLUDE THE AMOUNT OF THE MORTGAGE WHEN COMPUTING THE AMOUNT REALIZED ON THE SALE

■ **INSTANT FACTS** Mrs. Crane (P) sold her property subject to a nonrecourse mortgage for $2,500, and realized a gain on the sale in the amount of the mortgage plus the additional consideration.

■ **BLACK LETTER RULE** A taxpayer who acquires depreciable property subject to an unassumed mortgage and later sells it still so encumbered and for additional consideration realizes a taxable gain on the sale in the amount of the mortgage plus any equity.

■ **PROCEDURAL BASIS**

Review by United States Supreme Court from decision of Court of Appeals, which reversed decision of Tax Court, in action challenging tax deficiency.

■ **FACTS**

Mrs. Crane (P) inherited land and an apartment building from her husband. It was subject to a nonrecourse mortgage (one that she was not personally liable to repay), with an unpaid balance of $262,042.50. The property was appraised at exactly the same value. For over six years, Crane (P) claimed depreciation deductions for the building. Thereafter, she transferred the property, still subject to the mortgage, to a third party for the sum of $2,500. When Crane (P) reported this transaction for income tax purposes, she claimed that the property consisted only of the equity, i.e., the $2,500. Thus, she contended that the amount realized on the sale was $2,500 and her basis was zero. The Commissioner (D) argued that the property was not limited to the equity interest, and that the amount of the mortgage should be included. After doing its own computations, the Commissioner (D) claimed that the gain from the sale of the property was $23,502.60. [Crane probably wishes her husband had gotten rid of thing before he died.]

■ **ISSUE**

Does a taxpayer who acquires depreciably property subject to an unassumed mortgage and later sells it still so encumbered realize a taxable gain on the amount of the mortgage plus any equity?

■ **DECISION AND RATIONALE**

(Vinson, J.) Yes. We hold that a taxpayer who acquires depreciably property subject to an unassumed mortgage and later sells it still so encumbered and for additional consideration realizes a taxable gain on the sale in the amount of the mortgage plus any equity. Section 1001(a) defines the gain from "the sale or other disposition of property" as "the excess of the amount realized therefrom over the adjusted basis provided in section [1011(a)] ..." The amount realized from the sale or other disposition of property is defined as "the sum of any money received plus the fair market value of the property (other than money) received." (§ 1001(b)). The adjusted basis for determining the gain or loss from the sale or other disposition of property is declared to be "the basis determined under subsection (a), adjusted ... for exhaustion, wear and tear, obsolescence, amortization ... to the extent allowed (but not less than the amount allowable) ..." (§ 1016). The basis of the property was acquired by devise or by the decedent's estate from the decedent, is the "the fair market value of such property at the time of such acquisition." (§ 1014). [Did you get all that?] We must first determine the unadjusted basis of the property under § 1014. The term "property," we conclude, means the land and building themselves, undiminished by the mortgage. Thus, the applicable provisions of the Act expressly preclude an equity basis. The proper basis under § 1014 is the value of the property, undiminished by mortgages thereon. Next we must determine what adjustments are required under § 1016. This section provides that "proper adjustment in respect of the property shall in all cases be made ... for exhaustion, wear and tear ... to the extent allowed (but not less than the amount allowable.)" We agree that the apartment house was property of a kind subject to physical exhaustion, and that the taxpayer would have been entitled to a depreciation allowance. Crane (P) urges to the contrary that she was not entitled to depreciation deductions, because the law allows them only to one who actually bears the capital loss, and here the loss was not hers but the mortgagee's. We disagree with such a contention. We finally must determine the "amount realized" on the sale. We think that a mortgagor, not personally liable on the debt, who sells the property subject to the mortgage and for additional consideration, realizes a benefit in the amount of the mortgage as well as the boot. Thus, we conclude that the Commissioner (D) was right in determining that Crane (P) realized $257,500 on the sale of the property. Affirmed.

■ DISSENT

(Jackson, J.) We do not believe that it was not within the province of the Tax Court to find that Crane (P) received an equity which at that time had a zero value. The taxpayer never became personally liable for the debt, and hence when she sold she was released from no debt. The mortgage debt was simply a subtraction from the value of what she did receive, and from what she sold. The subtraction left her nothing when she acquired it and a small margin when she sold it. She acquired a property right equivalent to an equity of redemption and sold the same thing. It was the "property" bought and sold as the Tax Court considered it to be under the Revenue Laws. We would reverse the Court of Appeals and sustain the decision of the Tax Court.

Analysis:

The main holding of this case concerns its ruling on the "amount realized" on the sale. Crane's (P) goal was to not have to include the amount of the mortgage in computing the amount realized on the sale. Unfortunately for Crane (P), the Court held that she must include the amount of the mortgage in computing the gains. Note that in this case, the value of the property was equal to the amount of the nonrecourse mortgage. In the case that follows, *Commissioner v. Tufts*, the issue is whether the rule in *Crane* applies when the property sold has a fair market value that is less than the unpaid balance on a nonrecourse mortgage. The Court held that it did, and that the taxpayer had realized an amount equal to the unpaid mortgage balance.

■ CASE VOCABULARY

BOOT: The additional money or property in a transaction that is subject to tax in an otherwise tax-free exchange.

PENDENTE LITE: Latin for, "while the action is pending."

RECEIVER: One appointed by a court to oversee the collection and payment of monies of a company in order to preserve the assets.

Commissioner v. Tufts

(Commissioner of Internal Revenue) v. *(Taxpayer)*
461 U.S. 300, 103 S.Ct. 1826 (1983)

FOR DETERMINING THE GAIN REALIZED FROM DEALINGS IN PROPERTY, NONRECOURSE DEBTS WILL BE TREATED AS TRUE DEBTS FOR TAX PURPOSES

■ **INSTANT FACTS** A partnership reported a loss on the sale of property encumbered by a nonrecourse mortgage equal to the excess of the balance on the mortgage over the fair market value of the property, an amount of $55,740.

■ **BLACK LETTER RULE** When a party transfers property encumbered by a nonrecourse mortgage with an unpaid balance that exceeds the fair market value of the property, the transferor has realized, for tax liability puposes, an amount equal to the unpaid mortgage balance.

■ **PROCEDURAL BASIS**

Appeal to the United States Supreme Court, challenging the Court of Appeals' reversal of the Tax Court's decision to uphold the deficiencies against the taxpayers.

■ **FACTS**

Mr. Tufts (P) was the member of a general partnership formed in 1970 for the purpose of constructing an apartment complex. The partnership took out a $1,851,500 nonrecourse mortgage loan. The partnership's claimed adjusted basis in the property in 1972 was $1,455,740. The partnership became unable to make the payments due on the mortgage. Each partner sold his interest to a third party, who assumed the mortgage. The fair market value of the property on the date of transfer did not exceed $1,400,000. Each partner reported the sale on his income tax return and indicated a loss to the partnership of $55,740. The Commissioner (D) determined that the sale resulted in a partnership gain of approximately $400,000 based on the theory that the partnership had realized the full amount of the nonrecourse debt. The United States Tax Court agreed with the Commissioner (D), but the Court of Appeals reversed.

■ **ISSUE**

If the unpaid amount of a nonrecourse mortgage exceeds the fair market value of property sold, does the seller realize an amount equal to the unpaid mortgage balance?

■ **DECISION AND RATIONALE**

(Blackmun, J.) Yes. When a party transfers property encumbered by a nonrecourse mortgage with an unpaid balance that exceeds the fair market value of the property, the transferor has realized, for tax liability purposes, an amount equal to the unpaid mortgage balance. In *Crane v. Commissioner* this Court held that a taxpayer who sells property encumbered by a nonrecourse mortgage must include the unpaid balance of the mortgage in the computation of the amount realized on the sale. But the Court expressly withheld a determination of whether that rule would apply where the fair market value of the property transferred was less than the balance on the unpaid mortgage. We read *Crane* as an approval of the Commissioner's (D) decision to treat nonrecourse mortgages in this context as a true loan, and not merely resting on the theory of economic benefit. Because no difference between recourse and nonrecourse obligations is recognized in calculating basis, *Crane* teaches that the Commissioner may ignore the nonrecourse nature of the obligation in determining the amount realized upon disposition of the property. This treatment balances the fact that the mortgagor may exclude the amount of the loan from gross income. A contrary rule would give the mortgagor untaxed income at the time the loan is extended, in addition to giving him an increase in the basis of the property. Moreover, this treatment avoids the situation where the taxpayer may claim a loss that he has not suffered, as was done here. In this case it was the bank who was at risk when the market value of the property fell below the unpaid balance on the mortgage. The partners lost nothing, yet they reported a tax loss of over $55,000. We, therefore hold that the Commissioner (D) properly required the partners to include among the assets realized the outstanding amount of the obligation. Reversed.

■ CONCURRENCE

(O'Connor, J.) I concur with the Court. Were we writing on a dean slate except for the *Crane* decision, I would take a different approach. Instead of treating a nonrecourse debt as a true loan, I would bifurcate the transaction and treat the acquisition and sale of the property separate from the arrangement and retirement of the loan. The first part of the analysis would give the taxpayer a basis in the property equal to the purchase price or the fair market value of the property on the date of acquisition. Upon disposition of the property the taxpayer would realize a gain or loss that is dependent on the fate of the property. In the separate borrowing transaction the taxpayer received cash from the mortgagee, at which time he need not recognize income. If he later surrenders the property when it is worth less than the unpaid balance on the loan, we have the classic situation of cancellation of indebtedness, requiring the taxpayer to recognize income in the amount of the difference between the proceeds of the loan and the value of the property. The reason we should treat the two aspects of the transaction separately is that different forms of income carry with them different tax consequences. The logic of this approach notwithstanding, I do not agree it should be adopted judicially in light of *Crane* and countless lower court cases that have applied the rule announced by the Court today.

Analysis:

This case addresses the issue the Court left open in *Crane*, whether the rule adopted in that case also applies when the property sold has a fair market value that is less than the unpaid balance on a mortgage secured by the transferred property. The Court here holds that it does. The lesson to be taken from this case lies in the Court's reading of *Crane*. In the Court's view, *Crane* established the proposition that nonrecourse mortgages should be treated as true loans for tax purposes. The Court reasons that treating a nonrecourse loan any differently would give the taxpayer untaxed income upon receiving the loan proceeds and would give the taxpayer an increased basis. The policy behind the Court's holding is sound, but not grounded in "real-world" economics. To solve the inconsistency, Justice O'Connor's concurring opinion suggests treating the transaction in two parts: a loan, and a disposition of property. This treatment makes sense, but unfortunately it was not adopted, probably because the Court felt bound to follow *Crane*.

Gilbert v. Commissioner

(*Embezzling Taxpayer*) v. (*IRS*)

552 F.2d 478 (2d Cir.1977)

COURT HOLDS THAT CONSENSUAL RECOGNITION OF AN OBLIGATION TO REPAY IN AN EMBEZ-ZLEMENT CASE EXISTS SO THAT TAXPAYER DOES NOT REALIZE INCOME ON THE WITHDRAWN FUNDS

■ **INSTANT FACTS** Gilbert (P) plead guilty to embezzling funds, and he appealed tax court's decision that he realized income from the unauthorized withdrawal of corporate funds.

■ **BLACK LETTER RULE** Where a taxpayer withdraws funds from a corporation which he fully intends to repay, and which he expects with reasonable certainty he will be able to repay, where he believes that his withdrawals will be approved by the corporation, and where he makes a prompt assignment of assets sufficient to secure the amount owed, he does not realize income on the withdrawals.

■ **PROCEDURAL BASIS**

Appeal from decision by tax court in action challenging tax deficiency.

■ **FACTS**

Mr. Gilbert (P) was found by the tax court to have realized taxable income on certain unauthorized withdrawals of corporate funds made by him. He was president, principal stockholder and a director of E.L. Bruce Company, Inc. (Bruce Co.). Gilbert (P) acquired on margin a substantial ownership of stock in another company, intending to ultimately bring about a merger of the two companies, which would have benefited Bruce Co. He convinced others, including Bruce Co., to purchase the stock as well, so that the other company was 56 % controlled by Gilbert (P) and Bruce Co. When the stock market declined, he was called upon to furnish additional margin [this means money]. He did not have sufficient cash of his own, so he used Bruce Co. funds [to the tune of $1,958,0000] to supply the necessary margin. Gilbert (P) intended to repay the money, and he promptly informed several other corporate officers and directors of the withdrawals. He went to the attorneys for Bruce Co. and they initiated negotiations to sell the shares of the other company to Ruberoid Co. Gilbert (P) also executed promissory notes to Bruce Co., secured by an assignment of most of his property, with the net value of the assets assigned substantially exceeding the amount Gilbert (P) owed. Thereafter, Bruce Co.'s board of directors refused to ratify Gilbert's (P) unauthorized withdrawals. The board was notified that Ruberoid Co. had rejected the price offered for the sale of the other company's stock. Thereupon, the Bruce Co. board obtained Gilbert's (P) resignation. The IRS filed tax liens against Gilbert (P). Several years later, Gilbert (P) pled guilty of unlawfully withdrawing the funds from Bruce Co. The tax court determined that Gilbert (P) realized income when he made the unauthorized withdrawals of funds from Bruce Co., and that his efforts at restitution did not entitle him to any offset against this income. Gilbert (P) appealed.

■ **ISSUE**

Does a taxpayer realize income for tax purposes when he makes an illegal and unauthorized withdrawal of funds from a corporation?

■ **DECISION AND RATIONALE**

(Lumbard, J.) No. As long as there is consensual recognition of the obligation to repay, there is no realized income on the withdrawals. In *James v. United States*, the Supreme Court established that embezzled funds could constitute taxable income to the embezzler. It said, "When a taxpayer acquires earnings, lawfully or unlawfully, without the consensual recognition, express or implied, of an obligation to repay and without restriction as to their disposition, 'he has received income which he is required to return, even though it may still be claimed that he is not entitled to the money, and even though he may still be adjudged liable to restore its equivalent.' . . ." In *Buff v. Commissioner*, the court held that if an embezzler repays the money during the same taxable year, he would not be taxed. The Commissioner (D) contends that there can never be "consensual recognition . . . of an obligation to repay" in an embezzlement case. This however is not a typical embezzlement case. For instance, when Gilbert (P) withdrew the corporate funds, he recognized his obligation to repay and intended to do so. The funds were to be used not only for his benefit but also for the benefit of Bruce Co. He immediately informed several officers and directors and when he executed the assignment of his assets, the net market value of the assets was substantially more than the amount owed. [But Gilbert (P) flew to Brazil for a few months, the assets took a dive, and Bruce Co. was unable to collect its money.] We therefore conclude that where a taxpayer withdraws funds from a corporation which he fully intends to repay and which he expects with reasonable certainty he will be able to repay, where he believes that his withdrawals will be approved by the corporation, where he makes a prompt assignment of assets sufficient to secure the amount owed, he does not realize income on the withdrawals under the *James* test. When Gilbert (P) acquired the money, there was an express consensual recognition of his obligation to repay. Reversed.

Analysis:

The court was able to distinguish the facts of this case from *James* and *Buff v. Commissioner* because Gilbert (P) recognized his obligation and intended to repay; the funds withdrawn benefited Bruce Co., "meeting the margin call was necessary to maintain the possible merger," Gilbert (P) expected his decision to be ratified, he did not intend to retain the funds, he advised the officers and directors of the withdrawals, he disclosed his actions to the law firm, and he signed promissory notes secured by most of his assets. The court concluded that, based upon these facts, the *James* test had not been met. Accordingly, Gilbert (P) did not realize income on the withdrawals.

■ CASE VOCABULARY

MARGIN CALL: Where a securities broker finances the purchase of securities and then demands that the customer pay money or stock as collateral for the purchase.

CHAPTER THREE

Problems of Timing

Eisner v. Macomber

Instant Facts: A shareholder who received a stock dividend was taxed on the fair market value of the stock even though the dividend did not increase the shareholder's wealth or provide the shareholder with any cash.

Black Letter Rule: Stock dividends are not taxable.

Helvering v. Bruun

Instant Facts: The government sought to tax a landlord who regains possession of his property after his tenant made improvements that increased the value of the land by $51,434.25.

Black Letter Rule: A landlord realizes income upon regaining possession of land with an increased value due to improvements made by a tenant.

Woodsam Associates, Inc. v. Commissioner

Instant Facts: The debtor on a nonrecourse mortgage sought to avoid paying a tax on the difference between her basis in the property and the amount owing upon foreclosure by claiming that she disposed of the property when she executed a mortgage for an amount greater than her basis in the property.

Black Letter Rule: The basis for determining gain or loss upon the sale or other disposition of property is not increased, when subsequent to acquiring the property, the owner executes a nonrecourse mortgage in an amount greater than her adjusted basis.

Cottage Savings Association v. Commissioner

Instant Facts: A savings and loan institution exchanged participation interests in various mortgages with lenders in order to realize tax-deductible losses sustained as a result of a surge in interest rates which caused the mortgages to lose significant value.

Black Letter Rule: An exchange of similar property is a realizing event so long as the properties carry different legal entitlements.

Burnet v. Logan

Instant Facts: When a shareholder in a mining company sold her stock for cash and the promise of future payments to be based on the amount of ore extracted, the government sought tax the shareholder on the present value of the payments it estimated she would receive.

Black Letter Rule: The gain realized in an open transaction one where the consideration received has no ascertainable fair market value is not recognized until the taxpayer has ascertainably received an amount over her basis in the property transferred.

Amend v. Commissioner

Instant Facts: The government sought to tax a farmer on the gain from the sale of wheat in the year the contract for sale was executed and the wheat was delivered, even though the farmer had contracted for and could not receive payment until the following year.

Black Letter Rule: The doctrine of constructive receipt does not apply where the seller of property receives as consideration from the buyer only a promise to pay in the following year so long as the sale was bona fide and conducted at arm's-length.

Pulsifer v. Commissioner

Instant Facts: The government sought to tax three minor children on their share of lottery proceeds, even though their father did not apply for release of the funds.

Black Letter Rule: An individual on the cash receipts and disbursements method of accounting is currently taxable on the economic and financial benefit derived from the absolute right to income in the form of a fund which has been irrevocably set aside for him in trust and is beyond the reach of the creditors.

Minor v. United States

Instant Facts: The government sought to tax a physician on amounts paid into a fund by his employer pursuant to a deferred compensation plan whereby the physician and his employer agreed the physician would be paid 10 percent of his fees at the time the services were rendered and the rest would be deferred for payment at a later date.

Black Letter Rule: Deferred compensation is not taxable to the employee in the year services are rendered if the compensation plan is unfunded and unsecured and the employee faces a substantial risk of forfeiture.

Cramer v. Commissioner

Instant Facts: Seeking capital gains treatment of stock options granted to them, three corporate officers included in their gross income the value of the options, which they claimed had no value, in contravention of Treasury Regulations in place at the time.

Black Letter Rule: Options to purchase non-publicly traded stock which are granted to corporate employees with vesting and transfer restrictions have no readily ascertainable market value under § 83(e).

United States v. Davis

Instant Facts: The government sought to tax a husband on the appreciated value of stock he transferred to his wife pursuant to their divorce.

Black Letter Rule: The transfer of appreciated property between spouses pursuant to a separation or divorce must be taxed as a gain to the transferor spouse in an amount equal to the difference between the fair market value of the property and his or her basis therein.

Farid-Es-Sultaneh v. Commissioner

Instant Facts: A taxpayer sought to have her basis in corporate stock determined by the value of the shares when she acquired them in exchange for the release of marital rights pursuant to an antenuptial agreement.

Black Letter Rule: A transfer which should be classed as a gift under the gift tax law is not necessarily to be treated as a gift income-tax-wise.

Diez–Arguelles v. Commissioner

Instant Facts: A married couple sought to deduct as a short-term capital loss child support payments that were not made by the wife's former husband.

Black Letter Rule: Amounts due for child support are not deductible under § 186 as nonbusiness bad debts.

Georgia School–Book Depository v. Commissioner

Instant Facts: An accrual-method taxpayer failed to include in its gross income earned commissions which remained currently unpaid by the appropriate state agency, due to a lack of funds.

Black Letter Rule: A taxpayer has a reasonable basis for not accruing earned income only when there is an unresolved and allegedly intervening right which makes receipt of the income contingent or the insolvency of the debtor makes payment improbable.

American Automobile Association v. United States

Instant Facts: The government sought to challenge an automobile club's accounting methods, arguing that the club could not postpone the inclusion in gross income of prepaid membership dues.

Black Letter Rule: The government may reject a taxpayer's accounting method and require the taxpayer to include in gross income for the current year prepaid dues received from services to be rendered in a subsequent year.

Westpac Pacific Food v. Commissioner

Instant Facts: A grocery store partnership received volume discounts on purchases in the form of cash advances that would have to be repaid if the full volume was not purchased, and the IRS deemed the advances "gross income"; the taxpayer appealed.

Black Letter Rule: Cash advances in exchange for volume purchase commitments, subject to pro rata repayment if the volume commitments are not met, are not gross income when received.

Eisner v. Macomber

(*Internal Revenue Commissioner*) v. (*Taxpayer Who Received Stock Dividend*)

252 U.S. 189, 40 S.Ct. 189 (1920)

GAINS MUST BE REALIZED BEFORE THEY ARE TAXED

■ **INSTANT FACTS** A shareholder who received a stock dividend was taxed on the fair market value of the stock even though the dividend did not increase the shareholder's wealth or provide the shareholder with any cash.

■ **BLACK LETTER RULE** Stock dividends are not taxable.

■ **PROCEDURAL BASIS**

Not Provided.

■ **FACTS**

In 1926 the Standard Oil Company of California declared a 50 percent stock dividend, giving the company's shareholders one extra share with a par value of $100 for every two shares they owned. Myrtle Macomber (P), who owned 2,200 shares with a par value of $100 at the time the dividend was announced, received an extra 1,100 shares, each also with a par value of $100. Before the stock dividend, Mrs. Macomber's (P) 2,200 shares had a fair market value of $360 to $382 and, after the dividend, the 3,300 shares had a value of $234 to $268. The drop in market value caused no significant change to Mrs. Macomber (P) wealth. The government sought to tax Mrs. Macomber (P) for the par value of the shares transferred to her as part of the dividend after the income tax became effective.

■ **ISSUE**

May Congress constitutionally tax stock dividends received by a shareholder?

■ **DECISION AND RATIONALE**

(Pitney, J.) No. Stock dividends are not taxable. The Sixteenth Amendement gives Congress the "power to lay and collect taxes on *incomes* from whatever source derived without apportionment...." The Amendment did not alter the apportionment requirement when Congress elects to tax property. Therefore, it becomes essential to determine the meaning of the word "income," as it is used in the Amendment. The congressional adoption of a particular definition does not settle the issue, for Congress' power to legislate derives from the Constitution. The difference between "capital" and "income" has been likened to the relationship between a tree and its fruit—one flows from the other. This Court has defined the term income to mean "the gain derived from capital, labor or both, including gains through a sale or conversion of capital assets." In this case the modifying phrase "derived from capital" is significant. A gain derived from capital is not a gain accruing to capital nor an increase or growth in the value of capital; rather, it is a profit or something of exchangeable value that proceeds from the capital and is received by the taxpayer. We do not believe that a stock dividend fits such a definition of income. The shareholder has no right to withdraw any part of either capital or profits from the corporation. In fact the shareholder's interest in the assets of the corporation is only indirect, meaning that he has full title to the corporation but not to any particular asset or group of assets. When a corporation realizes profits, it accounts for them as a liability to the shareholder. However, shareholders have a right to enjoy their share in those profits only when management decides to declare a cash dividend. A stock dividend, on the other hand, only means that the corporation has capitalized the profits. The essential and controlling fact is that the stockholder receives nothing for his separate use upon the announcement of a stock dividend. The stock dividend is only evidence of the corporation's accumulation of profits, showing that the stockholder has not realized any income. Looking at the substance of the relationship between the shareholder and the corporation and the substance of the transaction, Mrs. Macomber (P) received nothing within the Amendment's meaning of the word income. We reject the government's argument that Mrs. Macomber should be taxed because the dividend has made her richer. The problem with this view is that the extent of the enrichment would depend on how long the shareholder held the stock. More importantly, an increase in the value of capital investment is not income in any proper meaning of the term. The Government (D) claims that there is no difference between receiving a stock dividend and receiving a cash dividend to purchase more shares. We believe the difference is that the shareholder gets to do what she wants with the cash dividend. We also find unpersuasive the government's argument that the government really seeks to tax the stockholder's share of the undivided profits accumulated by the corporation. If that were true, it means that the government would be seeking to tax property, as opposed to income. A tax on property is a tax that must be apportioned amongst the several States. Affirmed.

■ **DISSENT**

(Holmes, J.) The word income should be read according to its most common understanding, especially since it is the public who adopts constitutional amendments. The Sixteenth Amendment justifies the tax.

■ **DISSENT**

(Brandeis, J.) Corporations have at their disposal two methods for, paradoxically, keeping accumulated profits for corporate purposes and distributing to shareholders those same profits. The method employed here was an increase in capital stock paid up with the profits and distributed pro rata amongst the shareholders. If Mrs. Macomber (P) wanted the money she could simply sell the new shares. Under the other method, the corporation arranges to issue new stock to be offered to the shareholders and gives the shareholder the money to pay for that stock, which is priced below its fair market value to ensure that the shareholders will subscribe for their pro rata share. If the shareholder wants the money he sells the right to a third party to purchase shares priced below the fair market value. Both these methods were in place prior to the adoption of the Amendment and both are thought to be equal. However, under the Courts holding the shareholder under the first method is not taxed, while the shareholder who takes the corporation's money to buy new stock is taxed. If the substance of the transactions is the same, a difference in taxation cannot flow from the difference in their form.

Analysis:

It remains true today that stock dividends are non-taxable. That ruling is now codified in § 305(a), subject to certain limitations set forth in § 305(b). However, the reason stock dividends remain non-taxable has little to do with the Court's pronouncement as to the constitutionality of taxing such dividends. The Court's ruling here was based on its belief that an increment in the value of capital is not income within the Sixteenth Amendment. Basically, the Court's holding evokes an awareness that income should (not must) be realized before it is taxed. The government today does not, as a general matter, tax unrealized gains in property. However, the reason for withholding an imposition of tax until realization has nothing to do with the Sixteenth Amendment. Rather, the realization requirement is based on notions of convenience and fairness.

■ **CASE VOCABULARY**

STOCK DIVIDEND: A dividend which a corporation pays by issuing more shares to the stockholders.

Helvering v. Bruun

(Commissioner of Internal Revenue) v. *(Landlord Who Took Possession of Buildings Erected by Tenant)*

309 U.S. 461, 60 S.Ct. 631 (1940)

AN INCREASE IN THE VALUE OF A CAPITAL ASSET MAY BE TAXED AS REALIZED INCOME

■ **INSTANT FACTS** The government sought to tax a landlord who regains possession of his property after his tenant made improvements that increased the value of the land by $51,434.25.

■ **BLACK LETTER RULE** A landlord realizes income upon regaining possession of land with an increased value due to improvements made by a tenant.

■ PROCEDURAL BASIS

Certiorari to the United States Supreme Court to review the decisions of the Circuit Court of Appeals and Board of Tax Appeals, both of which overruled the Commissioner's determination that the taxpayer realized a gain upon repossessing his land.

■ FACTS

Bruun (P) leased an improved lot for a term of 99 years. In accordance with lease provisions which permitting him to do so, the tenant razed the building existing on Bruun's (P) lot and erected a new building. A few years thereafter, Bruun (P) canceled the lease for default in payment and regained possession. Both the Commissioner (D) and Brunn (P) stipulated that the original building had an adjusted basis of $12,811.43 and that the new building had a fair market value of $64,245.68. The Commissioner determined that the difference between these two figures gave Brunn (P) a realized gain of $51,434.25. The Board of Tax Appeals overruled the Commissioner's finding and the Court of Appeals affirmed the Board.

■ ISSUE

Does a landlord realize a gain upon regaining possession of land with an increased value due to improvements made by a tenant?

■ DECISION AND RATIONALE

(Roberts, J.) Yes. A landlord realizes income upon regaining possession of land with an increased value due to improvements made by a tenant. Bruun (P) argues that the improvements made were not a gain realized upon his retaking of possession, because the building erected became part of and inseparable from his capital asset—the realty; that the improvements cannot be separately valued or treated as received in exchange for the old building; and that the improvements made by his tenant have the same character as if he would have made them. Relying heavily on *Eisner v. Macomber* [Supreme Court holds that a stock dividend is merely an increase in the value of a capital assets, and therfore, not income within the meaning of the Sixteenth Amendment] Bruun's (P) argument is, essentially, that the economic gain represented by the increased value to his land is not gain derived from capital or realized within the meaning of the Sixteenth Amendment. We disagree. The expression found in *Eisner* to the effect that the gain must be something of exchangeable value, separately disposable from the capital asset is inapposite. The Court in *Eisner* was clarifying the distinction between an ordinary dividend and a stock dividend to show that a stock dividend is inseparable from and does not change a shareholder's interest in the corporation. It is well settled that the realization of gain need not be in cash derived from the sale of an asset. The fact that the gain is a portion of the value of property received by the taxpayer does not negate its realization. Thus, it was not a necessary condition of realization that Bruun (P) be able to sever the building from his original capital. If that were the case, exchanges of property could never be taxed. Reversed.

Analysis:

The point of this case is that nothing (including the Constitution) prevents an increase in the value of an asset from being taxed as a gain. In other words, the concept of realization does not define income or limit what economic gains may be taxed. Rather, realization goes to the issue of *when* income can be taxed. The Court holds that the value added to a capital asset need not be separable from that asset in order to be taxed. This conclusion seems a bit at odds with *Eisner*. The *Bruun* Court does attempt to distinguish *Eisner* on this point by stating that the *Eisner* Court wrote of "separation" not as a requirement for realization, but as a way to differentiate stock and cash dividends. Whether or not *Bruun* implicitly overrules *Eisner*, it is clear that the effect of the former is to limit application of the latter. The *Bruun* Court takes the concept of realization out of the definition of income.

Woodsam Associates, Inc. v. Commissioner

(Mortgagor/Taxpayer) v. *(Commissioner of Internal Revenue)*
198 F.2d 357 (2d Cir. 1952)

THE EXECUTION OF A NONRECOURSE MORTGAGE IS NOT A REALIZING EVENT

■ **INSTANT FACTS** The debtor on a nonrecourse mortgage sought to avoid paying a tax on the difference between her basis in the property and the amount owing upon foreclosure by claiming that she disposed of the property when she executed a mortgage for an amount greater than her basis in the property.

■ **BLACK LETTER RULE** The basis for determining gain or loss upon the sale or other disposition of property is not increased, when subsequent to acquiring the property, the owner executes a nonrecourse mortgage in an amount greater than her adjusted basis.

■ **PROCEDURAL BASIS**

Appeal to the Second Circuit Court of Appeals to review the decision of the Tax Court affirming the Commissioner's denial of a refund and determination of a deficiency.

■ **FACTS**

Mrs. Wood (P) owned a parcel of improved land which cost her $296,400. Over the span of nine years Mrs. Wood (P) borrowed nearly $325,000, the loans secured by recourse mortgages on the property. In 1931, Mrs. Wood (P) borrowed an additional $75,000 and executed a consolidated nonrecourse mortgage in the amount of $400,000. In 1943, after the bank had foreclosed on the property, the government sought to tax as a gain to Mrs. Wood (P) the difference between her basis in the property and $381,000, the amount owing on the mortgage. Mrs. Wood (P) sought to avoid the tax by claiming that she realized a gain in 1931, a tax year no longer subject to review, when she executed a nonrecourse mortgage in excess of her basis, and that such gain increased her basis in the property.

■ **ISSUE**

When a taxpayer executes a nonrecourse mortgage on property in excess of the taxpayer's basis in the property, does the taxpayer realize a gain equal to the difference between her basis and the amount of the mortgage, so that her basis in the property is increased by the amount of that "gain"?

■ **DECISION AND RATIONALE**

(Chase, Cir. J.) No. The basis for determining gain or loss upon the sale or other disposition of property is not increased, when subsequent to acquiring the property, the owner executes a nonrecourse mortgage in an amount greater than her adjusted basis. The problem with Mrs. Wood's (P) theory is that it is based on the mistaken premise that she made a taxable disposition of property when she executed the nonrecourse mortgage and freed herself from any personal liability on the mortgage. All Mrs. Wood (P) did was borrow money. She did not dispose of property to create a taxable event which the Code makes a condition precedent to the taxation of a gain. "Disposition," within the meaning of the statute is to get rid of or relinquish anything. Mrs. Wood (P) was at all times the owner of the property. Therefore, realization of a gain was postponed until there was a final disposition, which did not occur until the foreclosure sale. Affirmed.

Analysis:

Mrs. Wood's (P) argument was twofold. First, she claimed that when she executed the $400,000 nonrecourse mortgage, she essentially sold the property for the amount of the mortgage. Upon this sale she recognized a "gain" equal to the difference between the mortgage and her original basis in the property. It is at this point that Mrs. Wood (P) claims her tax was due. Mrs. Wood's argument continues with the assertion that this "gain," (which, coincidentally, was no longer taxable due to the statute of limitations) was simultaneously used to "repurchase" the property, increasing her basis. Thus, upon foreclosure her basis was the amount of the mortgage. If you take a look at the justifications for the realization requirement, however, you will see that they are inapplicable to Mrs. Wood's (P) situation: (1) The appreciation is not hard to value because it is equal to the difference between the basis and amount of the mortgage; (2) she has the cash available to pay for the tax because the bank just loaned her almost $200,000; and (3) she faces no risk of loss because she signed a nonrecourse mortgage.

Cottage Savings Association v. Commissioner

(*Savings & Loan Association*) v. (*Commissioner of Internal Revenue*)

499 U.S. 554, 111 S. Ct. 1503 (1991)

AN EXCHANGE OF TWO PROPERTIES IS A REALIZING EVENT ONLY IF THE TWO PROPERTIES ARE, FROM A LEGAL POINT OF VIEW, MATERIALLY DIFFERENT

■ **INSTANT FACTS** A savings and loan institution exchanged participation interests in various mortgages with lenders in order to realize tax-deductible losses sustained as a result of a surge in interest rates which caused the mortgages to lose significant value.

■ **BLACK LETTER RULE** An exchange of similar property is a realizing event so long as the properties carry different legal entitlements.

■ **PROCEDURAL BASIS**

Writ of certiorari from the United States Supreme Court to review the decision of the Sixth Circuit, which reversed the holding of the Tax Court recognizing a loss when a bank exchange participation in mortgages with another lender.

■ **FACTS**

Cottage Savings Association (Cottage) (P) held several long-term, low-interest mortgages which had depreciated in value due to a surge in interest rates. Bank regulations made it impractical to sell the mortgages and claim loss deductions because the thrifts would have to record the loss on their books, bringing the thrift one step-closer to closure. However, the Federal Home Loan Bank Board (FHLBB) permitted thrifts holding these depreciated mortgages to exchange them with each other without having to record the losses on their books. The mortgages had to be "substantially identical," a characteristic requiring the exchanged mortgages to be equal in ten different areas, including maturity, interest rates and fair market value, et al.. The exchanges had the practical advantage of providing a realizing event to claim loss deductions, but the thrifts would hold virtually the same property. Pursuant to the new regulations, Cottage (P) exchanged "90% participation" in 252 mortgages for "90% participation" in 305 mortgages. The fair market value of each group of mortgages was approximately $4.5 million. The face value of the mortgages relinquished by Cottage (P) was approximately $6.9 million. Accordingly, Cottage (P) claimed a loss deduction of nearly $2.5million. The Commissioner disallowed the deductions.

■ **ISSUE**

If an exchange of properties is to qualify as a realizing event, must the properties have material economic differences?

■ **DECISION AND RATIONALE**

(Marshall, J.) Yes. An exchange of similar property is a realizing event so long as the properties carry legal entitlements that differ in kind or extent. Before a gain or loss in the value of property can be realized, § 1001 of the Internal Revenue Code requires that there be a "sale or other disposition of the property." The issue before us turns on whether the exchange of mortgages constitutes a "disposition of property." First, we find that we must defer to the Commissioner's interpretation, as it is embodied in

Treas. Reg. § 1.1001–1, providing that an exchange of property can be treated as a disposition only if the properties exchanged are "materially different." We find this interpretation supported by case law and congressional intent. However, the more complicated question we are asked to answer is: What constitutes a "material difference" for purposes of § 1001? The Commissioner argues that to determine whether the participation interests were "materially different" we look to the attitude of the parties, the evaluation of the interests by the secondary mortgage market and the views of thrift regulators. Unlike with the previous question, we cannot defer to the Commissioner on this point because he had promulgated no applicable regulation prior to this litigation. Upon examining our prior cases, we find that they stand for the proposition that properties are "materially different" under the Code so long as their respective possessors enjoy legal entitlements that are different in kind or extent. The "material difference" test demands nothing more. The Commissioner's test would require identification of the relevant market, the establishment of whether there is a regulatory agency with a pertinent view and an assessment as to how the parties treat the transaction. The cases belie the Commissioner's stance which would require a subjective test. Moreover, the Commissioner's formulation ill serves the goal of administrative convenience that is at the heart of the realization requirement. Also the Code contains nonrecognition provisions which serve as evidence that, had Congress wanted to provide that the exchange of similar properties would not count as realization, it could have done so. Applying these principles to the facts we find that the exchange was a realizing event. The mortgages were different because they involved different debtors and secured different homes. The fact that these mortgages were "substantially identical" for regulatory purposes does not mean that they could not be "materially different" for tax purposes. Finally, we reject the contention that these losses were not sustained in the applicable tax year, as required by § 165(a). Because these transactions were made at arm's length and Cottage (P) did not retain de facto control over the mortgages, we find that the losses were sustained within the meaning of § 165(a). Reversed.

■ **DISSENT**

(Blackmun, J.) I believe that a "material difference" is one that has the capacity to influence a decision. Application of this standard can only lead one to conclude that the mortgages exchanged were not "materially different." The thrift regulators came up with ten factors that, when satisfied, ensured the mortgages were "substantially identical." In fact, material differences is exactly what the FHLBB sought to avoid. The conclusion that the mortgages were not materially different is also supported by several other factors: That Cottage (P) kept a 10% interest to enable the thrift to service the loan; that Cottage (P) collected payments from its original borrowers; nothing really changed, except for names on a piece of paper; that the parties treated the mortgages as fungible; the identity of the borrowers was a non-issue in the transaction; the files were exchanged years after the transaction; and the mortgages were all in the same State. In sum, the substance of the transaction negates a finding of material differences. The Supreme Court's decision in this case goes to the heart of the realization requirement.

Analysis:

The major issue of contention between the majority opinion and the dissent is whether a "material difference" in property relates to economic characteristics or legal characteristics. By adopting a legal definition of material difference, the Court seems to eschew the long-established principle that the tax law looks at the economic substance of a transaction, as opposed to the legal formalities. To grasp the fundamental issues presented by this case it is necessary to understand that realization has two components, the economic loss and the accounting of that loss. An issue with the holding in this case is that while Cottage (P) experienced an economic loss, that loss was not realized in the year in question because there was no transaction of any substance to account for its loss. The policies behind realization may raise questions about the recognition of this kind of transaction.

■ **CASE VOCABULARY**

FHLBB: Federal Home Loan Bank Board, the agency charged with regulating thrifts and savings and loan associations prior to the 1990s, when the Office of Thrift Supervision took over those duties.

Burnet v. Logan

(*Commissioner of Internal Revenue*) v. (*Shareholder Who Sold Stock for Cash and Mining Interests*)
283 U.S. 404, 51 S.Ct. 550 (1931)

WHERE THE TOTAL VALUE OF THE CONSIDERATION TO BE RECIVED BY A TAXPAYER IS UNCERTAIN, A GAIN IS NOT RECOGNIZED UNTIL THE PAYMENTS RECEIVED EXCEED THE BASIS

■ **INSTANT FACTS** When a shareholder in a mining company sold her stock for cash and the promise of future payments to be based on the amount of ore extracted, the government sought tax the shareholder on the present value of the payments it estimated she would receive.

■ **BLACK LETTER RULE** The gain realized in an open transaction—one where the consideration received has no ascertainable fair market value—is not recognized until the taxpayer has ascertainably received an amount over her basis in the property transferred.

■ **PROCEDURAL BASIS**

Not provided.

■ **FACTS**

Mrs. Logan had a $180,000 basis in 1,000 shares she owned in the Andrews and Hitchcock Mining Company. In 1916, Mrs. Logan and her fellow shareholders were bought out by the Youngstown Sheet & Tube Company (Youngstown). For her 1,000 shares, Mrs. Logan received $120,000 and the right to receive additional payments based on the amount of ore extracted by Youngstown. The government estimated that Mrs. Logan would receive $9,000 a year for 25 years under the contract, the present value of these payments being $100,000. Based on this calculation, the government sought to tax Mrs. Logan on a $40,000 gain and provide her with a $100,000 basis in the right to receive payments. The basis would be recoverable at the rate of $4000 per year for the next 25 years. Mrs. Logan's argument for open-transaction treatment had two aspects. First, she claimed that the additional payments should be ignored in the year of the sale because they had no ascertainable value. She then claimed that she should be allowed to recover her remaining basis ($60,000) before reporting any gain.

■ **ISSUE**

Is a taxpayer allowed to recover her basis in property sold before reporting a gain from a transaction where the value of the consideration received is unascertainable at the time of the sale?

■ **DECISION AND RATIONALE**

(McReynolds, J.) Yes. The gain realized in an open transaction—one where the consideration received has no ascertainable fair market value—is not recognized until the taxpayer has, ascertainably, received an amount over her basis in the property transferred. As the annual payments are made by Youngstown tax liability can be assessed without resort to estimates, assumptions and speculation. However the promise to pay was not equivalent to cash and had no ascertainable value. A promise to pay is not necessarily taxable income. The transaction was not a closed one. Mrs. Logan might not ever recover her basis. A gain is realized only when the taxpayer receives value over her basis in the property sold. Mrs. Logan correctly demanded that she recoup her capital before having to report a gain.

Analysis:

The Court here adopts the open transaction doctrine and takes a "wait and see" approach to future payments that are contingent. This approach is also known as the cost-recovery method of recognizing gains. Under cost-recovery, the taxpayer is not taxed on any payments up to the amount of basis. Once the basis has been recovered, all receipts thereafter are treated as taxable gains. The reason for open transaction treatment can be found in some of the justifications for the realization requirement. First, a promise to make contingent payments is difficult to value at any time. Second, although Mrs. Logan received a large cash payment, there remains the possibility that a taxpayer would not have the cash on hand to pay his tax liability if the contingent future payments make up the bulk of the consideration. Under current regulations, the cost-recovery method is available only in the rarest of circumstances, where the consideration has no fair market value.

Amend v. Commissioner

(Farmer) v. *(Commissioner of Internal Revenue)*
13 T.C. 178 (1949), acq., 1950–1 C.B. 1

THE DOCTRINE OF CONSTRUCTIVE RECIEPT DOES NOT APPLY WHEN THE TAXPAYER CHOOSES NOT TO BARGAIN FOR THE RIGHT TO DEMAND IMMEDIATE PAYMENT

■ **INSTANT FACTS** The government sought to tax a farmer on the gain from the sale of wheat in the year the contract for sale was executed and the wheat was delivered, even though the farmer had contracted for and could not receive payment until the following year.

■ **BLACK LETTER RULE** The doctrine of constructive receipt does not apply where the seller of property receives as consideration from the buyer only a promise to pay in the following year so long as the sale was bona fide and conducted at arm's-length.

■ **PROCEDURAL BASIS**

Not provided.

■ **FACTS**

In August of 1944, Amend (P) sold his wheat crop to Burrus for delivery in January of 1945. However, Amend (P) and Burrus agreed that Amend (P) would deliver the wheat in August and Burrus would pay for it in January of the following year. On August 2, Amend shipped the wheat to Burrus. On January 17, 1945, Burrus paid Amend (P) with a check for $40,164.08. The testimony of all the parties involved, including Amend's (P) attorney, was that Amend (P) would not have the right to demand payment until 1945. Amend testified that he structured his sales this way in order to counter the uncertainties involved in farming by making his income "more uniform and even."

■ **ISSUE**

Does the doctrine of constructive receipt apply when, in a bona fide arm's length transaction, the seller of property receives only a promise to pay at a future date?

■ **DECISION AND RATIONALE**

(Black, J.) No. The doctrine of constructive receipt does not apply where the seller of property receives as consideration from the buyer only a promise to pay in the following year so long as the sale was bona fide and conducted at arm's-length. It is well settled that a cash basis taxpayer does not realize income at the time a promise to pay in the future is made. The reason for this is that there is an element of uncertainty in the transaction and the promise has no "market value." The plain facts of this case belie the Commissioner's (D) argument that Amend (P) had the unqualified right to receive his money for the wheat and all he had to do was ask for it. The sale between Amend (P) and Burrus was bona fide in all respects. Furthermore, Amend (P) had been structuring his sales this way for several years, and has continued to do so. For these reasons we find the doctrine of constructive receipt inapplicable.

Analysis:

A cash basis taxpayer is taxed as he receives income, not when he earns the right to it. As its name implies, the constructive receipt doctrine expands the notion of when income is "received." The doctrine is now embodied by Treas. Reg. 1.451–2(a), which provides: ''Income although not actually reduced to a taxpayer's possession is constructively received by him in the taxable year during which it is credited to his account, set apart for him, or otherwise made available so that he may draw upon it at any time, or so that he could have drawn upon it during the taxable year if notice of intention to withdraw had been given.'' This case stands for the proposition that the doctrine is inapplicable where the taxpayer failed or chose not to bargain for the immediate right to demand payment.

■ **CASE VOCABULARY**

CONSTRUCTIVE RECEIPT OF INCOME: The rule whereby a cash-method taxpayer is required to pay taxes on income that he has the unqualified right to receive, whether or not the income is actually received by him in cash.

Pulsifer v. Commissioner

(*Under–Aged Lottery Winners*) v. (*Commissioner of Internal Revenue*)

64 T.C. 245 (1975)

A TAXPAYER REALIZES INCOME WHEN HE HAS THE IRREVOCABLE RIGHT TO RECEIVE MONIES SET ASIDE IN THE FORM OF A FUND OR TRUST

■ **INSTANT FACTS** The government sought to tax three minor children on their share of lottery proceeds, even though their father did not apply for release of the funds.

■ **BLACK LETTER RULE** An individual on the cash receipts and disbursements method of accounting is currently taxable on the economic and financial benefit derived from the absolute right to income in the form of a fund which has been irrevocably set aside for him in trust and is beyond the reach of the creditors.

■ **PROCEDURAL BASIS**

Petition to the Tax Court for a review of the Commissioner's determination of deficiencies.

■ **FACTS**

In 1969, Gordon Pulsifer entered into an Irish sweepstakes on behalf of himself and his three minor children, Stephen (P), Susan (P) and Thomas (P). The Pulsifer's (P) ticket came up a winner, earning $48,000. When Gordon applied for the winnings he was told that three-fourths of the proceeds could not be released until his children reached the age of 21 or an appropriate party applied for the funds on their behalf. The money was set aside in the Bank of Ireland earning interest in the account of the Accountant of the Courts of Justice.

■ **ISSUE**

May the government tax unclaimed cash winnings held in trust for the winner, who has an absolute right to obtain the winnings, in the year the money is won?

■ **DECISION AND RATIONALE**

(Hall, J.) Yes. Under the economic benefit rule, an individual on the cash receipts and disbursements method of accounting is currently taxable on the economic and financial benefit derived from the absolute right to income in the form of a fund which has been irrevocably set aside for him in trust and is beyond the reach of the creditors. Under the economic benefit rule, the Tax Court has held a taxpayer currently taxable on fund's placed in to a trust by his employer for the taxpayer's sole benefit in consideration of services already rendered. In that case, the employee had an absolute right to the funds, which were beyond the reach of his employer. Stephen (P), Susan (P) and Thomas (P) all had an absolute nonforfeitable right to their winnings on deposit. All that they needed to do was to have their father apply for the funds. For these reasons we find that the Commissioner correctly determined that the brothers and sister were taxable in 1969, the year the money was won.

Analysis:

Courts often ignore the distinctions between the economic benefit doctrine and constructive receipt. Generally, the economic benefit rule is applicable when the taxpayer earns the right to a future cash payment that is nonforfeitable and is placed in a fund or set aside for payment. The constructive receipt doctrine, on the other hand, focuses on whether the taxpayer has the power to obtain possession of the income. This case could likely have been decided on the basis of either doctrine.

■ **CASE VOCABULARY**

ECONOMIC BENEFIT DOCTRINE: A rule which acts to tax a cash-method taxpayer on income which he has the irrevocable right to receive at a future time and which has been funded or placed in trust for the taxpayer's benefit.

Minor v. United States

(Physician Who Deferred Compensation) v. *(Internal Revenue Service)*
772 F.2d 1472 (9th Cir. 1985)

DEFERRED COMPENSATION IS NOT TAXABLE TO THE EMPLOYEE IN THE YEAR SERVICES ARE RENDERED IF THE COMPENSATION PLAN IS UNFUNDED AND UNSECURED AND THE EMPLOYEE FACES THE RISK OF FORFEITURE

■ **INSTANT FACTS** The government sought to tax a physician on amounts paid into a fund by his employer pursuant to a deferred compensation plan whereby the physician and his employer agreed the physician would be paid 10 percent of his fees at the time the services were rendered and the rest would be deferred for payment at a later date.

■ **BLACK LETTER RULE** Deferred compensation is not taxable to the employee in the year services are rendered if the compensation plan is unfunded and unsecured and the employee faces a substantial risk of forfeiture.

■ **PROCEDURAL BASIS**

Appeal to the Ninth Circuit Court of Appeals for a review of a judgment of the district court, which held that contributions to a deferred compensation plan were not currently taxable to the employee.

■ **FACTS**

Dr. Ralph Minor (P) entered into a deferred compensation plan with his employer, Snohomish County Physicians Corporation (Snohomish). Under the plan, Dr. Minor (P) was to be paid 10 percent of his fees in the year they were earned, the balance to be paid upon Dr. Minor's (P) death, disability, retirement or relocation to another practice area. To fund the plan, Snohomish established a trust, naming itself as settlor and sole beneficiary. The trustees were three physicians, one of whom was Dr. Minor (P). As part of the plan Dr. Minor (P) agreed to continue to perform services until the benefits became payable, to limit his practice after retirement, to continue to provide some services upon Snohomish's request and to refrain from providing services to competitors. Based on the economic benefit rule, the IRS (D) argued that Dr. Minor (P) should have included in his gross income the amounts paid into the trust by Snohomish. Dr. Minor (P) argued that he was not taxable on those amounts because he had no right, title or interest in the trust and the payments therefrom had not vested in him.

■ **ISSUE**

Is deferred compensation currently taxable to the employee when the plan calls for his employer to place funds in a trust in which the employee has no right, title or interest and the plan makes future payments contingent?

■ **DECISION AND RATIONALE**

(Judge Not Named) No. Deferred compensation is not taxable to the employee in the year services are rendered if the compensation plan is unfunded and unsecured and the employee faces a substantial risk of forfeiture. It is settled that an employer's unsecured promise to pay funds does not constitute the constructive receipt of compensation on which the employee is currently taxable. The IRS (D) concedes that Dr. Minor (P) did not constructively receive the payments made by Snohomish into the fund. Instead, the IRS (P) bases its argument on the economic benefit doctrine. That doctrine provides that an employer's promise to pay deferred compensation in the future is taxable if the current value of the promise can be ascertained. This valuation is ascertainable where the employer makes a contribution to an employee's deferred compensation plan which is nonforfeitable, fully vested in the employee and secured against the employer's creditors by a trust arrangement. The trust established by Snohomish is, superficially, secured against its creditors, but the plan makes Dr. Minor's (P) benefits forfeitable by placing conditions upon his receipt of them. We believe the plan does not really protect against Snohomish's creditors because the assets remain the sole property of Snohomish. We also find the deferred compensation plan is unfunded because the trust names Snohomish as settlor and beneficiary and Dr. Minor (P) has neither substantial control over nor interest in that trust. Therefore, Dr. Minor (P) has not received an economic benefit. The facts also show that Dr. Minor's (P) receipt of the money is contingent upon his complying with the non-compete provisions of the agreement. Section 83(a) of the Code requires an employee to include in his gross income any property transferred in connection with his performance of services, unless the property is subject to a "substantial risk of forfeiture." Although the district court did not make any findings as to the substance of the risk of forfeiture, we find that Minor's (P) benefits are not property within the meaning of § 83(a) because the plan is not secured from Snohomish's creditors.

Analysis:

The court held (and the IRS conceded) that Dr. Minor (P) did not constructively receive the payment at issue here because he had no existing right to demand immediate payment. The court goes on to hold that the plan at issue here failed the security requirements. The fund was held to be unsecured, because, according to the court, the fact that Snohomish was the settlor and beneficiary made the trust's assets subject to Snohomish's creditors. The court also held as inapplicable § 83 of the Code, which includes in gross income property transferred to another for services rendered to the transferor. The court's holding as to the inapplicability of § 83 was based on the fact that it believed that § 83's use of the word "property" did not include funds set aside in an unsecured trust.

■ CASE VOCABULARY

SETTLOR: The person who creates or establishes a trust.

Cramer v. Commissioner

(Corporate Directors) v. *(Commissioner of Internal Revenue)*
64 F.3d 1406 (9th Cir. 1995)

AN EMPLOYEE DOES NOT REALIZE GROSS INCOME WHEN HE RECIEVES STOCK OPTIONS WITH NO ASCERTAINABLE VALUE

■ **INSTANT FACTS** Seeking capital gains treatment of stock options granted to them, three corporate officers included in their gross income the value of the options, which they claimed had no value, in contravention of Treasury Regulations in place at the time.

■ **BLACK LETTER RULE** Options to purchase non-publicly traded stock which are granted to corporate employees with vesting and transfer restrictions have no readily ascertainable market value under § 83(e).

■ **PROCEDURAL BASIS**

Appeal to the Ninth Circuit Court of Appeals to review a decision of the Tax Court, which upheld deficiencies determined and penalties imposed by the Commissioner against three corporate officers for their disregard of Treasury Regulations.

■ **FACTS**

Richard Cramer (P), Warren Boynton (P) and Kevin Monaghan (P) were officers and directors in IMED Corporation. In 1978, IMED issued to Cramer (P) an option to purchase IMED stock at $50 per share. The terms of the option stated that Cramer (P) could exercise the option only while he remained an officer of the company and only in 20% annual increments over 5 years. The options could only be transferred to persons approved by the board and the transferee would have to take the option subject to the vesting restrictions. In 1979, IMED issued to Cramer (P), Boynton (P) and Monaghan (P) differing amounts of options with the same vesting and transfer restrictions as the 1978 options. At the time of the transfers, IMED stock was not publicly traded. All three men were informed that in order to treat the gain from the disposition of the options as a capital gain, § 83(b) required them to include the fair market value of the options in their gross income for the year they received the options. They were also informed that the Treasury Regulations did not seem to permit them to include the options in gross income because they had no "readily ascertainable fair market value," as required by § 83(e). Notwithstanding these warnings, Cramer (P), Boynton (P) and Monaghan (P) all reported as gross income the fair market value of the options, which they reported as having zero value, even though they all believed the options to be valuable. When IMED was purchased by Warner–Lambert Corp., Cramer (P) received $25,945,506 for his options, while Boynton (P) and Monaghan (P) each received $7,714,800 and $2,274,895, respectively. Even though they knew they had no basis in the options, Cramer (P) reported a basis of $7,535,620 and proceeds of $32,191,129 and Monaghan (P) reported a basis of $2,558,500 and proceeds of $4,832,395. All three listed the gains as long-term capital gains. After auditing all three men, the IRS (D) determined that the sale of the options were ordinary income in the year they were sold. The IRS (D) also assessed penalties for the intentional disregard of tax rules and regulations. The Tax Court upheld both the deficiencies and the penalties.

■ **ISSUE**

Do options to purchase non-publicly traded stock granted to employees with vesting and transfer restrictions have a readily ascertainable market value under § 83(e)?

■ DECISION AND RATIONALE

(Judge's Name Not Provided) No. Options to purchase non-publicly traded stock which are granted to corporate employees with vesting and transfer restrictions have no readily ascertainable market value under § 83(e). Treasury Regulation § 1.83–7(b)(2) provides that, under § 83(e), stock options have no ascertainable fair market value unless they: (1) Are transferable by the optionee; (2) are exercisable immediately in full by the optionee; (3) are subject to any restriction or condition that has a significant effect on their fair market value; and (4) have a fair market value readily ascertainable under subsection (b)(3). It is clear that the options granted by IMED failed to fulfill the regulation's first three requirements. In their defense, Cramer (P) and the others argue that Reg. § 1.83–7(b)(2) improperly interprets § 83(c). As support for this argument they point to the fact that paragraphs (a) and (b) of § 83 mandate that such restrictions should be disregarded when determining whether the property transferred has a "readily ascertainable fair market value." From this they conclude that the same restrictions should be disregarded under paragraph (e). The argument is disingenuous, for it is a principle of statutory construction that where one section of a statute includes a specific term, that same term will not be implied in another section of the same statute. Furthermore, Congress has had the opportunity to amend the statute, but has failed to do so. We also believe that the legislative history is irrelevant because resort to it should only occur to resolve, not create, an ambiguity. We also agree that the penalties assessed by the Commissioner were correctly affirmed by the Tax Court. A taxpayer cannot claim that he had a plausible argument that a regulation was invalid to negate the fact he intentionally disregarded that regulation. Even a reasonable basis for that belief would not act to exonerate a willful violation. Under such circumstances, the proper route is pay the tax and file suit for a refund. We also find that the penalties for substantial understatement of tax were warranted. An understatement of tax may be reduced by an amount attributable to tax treatment supported by substantial authority or tax treatment about which there was supporting documentation. However, we believe that Cramer (P), Boynton (P) and Monaghan (P) neither had substantial authority for their positions nor did they support those positions with documentation. In fact, two of the men claimed to have had a basis in the options, even though they knew they had claimed a value of zero as gross income from receipt of the options. The finding that the returns were filed in bad faith was correct. Affirmed.

Analysis:

The point of this case is simple. When a corporation grants non-statutory stock options that have no "readily ascertainable fair market value," any gain realized on their disposition must be treated as ordinary income in the year they are exercised. Cramer (P), Boynton (P) and Monaghan (P) were attempting to obtain capital gains tax treatment for their option. Capital gains are taxed at lower rates than ordinary compensation income. In order to obtain capital gains treatment, the directors were required by § 83(b) to claim the fair market value of the options as ordinary gross income in the year they were received. However, § 83(e) makes § 83(b) inapplicable when the property transferred to the employee is stock options with no "readily ascertainable market value." Consequently, the issue here turned on the question of how to define "readily ascertainable fair market value," as that term appears in § 83(e). The court upholds the Treasury Regulations' four-factor test, which the IMED stock options failed.

■ CASE VOCABULARY

NON–STATUTORY STOCK OPTIONS: Stock options that do not qualify for tax treatment under § 422, which allows a taxpayer to exclude stock options from gross income until they are exercised and the stock is sold.

United States v. Davis

(*Government*) v. (*Divorced Husband*)
370 U.S. 65, 82 S.Ct. 1190 (1962)

TRANSFERS PURSUANT TO A DIVORCE OR SEPARATION POSE QUESTIONS OF VALUATION, GAIN AND BASIS

■ **INSTANT FACTS** The government sought to tax a husband on the appreciated value of stock he transferred to his wife pursuant to their divorce.

■ **BLACK LETTER RULE** The transfer of appreciated property between spouses pursuant to a separation or divorce must be taxed as a gain to the transferor spouse in an amount equal to the difference between the fair market value of the property and his or her basis therein.

■ PROCEDURAL BASIS

Certiorari to the United States Supreme Court from the Court of Claims.

■ FACTS

In 1954, Thomas Davis (P) entered into a property settlement and separation agreement with his wife. Pursuant to the agreement, Mr. Davis (P) transferred 1,000 shares of stock to his wife in exchange for her release of all marital rights under state law. Under the law of Delaware, the property transferred belonged completely to Mr. Davis (P).

■ ISSUE

Is a property transfer between spouses pursuant to a divorce a taxable event?

■ DECISION AND RATIONALE

(Clark, J.) Yes. The transfer of appreciated property between spouses pursuant to a separation or divorce must be taxed as a gain to the transferor spouse in an amount equal to the difference between the fair market value of the property and his or her basis therein. Mr. Davis (P) takes the position his transfer of stock to his wife was akin to a nontaxable transfer of property between co-owners. The Government (D), on the other hand, contends that this is a property exchange for the release of a legal obligation. We cannot accept Mr. Davis' (P) position because the rights given to a wife under the law of Delaware are nowhere near those of ownership. Instead, a wife is given right of survivorship or, upon divorce, a reasonable share in the husband's property. We believe that these marital rights are more akin to a personal liability of the husband than to a property interest of the wife. Although this approach will lead to different tax treatment depending on the state, that issue is one for Congress to address. Having determined the taxability of the transfer the question becomes one of valuation. The Court of Claims in this case held that the gain on the transfer of the shares could not be determined because the wife's rights are incapable of being valued. We disagree. It is well settled that where two properties are exchanged in an arm's-length transaction, they are held to be equal in value. Accordingly, we may assume that the wife's rights had a value equal to that of the fair market value of the shares. It is this amount that should be used in calculating Mr. Davis' (P) gain and which gives the wife her basis in the newly acquired shares. Reversed in part and affirmed in part.

Analysis:

The editors have included this case to illustrate some of the issues that arise in the context of transfers pursuant to a divorce or separation. If such transfers are to be taxed as gains from dealings in property, it is necessary to ascertain the gain, the amount realized, and the basis of the parties. The Court here holds that marital rights that are released in a property settlement are presumed to have the same fair market value as the property received. This gives the transferor spouse an amount realized equal to the fair market value of the property transferred. The result of this decision has been overturned by Congress. Today, property settlements are treated as tax-neutral events. Section 1041 provides that no gain or loss is to be recognized on transfers of property between spouses pursuant to a divorce. Accordingly, the transferee spouse takes a carryover basis equal to the adjusted basis of the transferor spouse. Section 1041 applies to three different types of transfers of property. Those transfers that occur within one year of the cessation of the marriage are conclusively held to fall within the ambit of § 1041. Transfers that occur within six years are presumed to qualify for tax-neutral treatment, but the Commissioner may rebut the presumption. Those transfers that occur over six years after the cessation of the marriage are presumed not to be property settlements; however, the taxpayer may rebut the presumption that § 1041 does not apply.

Farid-Es-Sultaneh v. Commissioner

(*Taxpayer*) v. (*Commissioner of Internal Revenue*)
160 F.2d 812 (2d Cir. 1947)

A WIFE WHO TAKES PROPERTY PURSUANT TO AN ANTENUPTIAL AGREEMENT RECEIVES A BASIS EQUAL TO THE VALUE OF THE RIGHTS SHE GIVES UP

■ **INSTANT FACTS** A taxpayer sought to have her basis in corporate stock determined by the value of the shares when she acquired them in exchange for the release of marital rights pursuant to an antenuptial agreement.

■ **BLACK LETTER RULE** A transfer which should be classed as a gift under the gift tax law is not necessarily to be treated as a gift income-tax-wise.

■ **PROCEDURAL BASIS**

Appeal to the Second Circuit challenging the decision of the Tax Court.

■ **FACTS**

In 1924, Ms. Farid-Es-Sultaneh (P) received about $800,000 worth of shares of stock from Mr. Kresge, with whom she was contemplating marriage, to protect her in the event he should die prior to the marriage. Mr. Kresge's basis in the stock was 16¢ per share, which had a value of $10 each at the time of the transfer to Ms. Farid-Es-Sultaneh (P). Prior to their marriage, the two entered into an ante-nuptial agreement whereby Ms. Farid-Es-Sultaneh (P) agreed to release all dower and marital rights, including the right to her support, in consideration for those previously received shares, which the agreement expressly stated were a "gift." The couple married and then divorced. Ms. Farid-Es-Sultaneh (P) received no alimony, even though Mr. Kresge was worth about $375,000,000. In 1938, Ms. Farid-Es-Sultaneh (P) sold some of the shares for $19 per share. The Commissioner determined a deficiency on the ground that the stock was acquired by gift, and thus the basis in the hands of the Mr. Kresge carried over to Ms. Farid-Es-Sultaneh (P).

■ **ISSUE**

Is property received pursuant to an agreement releasing marital rights a gift for income tax purposes?

■ **DECISION AND RATIONALE**

(Chase, Cir. J.) No. A transfer made in consideration for the release of marital rights is not a gift for income tax purposes. The Supreme Court has held that property transferred in trust for the benefit of a prospective wife pursuant to an ante-nuptial agreement is a gift under the gift tax laws. The rule has also been held applicable in the estate tax context. In our opinion, however, income tax provisions are not to be construed as though they were in pari materia with either the estate tax law or the gift tax law. It is up to Congress to determine the legal effect a transfer made for consideration should have. We believe that the consideration given by Ms. Farid-Es-Sultaneh (P) is fair consideration. Although the transfers made before the ante-nuptial agreement were called a "gift" by the agreement, they were contingent upon the death of Mr. Kresge, an event which never occurred. Consequently, it seems no gift was made prior to the ante-nuptial agreement. Ms. Farid-Es-Sultaneh's (P) inchoate interest in the property of her affianced husband greatly exceeded the value of the stock. It was fair consideration under the ordinary legal concept of that term. The shares were held by way of purchase. Reversed.

■ **DISSENT**

(Clark, Cir. J.) The court has failed to give an adequate explanation why the term gift should be construed differently, depending on whether the Government is taxing gifts, estates or income. The purpose for requiring a carryover basis when property is transferred by gift is the same—to prevent the avoidance of taxes by way of judicious transfers within the family or intimate group. However, that point need not decide this case. The facts show that the shares were given prior to the marriage. At these times, Ms. Farid-Es-Sultaneh (P) had no marital rights to release. How could the release of nonexistent rights form consideration for the stock? Following the majority's point of view, Mr. Kresge would have realized a capital gain near $100,000,000, or one-third of Kresge's estate, to which his wife was entitled.

Analysis:

The court's rationale in this case raises some very interesting questions. First, if the exchange of marital rights for stock was a sale, should Ms. Farid-Es-Sultaneh (P) have been taxed on a gain? If so, how would you value her basis in those rights? Second, as Judge Clark points out, Mr. Kresge likely realized a gain in the year of the transfer. How would you value the consideration he received, i.e., the yet non-existent and very contingent marital rights? The majority assumes that those marital rights were more valuable than the stock. Does this mean that the court would not use the fair market value of the shares to determine the value of the rights? It is these types of questions that § 1041 was designed to eliminate. However, that section would not apply here, because this transfer was not between spouses or pursuant to a divorce or settlement.

Diez–Arguelles v. Commissioner

(*Ex–Spouse Entitled to Child Support*) v. (*Commissioner of Internal Revenue*)

48 T.C.M. 496 (1984)

UNPAID CHILD SUPPORT IS NOT A DEDUCTIBLE LOSS TO THE PAYEE SPOUSE

■ **INSTANT FACTS** A married couple sought to deduct as a short-term capital loss child support payments that were not made by the wife's former husband.

■ **BLACK LETTER RULE** Amounts due for child support are not deductible under § 186 as nonbusiness bad debts.

■ PROCEDURAL BASIS

Decision of the Tax Court which reviewed whether unpaid child support could be deducted as loss.

■ FACTS

Pursuant to a divorce decree, Christina Diez–Arguelles (Christina) (P) was to receive $300 per month in child support from her former husband Kevin Baxter. For six years Baxter failed to meet his full obligations, putting him in arrears by the amount of $4,325. Christina (P) and her new husband claimed this amount as a nonbusiness bad debt and deducted it from their gross income as a short-term capital loss. The following year, Baxter fell behind another $3,000. Christina (P) and her new husband again sought to deduct this amount in the same manner. Throughout this entire period Christina made diligent efforts to collect the money, but those efforts proved fruitless.

■ ISSUE

May a taxpayer deduct as a loss from a nonbusiness bad debt overdue child support payments?

■ DECISION AND RATIONALE

(Judge's Name Not Provided) No. Amounts due for child support are not deductible under § 186 as nonbusiness bad debts. Nonbusiness bad debts may be deducted only to the extent of the taxpayer's basis in the debts. The Board of Tax Appeals has held that uncollectible alimony was not a deductible bad debt because the taxpayer was not "out of pocket" anything due to the ex-husband's failure to pay. Christina and her husband argue that they are "out of pocket" the amount used to support Baxter's children. We have rejected this argument and, contrary to dictum stated by the Ninth Circuit, we maintain our position that capital used to make up for unpaid child support is not deductible.

Analysis:

Section 166 provides that nonbusiness bad debts may be deducted as a loss realized from the sale or exchange of capital assets held for less than one year. Thus, the court's decision turns on the question of whether Christina had any basis in the child support obligations. The court held that there was no basis in those debts because Christina and her husband were not "out of pocket" anything. Many have questioned the fairness of the ruling in this case, but the Tax Court has steadfastly maintained the nondeductibility of these debts.

HIGH COURT CASE SUMMARIES

69

Georgia School–Book Depository v. Commissioner

(Taxpayer Who Accrued Unpaid Commissions) v. *(Commissioner of Internal Revenue)*

1 T.C. 463 (1943)

A DELAY IN THE RECEIPT OF CASH DOES NOT PREVENT INCOME FROM ACCRUING FOR INCOME TAX PURPOSES

■ **INSTANT FACTS** An accrual-method taxpayer failed to include in its gross income earned commissions which remained currently unpaid by the appropriate state agency, due to a lack of funds.

■ **BLACK LETTER RULE** A taxpayer has a reasonable basis for not accruing earned income only when there is an unresolved and allegedly intervening right which makes receipt of the income contingent or the insolvency of the debtor makes payment improbable.

■ **PROCEDURAL BASIS**

(Not Provided)

■ **FACTS**

Georgia School–Book Depository (Depository) (P) (an accrual-method taxpayer) was, essentially, a school book broker for the State of Georgia, earning 8 percent commissions on all books sold to the state. The contract between the State and the Depository provided that the latter would receive its brokerage fees "at the time of settlement." In 1938 and 1939, the State of Georgia's "Free Textbook Fund (Fund)," from which the Depository (P) received its commissions, was underfunded. In its accounting the state treated the deficiencies not as liabilities, but as encumbrances on the textbook fund in the next year.

■ **ISSUE**

Does a delay in the receipt of cash mean that income has not accrued to the taxpayer?

■ **DECISION AND RATIONALE**

(Kern, J.) No. A taxpayer has a reasonable basis for not accruing earned income only when there is an unresolved and allegedly intervening right which makes receipt of the income contingent or the insolvency of the debtor makes payment improbable. Were we to hold otherwise, the taxpayer could shift income from year to year at his discretion. We reject the Depository's (P) argument that it had yet to earn the commissions; and for that reason, it had accrued no income. The facts clearly show that the Depository (P) performed all but one of the acts required of it in order to earn the commissions. The fact that the Depository had yet to receive money and pass it on to the publishers is immaterial. It is the right to receive money, not the right to actual payment, that justifies the accrual of income. As to the Depository's (P) argument that it had a reasonable basis for expecting that payment would not be made, we find its position untenable. Here, the Depository (P) could not have had such a reasonable expectation. The State of Georgia was not insolvent. The Fund was merely experiencing a shortage due to recent changes in the manner in which it was funded. The fact that the Depository (P) continued to do business with the state serves as evidence that it expected payment in full.

Analysis:

A delay in the receipt of cash will not prevent the accrual of income unless there is a reasonable expectation that payment will never be made. In other words, the collection of income is unrelated to the accrual of income. For purposes of taxation, it is the moment at which the right to income is earned that determines accrual. The moment payment is due is irrelevant under the accrual method. The reasonable expectations test applied by the court provides that a taxpayer is not required to accrue income if experience confirms a reasonable belief that the income will never be paid. Section 448(d)(5) now provides that an accrual-method taxpayer is not required to accrue income for services rendered if experience tells him it will not be collected.

■ **CASE VOCABULARY**

ACCRUED INCOME: Income which has been earned but not received.

American Automobile Association v. United States

(Accrual–Method Taxpayer That Received Unearned Income) v. *(Government)*

367 U.S. 687, 81 S.Ct. 1727 (1961)

INCOME MAY BE TAXED WHEN RECEIVED, EVEN IF IT IS NOT YET EARNED

■ **INSTANT FACTS** The government sought to challenge an automobile club's accounting methods, arguing that the club could not postpone the inclusion in gross income of prepaid membership dues.

■ **BLACK LETTER RULE** The government may reject a taxpayer's accounting method and require the taxpayer to include in gross income for the current year prepaid dues received from services to be rendered in a subsequent year.

■ PROCEDURAL BASIS

Certiorari by the United States Supreme Court to the Court of Claims, which held that prepaid membership dues were taxable income to a national automobile club in the years those dues were received.

■ FACTS

The American Automobile Association (AAA) (P) reported its income under the accrual-method of accounting. AAA's (P) income was realized primarily from prepaid annual membership dues. Essentially, members of the club would prepay annual dues which entitled them to various services over the following 12 months. Upon receipt of the dues, AAA (P) would deposit them in various accounts for use as general corporate funds. However, for AAA's (P) accounting purposes, the dues were treated in the club's books as income received ratably over the 12–month membership period. This system, a generally accepted accounting principle, was used so that AAA (P) could match income received in one year with the expenses incurred in earning dues in the following year. The Government (D) did not accept AAA's (P) accounting method, arguing that membership dues should have been reported in the year of their receipt, without regard to future expenses in the subsequent year.

■ ISSUE

May the government require that a taxpayer include in gross income for the current year prepaid dues received for services to be rendered in a subsequent year?

■ DECISION AND RATIONALE

(Clark, J.) Yes. The government may reject a taxpayer's accounting method and require the taxpayer to include in gross income for the current year prepaid dues received from services to be rendered in a subsequent year. In *Automobile Club of Michigan v. Commissioner* (a case involving almost identical facts) this Court held that the Commissioner had the authority to reject the pro rata allocation of the membership dues in monthly amounts as purely artificial. Based on this holding, the Court of Claims held that AAA's (P) treatment of dues was purely artificial and properly rejected by the Commissioner. AAA (P) attempts to distinguish *Michigan* on the fact that AAA (P) has provided adequate proof that its method of accounting is in accord with generally accepted accounting principles. However, the holding in *Michigan* was based upon the finding that the club performed the services only upon customer demand and that performance thus was not related to fixed dates after the taxable year in question. The same is true here. We also find as persuasive Congress' repeal of two sections that permitted the same practice employed by AAA (P). Furthermore, Congress has failed to extend a similar exception beyond the area of prepaid subscriptions to periodicals, newspapers and magazines. Affirmed.

■ DISSENT

(Stewart, J.) With this decision the Court effectively prevents an accrual basis taxpayer from making returns in accordance with an accepted and valid method of accounting which clearly reflects income. *Michigan* is not here dispositive because that case was decided on the ground that there was no proof of the correlation between the amounts deferred and the costs incurred by the taxpayer in carrying out its obligations. As evidence of Congress' intent to prohibit AAA's (P) method of accounting, the Court mistakenly relies on Congress' prior repeal of statutory provisions authorizing that method of accounting. The reason the Court mistakenly relies on that action is that Congress' sole concern was that the provisions would wreak disastrous results revenue-wise in the year of implementation. The effect of the decision is to require a hybrid accounting method—a cash basis for dues and an accrual basis for everything else. Such a method distorts actual income. For example, in a year were there are few deductions because the previous year yielded a low amount of dues there will be an inflated adjusted gross income. I believe that the statute requires the Commissioner to show that a method of accounting is faulty before he is allowed to reject it.

Analysis:

A taxpayer using the accrual method of accounting is required to report income when it is earned, as opposed to when it is received. The question here was, what should an accrual-method taxpayer do when the money is received before it is earned? What the court essentially does in this case is to uphold the power of the IRS to tax income as it is received, regardless of whether it has been earned or not. The outcome of this case has been undone by both statute and regulation. Section 456 permits membership organizations on the accrual method of accounting to defer income to years when it is earned. Treasury Regulation 1.451–5 provides a limited and qualified right to defer payments received to the year they are earned.

Westpac Pacific Food v. Commissioner

(*Grocery Store Partnership*) v. (*IRS Commissioner*)

451 F.3d 970 (9th Cir. 2006)

MONEY RECEIVED SUBJECT TO A REPAYMENT CONTINGENCY IS NOT GROSS INCOME

■ **INSTANT FACTS** A grocery store partnership received volume discounts on purchases in the form of cash advances that would have to be repaid if the full volume was not purchased, and the IRS deemed the advances "gross income"; the taxpayer appealed.

■ **BLACK LETTER RULE** Cash advances in exchange for volume purchase commitments, subject to pro rata repayment if the volume commitments are not met, are not gross income when received.

■ **PROCEDURAL BASIS**

Appeal by the taxpayer from a finding of the tax court that it underreported its gross income.

■ **FACTS**

Three grocery store chains organized as a partnership—Westpac (P)—to purchase and warehouse inventory. Westpac (P) entered into four contracts by which it promised to buy a certain volume of products from various suppliers, in exchange for a cash discount paid up front. That is, it negotiated a volume-discount price, but instead of paying the discounted price, it received the amount of the discount, up front, in cash. If Westpac (P) ultimately did not purchase the amount contracted for, the discount was adjusted. Westpac (P), an accrual-basis taxpayer, accounted for the cash advances at the time it received them, and then subtracted pro rata portions of the advance cash discounts from what it later paid for the inventory, which had the effect of reducing the cost of the goods sold and increasing the taxable profits from the sales by the amount of the cash advances attributable to the goods sold. The government took the position that Westpac (P) underreported over $5.5 million in gross income because it did not report the cash advances as gross income. The tax court agreed with the Commissioner, and Westpac (P) appealed.

■ **ISSUE**

Is cash paid in advance by a wholesaler to a retailer in exchange for a volume commitment—referred to in the grocery trade as an "advance trade discount"—gross income for federal income tax purposes?

■ **DECISION AND RATIONALE**

(Kleinfeld, J.) No. Cash advances in exchange for volume purchase commitments, subject to pro rata repayment if the volume commitments are not met, are not gross income when received. Although the definition of gross income is expansive, it does not go this far. Punitive damages received by a successful litigant, for instance, are gross income, because they are accessions to wealth, clearly realized, and over which the taxpayer has complete dominion. Here, however, although Westpac (P), the taxpayer, had complete dominion over the money, it did not become income until it was an "accession to wealth." That is why borrowed money is not income, even if the borrower has complete control over the cash. This case is like *Indianapolis Power*, in which utility customers' security deposits were not deemed income to the utility because of the obligation to repay the money when services ended. Here, because the taxpayer had to pay the money back if the volume commitments were not met, the money is not an accession to wealth, and it is therefore not income. Reversed.

Analysis:

The court helped explain that, although the facts of this case may seem complicated, there really are not, and it provided a hypothetical example to help clarify. Suppose Harry Homeowner goes to the furniture store and sees dining room chairs for $500 each. He says, "I'll take four if you give me a discount." He successfully negotiates a twenty-five percent discount and pays only $1,500 for the chairs. In such a case, he has not *made* $500, he has *spent* $1,500. Suppose, however, that Harry is short on cash and negotiates a deal whereby the furniture store gives him a discount in the form of a cash advance. According to this arrangement, Harry gets $400 cash back today, and then pays $2,000 for the four chairs next year. Still, he has not *made* $400, because the money is encumbered with a repayment obligation to the store. The latter scenario is like the present case, in that although Westpac (P) received cash, up front, in one fiscal year, there remained a possible obligation to pay it back in a later year, so it had not "made" the money either.

■ CASE VOCABULARY

ACCRUAL BASIS: An accounting method that records entries of debits and credits when the liability arises, rather than when the income or expense is received or disbursed.

CHAPTER FOUR

Personal Deductions, Exemptions and Credits

Dyer v. Commissioner

Instant Facts: A dispute between a taxpayer and the IRS arose when the taxpayer attempted to claim a casualty loss deduction for a vase destroyed by a cat's neurotic fit.

Black Letter Rule: The destruction of ordinary household equipment such as china or glassware through negligence of handling or by a family pet is not a casualty loss under § 165(c)(3) of the Internal Revenue Code (IRC).

Chamales v. Commissioner

Instant Facts: The taxpayers claimed a casualty loss deduction on their federal tax return after public interest in their celebrity neighbor's murder trial caused their neighborhood to become inundated with media and on-lookers and resulted in a sudden decline in the market value of their home.

Black Letter Rule: For purposes of qualifying as a casualty loss, there must be a permanent devaluation of the property for which the loss is claimed.

Blackman v. Commissioner

Instant Facts: A dispute between a taxpayer and the IRS arose when the taxpayer, who destroyed his own house when he set fire to some clothing inside of it, claimed a casualty loss of $97,853 on his tax return.

Black Letter Rule: Gross negligence on the part of a taxpayer that results in the destruction of property will bar any casualty loss deduction for the destroyed property.

Taylor v. Commissioner

Instant Facts: A dispute arose between the IRS and a taxpayer when the taxpayer attempted to claim the cost of paying someone to mow his lawn as a medical expense.

Black Letter Rule: The Internal Revenue Code specifically authorizes a deduction for medical care expenses paid during the taxable year which are not compensated for by insurance or otherwise; however, just because a doctor recommends an activity (or recommends abstention from an activity) does not mean that the cost of the activity can be deducted as a medical expense.

Henderson v. Commissioner

Instant Facts: The Hendersons (TP) claimed a medical expense deduction on their federal tax return related to the cost and modification of a van they purchased for the sole purpose of transporting their disabled son.

Black Letter Rule: Depreciation is not an "expense paid" or "amount paid" for purposes of the medical expense deduction under I.R.C. § 213.

Ochs v. Commissioner

Instant Facts: The taxpayer claimed as a medical expenses deduction the cost of sending his two daughters to boarding school.

Black Letter Rule: The fact that certain family expenses convey an indirect medical benefit on a family member is not enough to make those expenses deductible medical expenses under § 213 of the Internal Revenue Code (IRC).

Ottawa Silica Co. v. United States

Instant Facts: A dispute arose between a corporation and the IRS when the corporation was denied a charitable contribution deduction because its donation of land to the state carried with it significant benefits for the corporation.

Black Letter Rule: A contribution made to a charity is not made for exclusively public purposes if the donor receives or anticipates receiving a substantial benefit in return, and if the benefit received by the donor is greater than that which inures to the general public, no deduction can be taken.

Bob Jones University v. United States

Instant Facts: A dispute arose between the IRS (D) and Bob Jones University (P) when the IRS (D) decided that because of the University's (P) racially-discriminatory admissions practices, it no longer qualified as a tax-exempt charitable organization under IRC § 501(c)(3).

Black Letter Rule: A declaration that a given institution is not "charitable" should be made only where there can be no doubt that the activity in which the institution is involved is contrary to a fundamental public policy.

King v. Commissioner

Instant Facts: Lopez (P) and King (P), who were never married to each other, each claimed a dependency exemption deduction for their minor child on their 1998 and 1999 federal income tax returns.

Black Letter Rule: A noncustodial parent who never married and has lived apart from his child's mother during the last six months of a taxable year may claim a dependency exemption deduction if the child lives with one or both parents for more than half of the year, receives more than half of his support from his parents during the year, and the custodial parent signs a written declaration that she will not claim the dependency exemption deduction for the child.

Dyer v. Commissioner

(Taxpayer) v. *(IRS)*
20 T.C.M. 705 (1961)

ONLY THOSE LOSSES THAT RESULT FROM FIRE, SHIPWRECK, STORM, OR SUBSTANTIALLY SIMILAR OCCURRENCES CAN BE DEDUCTED AS CASUALTY LOSS UNDER IRC § 165(c)(3)

■ **INSTANT FACTS** A dispute between a taxpayer and the IRS arose when the taxpayer attempted to claim a casualty loss deduction for a vase destroyed by a cat's neurotic fit.

■ **BLACK LETTER RULE** The destruction of ordinary household equipment such as china or glassware through negligence of handling or by a family pet is not a casualty loss under § 165(c)(3) of the Internal Revenue Code (IRC).

■ **PROCEDURAL BASIS**

Appeal to the Tax Court of an IRS decision denying a casualty loss deduction for the destruction of a vase by a neurotic cat.

■ **FACTS**

Jean Dyer (P) owned both a cat and a vase. The vase, one of a matched pair, was valued at $100. Dyer's (P) cat (no value given) had neurosis. During the tax year of 1955, the cat had its first neurotic fit. [Do they make Valium for cats?] During the fit, it destroyed the vase. Dyer (P) claimed a casualty loss deduction of $100 for the broken vase on her 1955 income tax return. The IRS (D) did not approve of the deduction, and the matter was appealed to the Tax Court.

■ **ISSUE**

Can property loss caused by a neurotic cat's fit be deducted as a casualty loss?

■ **DECISION AND RATIONALE**

(Authoring Judge Not Stated) No. (Not even if it is the cat's first neurotic fit.) Dyer's (P) loss was not from fire, storm, or shipwreck, so if a deduction is to be allowed, it must fit within the definition of the phrase "other casualty." In construing that term, the rule of ejusdem generis is applicable, and in order that a loss may be deductible as a casualty loss, it must appear that the casualty was of a similar character to a fire, storm, or shipwreck. It does not have to be the same, but it must be similar. In this regard, the destruction of ordinary household equipment such as china or glassware through negligence of handling or by a family pet is not a casualty loss under § 165(c)(3). Dyer (P) does not disagree with this rule as a general statement. However, in her brief she argues that the broken vase was not a result of "the cat's ordinary perambulations on the top of the particular piece of furniture, but by its extraordinary behavior there in the course of having its first fit." We are not persuaded that the distinction which Dyer (P) endeavors to draw is a sound one, and it is, therefore, not sustained. The actions of the cat did not create a casualty loss within the meaning of the applicable statute. We find for the Commissioner (D).

Analysis:

Today (post–1983), casualty loss deductions are subject to two significant limitations. First, a taxpayer is only permitted to deduct that amount of aggregate loss that exceeds the amount of casualty gains for a year, plus 10% of a the taxpayer's adjusted gross income (AGI). IRC § 165(h)(2). This means that Dyer's (P) purported $100 loss would have to exceed 10% of Dyer's (P) AGI in order to be claimed (the nature of the loss aside). Thus, for example, if Dyer's (P) AGI was $500 (10% of which is $50), IRC § 165(h)(2) would only allow Dyer (P) to claim a $50 casualty loss. Needless to say, if her AGI were $1,000, no loss could be claimed. The second limitation, set forth in IRC § 165(h)(1), would actually preclude Dyer (P) from claiming the loss, even if her AGI was $1. Under subsection (h)(1), there is a $100 floor for each individual loss claimed, meaning that only the amount of a loss that exceeds $100 is potentially deductible. Thus, in this case, Dyer's (P) entire claim would be precluded (as her loss was valued at only $100). These two limitations have significantly reduced the amount of litigation involving the casualty loss deduction.

■ **CASE VOCABULARY**

CASUALTY LOSS: A loss caused by a fire, storm, shipwreck, or any other similar occurrence (the key word, under the rule of ejusdem generis, being "similar").

CASUALTY LOSS DEDUCTION: A tax deduction, codified in IRC § 165(c)(3), that is permitted when certain property is destroyed or lost as a result of a qualifying casualty.

EJUSDEM GENERIS: A rule of construction that applies when a general descriptive word follows a list of specific words; under the rule, the general word, though possibly encompassing many different things, is interpreted to mean only like things, or things similar to the specific words listed prior to the general word.

PERAMBULATIONS: Travels or movements.

Chamales v. Commissioner

(*Homeowners/Taxpayers*) v. (*Internal Revenue Service*)

T.C. Memo. 2000–33 (2000)

A TEMPORARY DECLINE IN HOME VALUE IS NOT A CASUALTY LOSS

■ **INSTANT FACTS** The taxpayers claimed a casualty loss deduction on their federal tax return after public interest in their celebrity neighbor's murder trial caused their neighborhood to become inundated with media and on-lookers and resulted in a sudden decline in the market value of their home.

■ **BLACK LETTER RULE** For purposes of qualifying as a casualty loss, there must be a permanent devaluation of the property for which the loss is claimed.

■ **PROCEDURAL BASIS**

Petition for a redetermination of the IRS's denial of the Chamales' casualty loss deduction and assignment of a federal income tax deficiency, as well as an accuracy-related penalty,

■ **FACTS**

The taxpayers bought a home in an exclusive neighborhood shortly after their celebrity neighbor who lived in an adjacent home was arrested for murder. Following the murders and the arrest, the neighborhood was inundated with media personnel, media equipment, and curiosity seekers. As a result, there was a significant decline in the value of the taxpayers' home. After consulting with their accountant, the taxpayers claimed a deduction for casualty loss on their federal income tax return. The IRS denied the deduction and then determined a federal income tax deficiency, along with an accuracy penalty.

■ **ISSUE**

Does the decline in the value of a home resulting from the attention drawn to the neighborhood after a celebrity neighbor's arrest for murder entitle homeowners to claim a net casualty loss deduction on their federal income tax return?

■ **DECISION AND RATIONALE**

(Nims, J.) No. The taxpayers' net casualty loss deduction was properly denied in this case because the decline in the value of their home was not the result of a casualty loss. A casualty loss arises when two circumstances are present: (1) the nature of the occurrence that precipitated the damage to the property must qualify as a casualty, and (2) the nature of the damage sustained must be such that it is deductible under I.R.C. § 165. The nature of the occurrence that caused the decline in the value of the taxpayers' home here did not qualify as a casualty because it was not an undesigned, sudden, and unexpected event, as required by the Code, but rather was the ongoing public attention generated by their celebrity neighbor's arrest and subsequent trials. Furthermore, the nature of the damage sustained was not deductible because it did not satisfy the Tax Court's interpretation of I.R.C. § 165 that only physical damage or permanent abandonment would be recognized as deductible. Since the decline in the value of the property was tied to public interest, which would likely decrease over time, the decline was temporary, and the position of the court has been to refuse to permit deductions based on a temporary decline in market value. The determination of the IRS as to the federal income tax deficiency is upheld. However, the determination of the IRS with regard to the accuracy-related penalty under

---

I.R.C. § 6662(a) is dismissed because the net casualty loss claim satisfied the "good faith" exception to the penalty.

Analysis:

The tax court's position that damage to a property has to be physical in order to be deductible under I.R.C. § 165 has not been universally accepted by the courts. The Court of Appeals for the Eleventh Circuit has permitted a deduction based on permanent buyer resistance, even in the absence of physical damage. However, the Eleventh Circuit's decision can be distinguished, since in *Chamales* the decline in value was temporary, while the decline in value of the home involved in the Eleventh Circuit case was permanent.

■ CASE VOCABULARY

EJUSDEM GENERIS: A canon of construction that when a general word or phrase follows a list of specific persons or things, the general word or phrase will be interpreted to include only persons or things of the same type as those listed.

CASUALTY LOSS: For tax purposes, the total or partial destruction of an asset resulting from an unexpected or unusual event, such as an automobile accident or tornado.

DEDUCTION: An amount subtracted from gross income, or from adjusted gross income, when calculating taxable income.

Blackman v. Commissioner

(Taxpayer) v. *(IRS)*
88 T.C. 677 (1987)

CASUALTY LOSS DEDUCTIONS WILL NOT BE ALLOWED WHERE ALLOWING THE DEDUCTION WILL FRUSTRATE PUBLIC POLICY

■ **INSTANT FACTS** A dispute between a taxpayer and the IRS arose when the taxpayer, who destroyed his own house when he set fire to some clothing inside of it, claimed a casualty loss of $97,853 on his tax return.

■ **BLACK LETTER RULE** Gross negligence on the part of a taxpayer that results in the destruction of property will bar any casualty loss deduction for the destroyed property.

■ **PROCEDURAL BASIS**

Appeal to the Tax Court of an IRS decision to deny a casualty loss to a taxpayer who negligently burned down his house.

■ **FACTS**

In 1980 Biltmore Blackman (P) discovered that his wife was not the woman he thought she was. One day when he arrived home unexpectedly early from being away on business, Blackman (P) discovered that another man was living with his wife (and five children). Neighbors told him the man had lived there before when Blackman (P) was away on business. When he returned again at a later date, Blackman (P) found his wife having a party. Her guests refused to leave when he asked them to do so, and Blackman (P) left angry. The next day, September 2, 1980, Blackman (P) once again went home, hoping to discuss the possibility of divorce. An argument ensued between Blackman (P) and his wife, and she left. Angry, Blackman (P) took some of his wife's clothes, put them on the stove, and lit them on fire. He then "took pots of water to dowse the fire, putting the fire totally out," and left. Obviously Blackman (P) was not as good at putting fires out as he thought, because the house eventually burned to the ground. Blackman (P) was charged with arson, destruction of property, and other crimes. By order of the court, the arson charge was placed on the "stet docket," and Blackmun was ordered to serve 24 months unsupervised probation on the malicious destruction charge. Blackman's (P) insurance company refused to cover the loss, so Blackman (P) claimed a $97,853 casualty loss deduction on his 1980 tax return (filed jointly with his wife [this is what might be called a dysfunctional family]). The IRS denied the deduction and the matter was taken to the Tax Court.

■ **ISSUE**

May a taxpayer whose property was destroyed in a fire that the taxpayer negligently started claim a casualty loss deduction for the value of the property destroyed?

■ **DECISION AND RATIONALE**

(Authoring Judge Not Stated) No. Section 165(a) allows a deduction for "any loss sustained during the taxable year and not compensated for by insurance or otherwise." Section 165(c)(3) provides, in pertinent part, that in the case of an individual, the subsection (a) deduction is to be limited to "losses of property not connected with a trade or business, if such losses arise from fire, storm, shipwreck, or other casualty, or from theft." The IRS (D) concedes that Blackman (P) sustained a loss through fire. However, it argues that he is not entitled to a deduction because to allow such a deduction when Blackman (P) set fire to his own house would be contrary to Maryland's public policy. Courts have traditionally disallowed casualty loss deductions where national or state public policy would be frustrated by allowing it. Conviction of a crime is not essential to a showing that the allowance would frustrate public policy. Moreover, it is well settled that the negligence of the taxpayer is not a bar to the allowance of the casualty loss deduction. On the other hand, gross negligence on the part of the taxpayer will bar a casualty loss deduction. "Needless to say, the taxpayer may not knowingly or wilfully sit back and allow himself to be damaged in his property or willfully damage the property himself." *White v. Commissioner.* Here, Blackman (P) was grossly negligent. He started the fire, and claims that he also attempted to extinguish it. Yet the firemen found clothing still on the stove and there is no evidence to corroborate Blackman's (P) claim that he attempted to dowse the flames. Further, the destruction of the house was a foreseeable result of Blackman's (P) actions. As such, he was grossly negligent, and we hold that this gross negligence bars him from deducting the loss claimed by him under § § 165(a) and (c)(3). In addition, allowing him a deduction would severely and immediately frustrate the articulated public policy of Maryland against arson and burning. Maryland has also articulated public policy against domestic violence, which would similarly be violated by allowing the deduction. We find for the Commissioner (D).

Analysis:

Blackman teaches two important lessons with respect to the casualty loss deduction available under IRC § 165(c)(3). First, gross negligence on the part of a taxpayer that results in the destruction of property will bar any casualty loss deduction. Second, casualty loss deductions will not be allowed where allowing the deduction will frustrate public policy. Certainly it makes sense that a taxpayer should not be permitted to profit from his or her own gross negligence or illegal acts. It is important to note that Blackman (P) first went to his insurance company for reimbursement. Had the insurance company paid for the loss, Blackman (P) would not have even been permitted to attempt a deduction, as the deduction only applies to losses not covered by insurance.

■ CASE VOCABULARY

STET DOCKET: A postponement of action on a particular criminal charge.

Taylor v. Commissioner

(Taxpayer) v. *(IRS)*
54 T.C.M. 129 (1987)

NOT ALL DOCTOR RECOMMENDED ACTIVITIES CONSTITUTE DEDUCTIBLE MEDICAL EXPENSES

■ **INSTANT FACTS** A dispute arose between the IRS and a taxpayer when the taxpayer attempted to claim the cost of paying someone to mow his lawn as a medical expense.

■ **BLACK LETTER RULE** The Internal Revenue Code specifically authorizes a deduction for medical care expenses paid during the taxable year which are not compensated for by insurance or otherwise; however, just because a doctor recommends an activity (or recommends abstention from an activity) does not mean that the cost of the activity can be deducted as a medical expense.

■ **PROCEDURAL BASIS**

Appeal to the Tax Court of an IRS denial of a medical deduction involving the cost of lawn mowing.

■ **FACTS**

Due to severe allergies, Taylor's (P) doctor instructed him not to mow his own lawn. In 1982, Taylor (P) paid $178 to have his lawn mowed. He then claimed a medical expense deduction in that amount, arguing that the lawn care costs were a direct result of his doctor's orders. The IRS (D) denied the deduction, and the matter was taken to the Tax Court.

■ **ISSUE**

Can the costs of all doctor-recommended activities be claimed as deductible medical expenses?

■ **DECISION AND RATIONALE**

(Authoring Judge Not Stated) No. Section 262 disallows deductions for personal, living, or family expenses. Section 213, however, specifically authorizes a deduction for medical care expenses paid during the taxable year which are not compensated by insurance or otherwise. Here Taylor (P), who bears the burden of proof, has not satisfactorily demonstrated that the apparently personal expense of lawn care is a medical expense. No authority has been cited in support of his position, and there had been no showing why other family members could not undertake the mowing or whether he would have paid others to mow his lawn even absent his doctor's direction not to do so himself. The mere fact that an activity is doctor-recommended does not mean that the costs of that activity are deductible medical expenses. To be deductible, the expenses must fall within the parameters of "medical care." The $178 deduction was improper.

Analysis:

IRC § 213(a) allows the deduction of any "medical care" expenses that exceed 7.5% of a taxpayer's AGI. The IRC defines "medical care" expenses as those incurred "for the diagnosis, cure, mitigation, treatment, or prevention of disease, or for the purpose of affecting any structure or function of the body." IRC § 213(d)(1)(A). *Taylor* shows that the IRS and the Tax Courts have adopted a somewhat narrow interpretation of this section. As such, not all costs for doctor recommended activities (or activities that a doctor says should be avoided) will be held to constitute deductible medical expenses.

■ CASE VOCABULARY

MEDICAL CARE: As defined by the IRC, medical care is anything that goes to "the diagnosis, cure, mitigation, treatment, or prevention of disease, or for the purpose of affecting any structure or function of the body."

MEDICAL EXPENSE DEDUCTION: A provision found in IRC § 213 which provides for the deduction of expenses outlaid for "medical care."

NONDEDUCTIBLE PERSONAL EXPENSES: Personal living expenses such as food and clothing that, under § 262 of the Internal Revenue Code, cannot be deducted in the absence of a contrary code provision.

Henderson v. Commissioner

(Parents of Disabled Child–Taxpayer) v. *(Internal Revenue Service)*

T.C. Memo. 2000–321 (2000)

THE DEPRECIATION OF A VAN USED TO TRANSPORT A DISABLED CHILD WAS NOT DEDUCTIBLE

■ **INSTANT FACTS** The Hendersons (TP) claimed a medical expense deduction on their federal tax return related to the cost and modification of a van they purchased for the sole purpose of transporting their disabled son.

■ **BLACK LETTER RULE** Depreciation is not an "expense paid" or "amount paid" for purposes of the medical expense deduction under I.R.C. § 213.

■ PROCEDURAL BASIS

Petition for redetermination of the IRS's denial of the Hendersons' (TP) medical expense deduction.

■ FACTS

The Hendersons (TP) purchased a van for the sole purpose of transporting their disabled son. To further meet their son's medical needs, the Hendersons (TP) modified the van by installing a wheelchair lift and by raising the roof of the van. On the recommendation of their accountant, they claimed a depreciation deduction for the purchase price and modification costs of the van. The IRS conceded that the cost to modify the van was a deductible medical expense for the year in which it was paid, but denied the depreciation deductions claimed by the Hendersons (TP).

■ ISSUE

Is the depreciation cost claimed by the Hendersons (TP) on their federal tax returns deductible as a medical expense under I.R.C. § 213?

■ DECISION AND RATIONALE

(Cohen, J.) No. The depreciation cost claimed by the Hendersons (TP) was not deductible as a medical expense under I.R.C. § 213. Section 213, which creates an exception to the general rule under I.R.C. § 262(a) that personal, living or family expenses are not deductible, limits deductions to "expenses paid" for medical care during a taxable year and defines medical expenses as "amounts paid" for transportation primarily for and essential to medical care. Depreciation is not an "expense paid" or "amount paid" and, therefore, not deductible as a medical expense. The determination of the IRS is upheld.

Analysis:

Henderson reiterates the IRS's position that depreciation is not deductible as a medical expense under IRC § 213, but that is not the only important point to be gleaned from the case. The decision is also about the need for uniform adherence to the Tax Code provisions, regardless of the facts and circumstances of a particular matter.

■ **CASE VOCABULARY**

DEDUCTION: An amount subtracted from gross income, or from adjusted gross income when calculating taxable income.

DEPRECIATION: A decline in an asset's value because of use, wear, or obsolescence.

STRAIGHT–LINE DEPRECIATION METHOD: A depreciation method that writes off the cost or other basis of the asset by deducting the salvage value from the initial cost of the capital asset, and dividing the difference by the asset's estimated useful life.

MEDICAL EXPENSE: An expense for medical treatment or healthcare.

Ochs v. Commissioner

(Taxpayer) v. *(IRS)*
195 F.2d 692 (2d Cir.1952)

THE MERE FACT THAT SENDING CHILDREN TO BOARDING SCHOOL PROVIDES A MEDICAL BENEFIT TO AN ILL PARENT DOES NOT MAKE THE COST OF BOARDING SCHOOL A DEDUCTIBLE MEDICAL EXPENSE

■ **INSTANT FACTS** The taxpayer claimed as a medical expenses deduction the cost of sending his two daughters to boarding school.

■ **BLACK LETTER RULE** The fact that certain family expenses convey an indirect medical benefit on a family member is not enough to make those expenses deductible medical expenses under § 213 of the Internal Revenue Code (IRC).

■ **PROCEDURAL BASIS**

Appeal to the Second Circuit Court of Appeals of a Tax Court decision denying as a medical expenses deduction the cost of boarding school.

■ **FACTS**

In December of 1943, a thyroidectomy and histological examination of Helen H. Ochs (P) disclosed cancer. The cancer resulted in severe nervousness, and as a result of this nervousness, a physician suggested that Helen's two daughters be sent away from their mother so that she might recover. The two girls were thereafter sent to boarding school at significant expense. Their father claimed a medical expense deduction for the cost of the girls' tuition. That deduction was denied by the IRS, and Ochs (P) appealed. The Tax Court affirmed the IRS' decision, and Ochs (P) appealed to the Second Circuit Court of Appeals.

■ **ISSUE**

Can family expenses that convey an indirect medical benefit on a sick family member be deducted as qualified medical expenses?

■ **DECISION AND RATIONALE**

(Hand, J.) No. The expenses incurred by Ochs (P) were nondeductible family expenses within the meaning of IRC § 262 rather than medical expenses. Concededly the line between the two is a difficult one to draw, but this only reflects the fact that expenditures made on behalf of some members of a family unit frequently benefit others in the family as well. The expenses here were made necessary by the loss of the wife's services, and the only reason for allowing them as a deduction is that the wife also received a benefit. We think it unlikely that Congress intended to transform family expenses into medical expenses for this reason. Affirmed.

■ **DISSENT**

(Frank, J.) I think that Congress would have said that Ochs' (P) expense fell within the category of "mitigation, treatment, or prevention of disease," and that it was for the "purpose of affecting [a] structure or function of the body." The IRS (D) seemingly admits that the deduction might be a medical expense if the wife were sent away from her children to a sanitarium for rest and quiet, but asserts that it never can be if, for the very same purpose, the children are sent away from the mother—even if a boarding-school for the children is cheaper than a sanitarium for the wife. I cannot believe that Congress intended such a meaningless distinction. The cure ought to be the doctor's business, not the Commissioner's (D). Moreover, here Ochs' (P) was compelled to go to the expense of putting the children away primarily for the benefit of his sick wife. He would not have sent them away otherwise. Expenses incurred solely because of the loss of the patient's services and not as a part of his cure are a different thing altogether.

Analysis:

Ochs v. Commissioner demonstrates the difficulties that can arise in interpreting the language of the medical expense deduction found in IRC § 213(a). In the end, the majority holds that the mere fact that certain family expenses convey an indirect medical benefit on a family member is not enough to make those expenses deductible medical expenses. Arguably this narrow interpretation of the Code provides less room for manipulation and characterization of everyday family expenses as medical expenses, and therefore benefits the IRS, in that fewer activities and expenses can be claimed as medical deductions.

■ CASE VOCABULARY

HISTOLOGICAL EXAMINATION: An examination of one's body tissues.

SANITARIUM: A place where a chronically ill person can go for rest and recuperation.

THYROIDECTOMY: The surgical removal of certain gland tissue from the thyroid.

Ottawa Silica Co. v. United States

(Taxpayer) v. *(IRS)*

699 F.2d 1124 (Fed.Cir.1983)

IF A PARTY RECEIVES A SUBSTANTIAL BENEFIT IN RETURN FOR A CHARITABLE CONTRIBUTION, THERE HAS BEEN A QUID PRO QUO AND NO DEDUCTION WILL BE ALLOWED

■ **INSTANT FACTS** A dispute arose between a corporation and the IRS when the corporation was denied a charitable contribution deduction because its donation of land to the state carried with it significant benefits for the corporation.

■ **BLACK LETTER RULE** A contribution made to a charity is not made for exclusively public purposes if the donor receives or anticipates receiving a substantial benefit in return, and if the benefit received by the donor is greater than that which inures to the general public, no deduction can be taken.

■ **PROCEDURAL BASIS**

Appeal to the Court of Appeals for the Federal Circuit of a Court of Claims decision denying a charitable contribution deduction.

■ **FACTS**

Ottawa Silica Co. (P) was in the business of mining, processing, and marketing silica. As a part of its business, Ottawa (P) acquired a significant area of property near Oceanside, California. Then, knowing that the property would someday be of significant value for residential and commercial purposes, Ottawa (P) acquired more property in the same area. In the mid–1960's Ottawa (P) was approached by the Oceanside–Carlsbad Union High School District about the possibility of donating 50 acres of property for the purpose of building a new high school. Eventually a donation was made, and Ottawa (P) claimed a charitable contribution deduction of $415,000 on its tax return. At the time of its donation, Ottawa (P) was aware that the building of a high school would significantly increase the value of its surrounding properties. Additionally, Ottawa (P) also contemplated that the building of the high school would be accompanied by the building of roads, which would increase Ottawa's (P) access to various parts of its land. Ottawa's (P) deduction was denied on the grounds that it would receive a "substantial benefit" from the donation. Ottawa (P) appealed.

■ **ISSUE**

Can the IRS deny a charitable contribution deduction to a party who receives a substantial benefit in return for its contribution?

■ **DECISION AND RATIONALE**

(Colaianni, J.) Yes. In *Singer Co. v. United States*, the Supreme Court, addressing the charitable contribution deduction, stated: "[I]f the benefits received, or expected to be received, [by the donor] are substantial, and meaning by that, benefits greater than those that inure to the general public from transfers for charitable purposes (which benefits are merely *incidental* to the transfer), then in such case we feel that the transferor has received, or expects to receive, a quid pro quo sufficient to remove the transfer from the realm of deductibility under section 170 [of the IRC]." The parties to the present case disagree as to the meaning of the above quotation. The plain language, however, clearly indicates that a "substantial benefit" received in return for a contribution constitutes a quid pro quo, which precludes a deduction. The court defined a substantial benefit as one that is "greater than those that inure to the general public from transfers for charitable purposes." To put it another way, it is only when the donor receives or expects to receive additional substantial benefits that courts are likely to conclude that a quid pro quo for the transfer exists and that the donor is therefore not entitled to a charitable deduction. Ottawa (P) argues that it received no benefits, except incidental ones, in return for its contribution of the site, and it is therefore entitled to a § 170 deduction for the transfer of its land to the school district. Having considered the testimony and the evidence adduced at trial, we conclude that the benefits to be derived by Ottawa (P) from the transfer were substantial enough to provide it with a quid pro quo for the transfer and thus effectively destroyed the charitable nature of the transfer. Specifically, Ottawa (P) knew that the construction of a school and the attendant roads on its property would substantially benefit the surrounding land, and it made the conveyance expecting its remaining property to increase in value. The receipt of these benefits at least partially prompted Ottawa (P) to make the conveyance. Under *Singer*, this is more than adequate reason to deny a charitable contribution deduction. Affirmed.

Analysis:

Sometimes contributions to qualifying charities provide benefits to the donor, as well as to the donee. Such contributions are referred to as "quid pro quo" contributions. As the Federal Circuit in *Ottawa* states, the IRC limits the amount of the charitable contribution deduction that can be taken for quid pro quo transactions. Citing *Singer*, the court sets forth the rule that if the benefit received by the donor from a charitable donation is greater than that which inures to the general public, no deduction can be taken. Such was the case in *Ottawa*. In some cases, however, the value that inures to the public from a contribution exceeds the value received by the donor. The amount of the deduction is then the difference between the value that the donor receives and the value of the donation. Thus, for example, if a participant in a charitable auction pays $5,000 for a certain item with a fair market value of just $500, the donor can take a charitable contribution deduction in the amount of $4,500. To make certain that the proper amount of any deduction is taken, IRC § 6115 requires that for any quid pro quo contribution of more than $75, the recipient charity must give the donor a writing directing that the full amount of the gift is not deductible. The writing must also contain a "good faith estimate of the value of [the] goods or services" received so that the proper deduction can be determined.

■ CASE VOCABULARY

QUID PRO QUO: An exchange of one thing for another thing of similar value.

Bob Jones University v. United States

(Nonprofit Corporation) v. *(IRS)*

461 U.S. 574, 103 S.Ct. 2017 (1983)

EDUCATIONAL INSTITUTIONS THAT EMPLOY RACIALLY–DISCRIMINATORY ADMISSIONS PRAC-
TICES DO NOT QUALIFY FOR TAX–EXEMPT STATUS UNDER IRC § 501(c)(3).

■ **INSTANT FACTS** A dispute arose between the IRS (D) and Bob Jones University (P) when the IRS (D) decided that because of the University's (P) racially-discriminatory admissions practices, it no longer qualified as a tax-exempt charitable organization under IRC § 501(c)(3).

■ **BLACK LETTER RULE** A declaration that a given institution is not "charitable" should be made only where there can be no doubt that the activity in which the institution is involved is contrary to a fundamental public policy.

■ **PROCEDURAL BASIS**

Appeal to the United States Supreme Court of a Fourth Circuit Court of Appeals decision denying tax exempt status to educational institutions that employ racially-discriminatory admissions practices.

■ **FACTS**

Bob Jones University (P), a nonprofit corporation located in South Carolina, was created "to conduct an institution of learning . . . , giving special emphasis to the Christian religion and the ethics revealed in the Holy Scriptures." One of the beliefs taught by the school was that interracial marriage and dating are prohibited by the Bible. As such, admissions decisions were made based on adherence to those ideas. Additionally, students at the school were prohibited from participating in interracial dating or marriage. Until 1970, the IRS (D) gave Bob Jones University (P) tax-exempt status under § 501(c)(3). In 1970, however, the IRS (D) notified the University (P) that it had decided to challenge the tax-exempt status of private schools practicing racial discrimination in their admissions policies. In federal district court, the tax-exempt status of the University (P) was upheld. The Court of Appeals reversed, and the University (P) appealed to the United States Supreme Court.

■ **ISSUE**

Can a nonprofit private school that adheres to racially discriminatory admissions standards on the basis of religious doctrine qualify as a tax exempt organization under IRC § 501(c)(3)?

■ **DECISION AND RATIONALE**

(Burger, J.) No. In Rev. Rul. 71–447, the IRS (D) formalized the policy first announced in 1970, that § 170 and § 501(c)(3) embrace the common law "charity" concept. Under that view, to qualify as a tax-exempt organization under § 501(c)(3), an institution must show, among other things, that its activity is not contrary to settled public policy. Section 501(c)(3) provides that "[c]orporations . . . organized and operated exclusively for religious, charitable . . . or educational purposes" are entitled to a tax exemption. The University (P) argues that the plain language of the statute guarantees its tax-exempt status. In doing so, it emphasizes the absence of any statutory language expressly requiring an organization to be "charitable" in the common law sense, and it also contends that the disjunctive "or" separating the categories in § 501(c)(3) precludes such a reading. Section 501(c)(3) must be analyzed and construed within the framework of the IRC and against the background of the Congressional purposes. Such an examination reveals unmistakable evidence that underlying all relevant parts of the

Code is the intent that entitlement to tax exemption depends on meeting certain common law standards of charity—namely, that an institution seeking tax-exempt status must serve a public purpose and not be contrary to established public policy. This "charitable" concept appears explicitly in § 170 of the Code. That section contains a list of organizations virtually identical to that contained in § 501(c)(3). It is apparent that Congress intended that list to have the same meaning in both sections. Further, tax exemptions for certain institutions thought beneficial to the social order are deeply rooted in our history. The origins of such exemptions lie in the special privileges that have long been extended to charitable trusts, and it is clear that the law has always recognized that the purpose of a charitable trust may not be illegal or violate established public policy. History also makes it clear that, to warrant exemption under § 501(c)(3), an institution's purpose must not be so at odds with the common community conscience as to undermine any public benefit that might otherwise be conferred. Determinations of public benefit and policy are sensitive matters with serious implications for the institutions affected; a declaration that a given institution is not "charitable" should be made only where there can be no doubt that the activity involved is contrary to a fundamental public policy. But there can be no doubt that racial discrimination in education violates the widely accepted views of elementary justice and fundamental national public policy. The University (P) contends that, regardless of whether the IRS (D) properly concluded that racially discriminatory private schools violate public policy, only Congress can alter the scope of § 170 and § 501(c)(3). As such, the University (P) argues that the IRS (D) overstepped its bounds. Yet ever since the inception of the tax code, Congress has allowed the IRS to interpret the tax laws. In an area as complex as the tax system, the agency Congress vests with administrative responsibility must be able to exercise its authority to meet changing conditions and news problems. Further, the actions and inactions of Congress since 1970 leave no doubt that the IRS (D) reached the correct conclusion in exercising its authority. In this respect, it is very clear that Congress was aware of the IRS's (D) decision. It is also clear that Congress, having this knowledge, chose not to act, thereby ratifying the IRS' (D) actions. Further, Congress affirmatively manifested its acquiescence in the IRS's (D) policy when it enacted the present § 501(i) of the Code. Finally, the University (P) contends that, even if the IRS's (D) policy is valid as to nonreligious private schools, that policy cannot constitutionally be applied to schools that engage in racial discrimination on the basis of sincerely held religious beliefs. As to such schools, it is argued that the IRS's (D) construction of § 170 and § 501(c)(3) violates their free exercise rights under the Religion Clauses of the First Amendment. The governmental interest at stake here is compelling. The Government has a fundamental, overriding interest in eradicating racial discrimination in education. That governmental interest substantially outweighs whatever burden denial of tax benefits places on the University's (P) exercise of its religious beliefs. The interests asserted by the University (P) cannot be accommodated with that compelling governmental interests, and no "less restrictive means" are available to achieve the governmental interest. Affirmed.

■ CONCURRENCE

(Powell, J.) I concur that tax-exempt status under §§ 170(c) and 501(c)(3) is not available to schools that are racially discriminatory. I do not agree, however, with the Court's more general explanation of the justifications for the tax exemptions provided to charitable organizations. First, I am unconvinced that the critical question is whether an individual organization provides a clear "public benefit" as that phrase is defined by the Court. Second, the Court asserts that an exempt organization must "demonstrably serve and be in harmony with the public interest," must have a purpose that comports with "the common community conscience," and must not act in a manner "affirmatively at odds with [the] declared position of the whole government." Taken together, these passages suggest that the primary function of a tax-exempt organization is to act on behalf of the government in carrying out governmentally approved policies. As such, there is no room for diversity of opinion, something that tax-exempt status should be used to promote.

■ DISSENT

(Rehnquist, J.) I agree that there exists a strong national policy against racial discrimination in education. But unlike the majority, I am convinced that while it certainly could do so, Congress simply has failed to take action on this matter, and as we have said over and over again, regardless of our view of the propriety of Congress' failure to legislate, we are not constitutionally empowered to act for them. With undeniable clarity, Congress has explicitly defined the requirements for § 501(c)(3) status, and nowhere is there to be found some additional, undefined public policy requirement. Whatever our views of racial discrimination, this court should not legislate for Congress.

Analysis:

Some entities are considered tax-exempt, meaning those entities are not required to pay taxes and will not be held liable for nonpayment. One provision of the IRC that provides such an exemption is § 501(c)(3), which exempts from tax liability any "[c]orporation[] . . . organized and operated exclusively for religious, charitable . . . or educational purposes." *Bob Jones* teaches that the plain language of the statute does not control. Instead, underlying the Code section is a "charitable" requirement, pursuant to which any organization seeking tax exempt status that in any way violates national public policy may not be given that status. Bob Jones University (P) was a corporation focused on religion-based instruction. This alone, however, was not enough, as the University (P) was not "charitable," as that term is defined in the common law. *Bob Jones* holds that the words "and charitable as that term is defined in the common law" have arguably been added to § 501(c)(3)'s list of exempt organizations. The second topic addressed by *Bob Jones* is that of personal deductions—the charitable contribution deduction in particular. In sum, the common law "charitable" requirement applies to both § § 170 and 501, meaning not only is Bob Jones University (P) not tax exempt, but also that donations to the University (P) arguably cannot be claimed as charitable contributions.

■ **CASE VOCABULARY**

CHARITABLE TRUST: A trust created for the purpose of benefitting either a specific charity or the public in general.

TAX–EXEMPT ORGANIZATION: An organization that is not required to pay taxes.

King v. Commissioner

(Taxpayer) v. *(Commissioner of Internal Revenue Service)*

121 T.C. No. 12 (2003)

NONCUSTODIAL PARENTS MAY BE ENTITLED TO A DEPENDENCY EXEMPTION DEDUCTION

■ **INSTANT FACTS** Lopez (P) and King (P), who were never married to each other, each claimed a dependency exemption deduction for their minor child on their 1998 and 1999 federal income tax returns.

■ **BLACK LETTER RULE** A noncustodial parent who never married and has lived apart from his child's mother during the last six months of a taxable year may claim a dependency exemption deduction if the child lives with one or both parents for more than half of the year, receives more than half of his support from his parents during the year, and the custodial parent signs a written declaration that she will not claim the dependency exemption deduction for the child.

■ **PROCEDURAL BASIS**

Tax Court consideration of the Commissioner's denial of dependency exemption deductions.

■ **FACTS**

Lopez (P) and King (P), who were never married to each other, were the father and mother, respectively, of a minor child born in 1986. In 1987, Lopez claimed a dependency exemption deduction for the child on his federal income tax return. In response, the Commissioner (D) requested that King (P) file a completed Form 8332, Release of Claim to Exemption for Child of Divorced or Separated Parents. On April 30, 1988, King (P) executed the form, which Lopez (P) timely filed for 1987 and each year thereafter. Beginning in 1993, however, King (P) and her husband began claiming a dependency exemption deduction for the child on their federal income tax returns. The child resided with the Kings (P) during tax years 1998 and 1999, and the Kings (P) provided more than one-half of the support for the child. Ms. King (P) never informed Lopez (P) of her intent to revoke the Form 8332 Release. In 2002, the Commissioner (D) issued notices of deficiency to King (P) and Lopez (P) for 1998 and 1999, denying both parties the deduction. Both parties sought a redetermination, and the cases were consolidated.

■ **ISSUE**

Does the special support test under IRC § 152(e) apply to parents who were never married to grant a noncustodial parent a dependency exemption deduction?

■ **DECISION AND RATIONALE**

(Judge undisclosed.) Yes. Generally, a taxpayer may take a dependency exemption deduction only if the taxpayer provided over half of the child's support during the tax year. When the child's parents are divorced, separated, or live apart during the last six months of the taxable year and the child is in the custody of one or both of his parents for more than half of the year, the custodial parent is treated as providing for more than half of the child's support under the special support test set forth in § 152(e). If, however, the custodial parent signs a written declaration that he or she will not claim the dependency exemption deduction, the noncustodial parent may claim the deduction by attaching the declaration to his or her income tax return. The written declaration may apply to one year, a set number of years, or all future years.

Here, Lopez (P) and King (P) lived apart during the last six months of 1998 and 1999, and the child was in the custody of King (P) for more than half of those years. Under ordinary circumstances, King (P) would be entitled to the dependency exemption deduction. However, King's (P) Form 8332 releasing the deduction for 1987 and all future years is a written declaration that she will not claim the child as a dependent, thus entitling Lopez (P) to the deduction. There is nothing in the statute nor the legislative history to suggest that the statute does not apply to individuals who were never married. Rather, the statute unambiguously applies to "parents" in three situations—divorce, legal separation, and those who live apart during the last six months of a calendar year. Nothing demands that the taxpayers be previously married.

The parties stipulated that King (P) had executed the Form 8332 "for the taxable year 1987 and all years thereafter," and her testimony does not reveal duress during the execution of the release in 1987. Despite King's (P) attempts to avoid the effect of this release, she must be bound by her stipulation. Lopez (P) is entitled to the deductions for 1988 and 1989.

Analysis:

Even attorneys who do not practice tax law face crucial taxation issues in their practices. For instance, in determining the support a divorced parent contributes toward a child, the label placed on the funds is telling. Only funds explicitly labeled as child support will be treated as such. Spousal maintenance paid to a former spouse but used for the support of a child will ordinarily be credited to the receiving spouse when apportioning the annual support of a child.

■ CASE VOCABULARY

CUSTODY: The care, control, and maintenance of a child awarded by a court to a responsible adult.

DEDUCTION: The amount subtracted from gross income when calculating adjusted gross income, or from adjusted gross income when calculating taxable income.

DEPENDENCY EXEMPTION: A tax exemption granted to an individual taxpayer for each dependent whose gross income is less than the exemption amount and for each child who is younger than 19 or, if a student, younger than 24.

NONCUSTODIAL: Of or relating to someone, especially a parent, who does not have sole or primary custody.

CHAPTER FIVE

Allowances for Mixed Business and Personal Outlays

Nickerson v. Commissioner

Instant Facts: The tax court determined that a wannabe farmer who bought a farm and operated at a loss for two years did not have a bona fide expectation of profit for tax purposes.

Black Letter Rule: A taxpayer need not expect an immediate profit from a business, and the existence of "start up" losses does not preclude a bona fide profit motive.

Popov v. Commissioner

Instant Facts: Popov (TP), a professional violinist, claimed a home office deduction for the living room of her apartment, which she used exclusively for practice.

Black Letter Rule: To claim a home office deduction, the home office must qualify as the taxpayer's principal place of business.

Moller v. United States

Instant Facts: The plaintiffs unsuccessfully attempted to deduct the expenses of operating home-offices from their taxes since they used them in order to manage their investments.

Black Letter Rule: When the only return is that of an investor, the taxpayer has not satisfied his burden of demonstrating that he is engaged in a trade or business since investing is not a trade or business.

Whitten v. Commissioner

Instant Facts: A contestant on "Wheel of Fortune" deducted his transportation, meals and lodging expenses from his game show winnings on his federal tax return, claiming they represent "gambling losses."

Black Letter Rule: Expenses incurred in participating as a contestant on a game show may not be characterized as wagering losses for tax purposes.

Henderson v. Commissioner

Instant Facts: A woman brought suit after she was not allowed to deduct amounts she spent in purchasing a picture and a plant to decorate her office, and the rental of a parking space.

Black Letter Rule: Amounts paid for a framed print and live plant used to decorate an office, and amounts paid to rent a parking space are nondeductible personal expenses under section 262.

Rudolph v. United States

Instant Facts: An insurance salesman and his wife were awarded an expenses-paid company trip to New York City for business/pleasure, and the Commissioner assessed its value to them as taxable income.

Black Letter Rule: When the purpose of the trip is primarily personal in nature, rather than related primarily to business, expenses for transportation, meals, and lodging are not deductible as "ordinary and necessary" business expenses under section 162.

Moss v. Commissioner

Instant Facts: The Commissioner (D) disallowed Moss' (P) federal income tax deductions representing his share of his law firm's daily lunch expense.

Black Letter Rule: Meals are deductible under section 162(a) when they are ordinary and necessary business expenses.

Danville Plywood Corporation v. United States

Instant Facts: A plywood company tried to deduct as a business expense the cost of taking 120 people away to New Orleans for the weekend to attend the Super Bowl.

Black Letter Rule: To qualify as an "ordinary and necessary" business expense under section 162(a), an expenditure must be both "common and accepted" in the taxpayer's community, as well as "appropriate" for the development of the taxpayer's business.

Churchill Downs, Inc. v. Commissioner

Instant Facts: Churchill Downs, Inc. (P) sought to deduct the full amount of expenses related to race-related entertainment events.

Black Letter Rule: Deductions for activities "generally considered to be entertainment" are limited to fifty percent of the amount of the expense, unless they are objectively integral to the taxpayer's business or occupation.

Smith v. Commissioner

Instant Facts: The plaintiffs claimed childcare expenses on their federal income taxes as business expenses, but the Commissioner disallowed the deduction.

Black Letter Rule: Nursemaids retained to care for infant children are expenses which are personal in nature and not deductible for federal income tax purposes.

Commissioner v. Flowers

Instant Facts: A lawyer unsuccessfully attempted to deduct the traveling expenses associated with his commuting from his home in Jackson, Mississippi to his work in Mobile, Alabama.

Black Letter Rule: Travel expenses in pursuit of business within the meaning of section 162(a)(2) can arise only when the business forces the taxpayer to travel and to live temporarily at some place other than his home, thereby advancing the interests of the business.

Hantzis v. Commissioner

Instant Facts: A law student living and attending law school in Massachusetts got a summer job in New York and attempted to deduct her living and traveling expenses for temporarily residing in New York from her taxes.

Black Letter Rule: For a taxpayer to be "away from home in the pursuit of a trade or business," she must establish the existence of some sort of business relation both to the location she claims as "home" and to the location of her temporary employment sufficient to support a finding that her duplicative expenses are necessitated by business exigencies.

Pevsner v. Commissioner

Instant Facts: A YSL salesperson deducted the cost of her YSL clothing and accessories, as well as the maintenance costs for the clothing, from her taxes as a business expense.

Black Letter Rule: The cost of clothing is deductible as a business expense only if the clothing is of a type specifically required as a condition of employment, is not adaptable to general usage as ordinary clothing, and is not so worn.

United States v. Gilmore

Instant Facts: A man deducted over $40,000 in legal expenses incurred in resisting his wife's community property claims in divorce proceedings from his income taxes.

Black Letter Rule: The only kind of expenses deductible under section 212(1) and (2) are those that relate to a "business," or profit-seeking, purpose.

Carroll v. Commissioner

Instant Facts: A police officer deducted the cost of attending college classes in preparation of attending law school as a business expense.

Black Letter Rule: The cost of education may be deducted as a business expense if there is a sufficient relationship between such an education and the particular job skills required.

Nickerson v. Commissioner

(Wannabe Farmer) v. *(Government)*

700 F.2d 402 (7th Cir.1983)

BUSINESS TAXPAYERS NEED ONLY PROVE THAT THEIR CURRENT ACTIONS WERE MOTIVATED BY THE EXPECTATION THAT THEY WOULD LATER REAP A PROFIT

■ **INSTANT FACTS** The tax court determined that a wannabe farmer who bought a farm and operated at a loss for two years did not have a bona fide expectation of profit for tax purposes.

■ **BLACK LETTER RULE** A taxpayer need not expect an immediate profit from a business, and the existence of "start up" losses does not preclude a bona fide profit motive.

■ **PROCEDURAL BASIS**

Appeal from the U.S. Tax Court's finding against the defendant.

■ **FACTS**

Nickerson (D) grew up working on his father's farm until he went to college and entered the field of advertising. At the age of forty, Nickerson (D) decided that his career in advertising would not last much longer, and he began to look for an alternative source of income for the future. He decided that dairy forming was the most desirable means of generating income and began searching for a farm. After several years, Nickerson bought an 80–acre farm in Wisconsin for $40,000. One year later, he bought an additional 40 acres adjoining the farm for $10,000. The farm was in a run-down condition, planted with alfalfa, which was at the end of its productive cycle. In an effort to improve things, Nickerson (D) leased the land to a tenant farmer for $20 an acre and an agreement that the farmer would convert an additional ten acres a year to the cultivation of a more profitable crop. This rent received from the farmer was the only income derived from the farm. Nickerson (D) visited the farm on most weekends during the growing season, and either worked on his land or assisted neighboring farmers. His efforts on his own land were in renovating an abandoned orchard and remodeling the farm house. In addition to learning about farming through his experience, Nickerson (D) read a number of trade journals and spoke with the area agricultural extension agent. Nickerson (D) did not expect to make a profit from the farm for approximately 10 years. He lost $8,668 the first year, and $9,873 the next. Although he did not keep formal books of account, Nickerson (D) did retain receipts and cancelled checks relating to farm expenditures. At the time of trial, Nickerson (D) had not yet acquired any livestock or farm machinery. The farm was similarly devoid of any recreational equipment and had never been used to entertain guests. The tax court decided that these facts did not support Nickerson's (D) claim that the primary goal in operating the farm was to make a profit.

■ **ISSUE**

Must a taxpayer have an immediate expectation of profits to deduct losses?

■ **DECISION AND RATIONALE**

(Pell, C.J.) No. Whether Nickerson (D) intended to run the dairy farm for a profit is a question of fact, and as such our review is limited to a determination of whether the tax court was "clearly erroneous" in determining that Nickerson (D) lacked the requisite profit motive. This standard of review applies

---

although the only dispute is over the proper interpretation of uncontested facts. This is one of those rare cases in which we are convinced that a mistake has been made. Our basic disagreement with the tax court stems from our belief that the court improperly evaluated Nickerson's (D) actions from the perspective of whether he sincerely believed that he could make a profit from the current level of activity at the farm. On the contrary, Nickerson (D) needs only prove that his current actions were motivated by the expectation that he would later reap a profit, in this case when he finished renovating the farm and began full-time operations. It is well established that a taxpayer need not expect an immediate profit; the existence of "start up" losses does not preclude a bona fide profit motive. The tax court found that the amount of time Nickerson (D) devoted to the farm was inadequate. In reaching this conclusion the court ignored his agreement with the tenant-farmer under which he would convert 10 acres a year to profitable crops in exchange for the right to farm the land. The court also rested its decision on the lack of a concrete plan to put the farm in operable condition. Once again, this ignores Nickerson's (D) agreement with the tenant-farmer whereby the majority of the land would be tillable by the time Nickerson (D) was prepared to begin full-time farming. The tax court also believed that Nickerson's (D) decision to renovate the farm house and orchard prior to obtaining farm equipment evidenced a lack of profit motive. As Nickerson (D) and his family planned to live on the farm when they switched careers, refurbishing the house would seem to be a necessary first step. Additionally, we fail to understand how renovating the orchard, a potential source of food and income, is inconsistent with an expectation of profit. While the Commissioner (P) need not prove that Nickerson (D) was motivated by goals other than making a profit, we think that more weight should be given to the absence of any alternative explanation for Nickerson's (D) actions. If this were a case in which wealthy taxpayers were seeking to obtain tax benefits through the creation of paper losses we would hesitate to reverse. Before us today, however, is a family of modest means attempting to prepare for a stable financial future. The amount of time and hard work invested by Nickerson (D) belies any claim that allowing these deductions would thwart Congress' primary purpose, that of excluding "hobby" losses from permissible deductions. Accordingly, we hold that the tax court's finding was clearly erroneous and reverse.

Analysis:

There is no basis for distinguishing Nickerson's (D) actions from a situation in which one absorbs larger losses over a shorter period of time by beginning full-time operations immediately. In either situation the taxpayer stands an equal chance of recouping start-up losses. In fact, it seems to be a reasonable decision by Nickerson (D) to prepare the farm before becoming dependent upon it for sustenance. Nickerson (D) was not seeking to simply supplement his existing income with his current work on the farm, but rather he was laying the ground work for a contemplated career switch. Since the court holds that Nickerson's (D) farm activity was a business and not a hobby, the losses incurred in running the farm are deductible and can be used to offset Nickerson's salary and other income.

■ CASE VOCABULARY

BONA FIDE: In or with good faith.

Popov v. Commissioner

(Professional Violinist–Taxpayer) v. *(Internal Revenue Service)*

246 F.3d 1190 (9th Cir. 2001)

A LIVING ROOM USED EXCLUSIVELY FOR MUSIC PRACTICE IS A "HOME OFFICE"

■ **INSTANT FACTS** Popov (TP), a professional violinist, claimed a home office deduction for the living room of her apartment, which she used exclusively for practice.

■ **BLACK LETTER RULE** To claim a home office deduction, the home office must qualify as the taxpayer's principal place of business.

■ **PROCEDURAL BASIS**

Appeal from the tax court's decision affirming a determination by the IRS that Popov (TP) was not entitled to claim a home office deduction for her living room, which she used exclusively for her violin practice.

■ **FACTS**

Popov (TP) was a professional violinist who performed at various studios and concert sites outside her home. Because she did not have access to a practice facility outside her home, she used the living room in her apartment exclusively for practice. Popov (TP) claimed a home office deduction for her living room and deducted a percentage of her rent and annual electricity bill on her federal income tax return. The IRS disallowed the deductions and Popov (TP) filed a petition for redetermination in the tax court. The tax court upheld the determination by the IRS.

■ **ISSUE**

Is Popov (TP) entitled to claim a home office deduction for the use of her living room as a practice area for her music?

■ **DECISION AND RATIONALE**

(Hawkins, J.) Yes. The IRS allows a deduction for a home office that is used exclusively as "the principal place of business for any trade or business of the taxpayer," and Popov's (TP) use of her living room as a practice area qualifies it as her principal place of business. Although the Tax Code does not define the phrase "principal place of business," in *Commissioner v. Soliman*, 506 U.S. 168 (1993), the Court established two factors for determining whether a home office qualifies as a taxpayer's principal place of business: (1) the "relative importance" factor and (2) the "amount of time" factor. The "relative importance" factor was not definitive, either way, in this case because the traditional "delivery of services test" (where goods and services are delivered) is not applicable to musical performances (how Popov (TP) earned her living). The "amount of time" factor (comparing the amount of time spent in the home office with the time spent in the business activity) weighed in favor of Popov (TP) because she spent more time practicing in her living room than she did performing at concert sites and music studios. Therefore, since the only factor in the *Soliman* test (the "amount of time" factor) weighed in favor of Popov's (TP) living room being her "principal place of business," Popov (TP) was entitled to claim a home office deduction for the use of her living room as a practice area. The decision of the tax court is reversed.

Analysis:

This case considers the "home office" outside of the ordinary context. The court's finding that the "delivery of services" framework did not apply to musicians, for purposes of determining the "relative importance" of the activities performed at each business location, potentially opened the door to deviations from that framework for any activity in which the creative content of the work product is developed in a place other than where it is eventually delivered.

■ CASE VOCABULARY

DEDUCTION: An amount subtracted from gross income, or from adjusted gross income when calculating taxable income.

SUB SILENTIO: Under silence; without notice being taken; without being expressly mentioned.

Moller v. United States

(Taxpayers) v. *(Government)*

721 F.2d 810 (Fed. Cir.1983)

MANAGING ONE'S OWN INVESTMENTS IN SECURITIES IS NOT THE CARRYING ON OF A TRADE OR BUSINESS, IRRESPECTIVE OF THE EXTENT OF THE INVESTMENTS OR THE AMOUNT OF TIME REQUIRED TO PERFORM THE MANAGERIAL FUNCTIONS

■ **INSTANT FACTS** The plaintiffs unsuccessfully attempted to deduct the expenses of operating home-offices from their taxes since they used them in order to manage their investments.

■ **BLACK LETTER RULE** When the only return is that of an investor, the taxpayer has not satisfied his burden of demonstrating that he is engaged in a trade or business since investing is not a trade or business.

■ **PROCEDURAL BASIS**

Appeal from the judgment of the Claims Court in favor of the plaintiffs.

■ **FACTS**

The Mollers (P) have relied almost entirely on the income from investments for their support for over ten years. Their only other sources of income have been two small pensions and social security payments. In 1976 and 1977, the Mollers (P) devoted their full time to their investment activities. Each spent forty to forty-two hours per week in connection with these activities. They kept regular office hours and monitored the stock market on a daily basis. They made all their investment decisions on their own. The total value of their portfolios was $13,500,000 in 1976 and $14,500,000 in 1977. They engaged in a variety of activities in managing their portfolios. The Mollers (P) did not purchase stocks for speculative purposes. They were primarily interested in long-term growth potential and the payment of interest and dividends, as that was over 98% of their gross income in 1976 and 1977. In 1976 their income from the sale of securities was only $612, while in 1977 their sales resulted in a loss of $223. The Mollers (P) also invested in Treasury Bills, but they did so to maintain liquidity and earn interest. The Mollers (P) maintained a summer and a winter residence. Each house had quarters in which they conducted their investment activities. They kept regular hours and used the quarters exclusively for investment activities. In managing their portfolios, the Mollers (P) incurred expenses of $22,659.91 in 1976 and $29,561.69 in 1977, and deducted these on their joint income tax returns. The expenses attributable to maintaining their two home-offices amounted to $7,439.65 in 1976, and $7,247.21 in 1977. The IRS disallowed the home-office expenses and asserted deficiencies against the Mollers (P) for 1976 and 1977. The Mollers (P) paid the deficiencies and filed claims for refunds. After these claims were disallowed, the Mollers (P) brought this action seeking recovery of the taxes paid, plus interest. The Claims Court held that the Mollers (P) were investors, not traders, but were nevertheless engaged in the trade or business of making investments and therefore entitled to deduct their home-offices expenses under section 280A of the Internal Revenue Code.

■ **ISSUE**

Are people who actively make long-term investments considered to be involved in a trade or business?

■ DECISION AND RATIONALE

(Kashiwa, C.J.) No. Section 280A of the Internal Revenue Code generally disallows all deductions for a taxpayer's use of a residence. There is, however, an exception to this rule for that portion of the residence used as "the principal place of business of the taxpayer." In order to get a deduction under section 280A, a taxpayer must conduct an activity which is in a trade or business, the principal office of which is in his home. The legislative history of section 280A makes clear that a taxpayer can no longer take a home-office deduction for an activity where it is for the production of income within the meaning of section 212, but it is not a "trade or business" under section 162. The principal question in the instant case is whether the Mollers' (P) investment activity was a trade or business. In determining whether a taxpayer who manages his own investments is engaged in a trade or business, the courts have distinguished between "traders," who are considered in a trade or business, and "investors," who are not. The Claims Court concluded that taxpayers were investors and not traders because they were primarily interested in the long-term growth potential of their stocks. We agree. The Claims Court, however, went on to hold that despite the fact that the Mollers (P) were investors, they were in the trade or business of making investments. The court distinguished between passive and active investors and concluded that the Mollers (P) were active investors engaged in a trade or business because their investment activities were regular, extensive, and continuous, and they involved the active and constant exercise of managerial and decision-making functions. We disagree. Managing one's own investments in securities is not the carrying on of a trade or business, irrespective of the extent of the investments or the amount of time required to perform the managerial functions. Additionally, when the only return is that of an investor, the taxpayer has not satisfied his burden of demonstrating that he is engaged in a trade or business since investing is not a trade or business. Although the Mollers' (P) investment activity was entered into for the production of income, it did not rise to the level of a trade or business. Section 280A restricts home-office deductions to expenses incurred in the carrying on of a trade or business. Therefore, the Mollers (P) were not entitled to a deduction under this section. Because we decide this case on the grounds that the Mollers (P) were not engaged in the trade or business of making investments, we need not and do not reach the issue of whether they could deduct the expenses of both their home-offices as their "principal place of business." Accordingly, the judgment of the Claims Court is reversed.

Analysis:

Neither the Internal Revenue Code nor the regulations define "trade or business." However, the concept of engaging in a trade or business, as distinguished from other activities pursued for profit, has been in the internal Revenue Code since its inception and has generated much case law. A taxpayer who merely manages his investments, seeking long-term gain, is not carrying on a trade or business irrespective of the extent or continuity of the transactions or the work required in managing the portfolio. In this case, the Mollers (P) were active investors in that their investment activities were continuous, regular, and extensive. However, this is not determinative of the issue and it is not the correct test. What is determinative is the fact that the Mollers' (P) return was that of an investor. They derived the vast majority of their income in the form of dividends and interest; their income was derived from the long-term holding of securities, not from short-term trading; and they were interested in the capital appreciation of their stocks, not short-term profits.

■ CASE VOCABULARY

CLAIMS COURT: This court has jurisdiction to render money judgments upon any claim against the United States.

TRUST CORPUS: The main body or principal of a trust.

Whitten v. Commissioner

(*"Wheel of Fortune" Contestant*) v. (*Government*)

T.C. Memo. 1995–508 (1995)

IT IS DOUBTFUL THAT CONGRESS EVER INTENDED TO ALLOW CASUAL GAMBLERS TO TREAT EXPENSES FOR TRANSPORTATION, MEALS, AND LODGING AS ANYTHING OTHER THAN EITHER MISCELLANEOUS ITEMIZED DEDUCTIONS OR NONDEDUCTIBLE PERSONAL EXPENSES

■ **INSTANT FACTS** A contestant on "Wheel of Fortune" deducted his transportation, meals and lodging expenses from his game show winnings on his federal tax return, claiming they represent "gambling losses."

■ **BLACK LETTER RULE** Expenses incurred in participating as a contestant on a game show may not be characterized as wagering losses for tax purposes.

■ FACTS

Whitten (P) applied for and received an invitation to compete to be a contestant on "Wheel of Fortune." At the conclusion of this process, Whitten (P) was one of 30 applicants selected to appear on the program. Whitten was contacted by the show and arrangements were made for him to take part in the taping of the program the following month in Los Angeles, California. Whitten (P) signed a contestant's release form that provided, among other things, that any travel undertaken by a contestant in connection with the contestant's appearance on the program shall be at the contestant's sole risk and expense. Whitten (P), his wife and three children, flew to California for the taping as scheduled. He won three consecutive games and was awarded cash prizes in the total amount of $14,850 and an automobile [Whoo Hoo!!]. Whitten (P) and his wife filed a joint federal income tax return, reporting his winnings as "other income" in the amount of $19,830. This entry represents the sum of the value of the car and his cash winnings, reduced by the expenses that he and his family incurred, namely $1,820 for transportation, meals, and lodging in order to participate as a contestant on the show. Whitten's (P) reporting position is premised on the theory that the expenses represent "gambling losses" that may be offset directly against his "gambling winnings" from the program. The Commissioner (D) determined a deficiency in Whitten's (P) Federal income tax for the year. Specifically, it determined that Whitten failed to report $1,820 in income from his winnings on the game show. In the Commissioner's (D) view, the expenses are properly characterized either as nondeductible personal expenses or as miscellaneous itemized deductions.

■ ISSUE

Can expenses incurred in participating as a contestant on a game show be characterized as wagering losses for tax purposes?

■ DECISION AND RATIONALE

(Not Stated) No. The parties have devoted a substantial amount of time and effort debating the issue of whether a contestant's appearance on the "Wheel of Fortune" game show constitutes a wagering transaction governed by the provisions of section 165(d). In our opinion it does not, however we will focus our attention on the more pertinent issue of whether the expenses in dispute can be characterized as wagering losses within the meaning of section 165(d). Wagering losses must be accounted for and reported separately from the expenses incurred by the taxpayer in order to engage in the underlying wagering transaction. In applying this rule to the facts presented herein, we hold that the expenses incurred by Whitten (P) in order to attend and participate in the "Wheel of Fortune" game show are at best expenses, deductible as a miscellaneous itemized deductions under section 67, rather than wagering losses under section 165(d). In so holding, we reject Whitten's (P) contention that the expenses in issue are tantamount to a bet or wager. Unlike a wager or bet, Whitten (P) incurred the expenses in question in exchange for specific goods and services, such as transportation, meals, and lodging. Further, we doubt that Congress ever intended to allow casual gamblers to treat expenses for transportation, meals, and lodging as anything other than either miscellaneous itemized deductions or nondeductible personal expenses. Consequently, we shall deny Whitten's (P) motion for summary judgment and grant the Commissioner's (D) cross motion.

Analysis:

The term "wagering losses" is not defined in the Internal Revenue Code, the regulations, or the legislative history underlying § 165(d). It is within this relative vacuum of authority that Whitten (P) relied on *Kozma v. Commissioner* as support for their position that the disputed expenses constituted wagering losses. However this reliance is misplaced, as *Kozma* stands for the narrow proposition that, in the case of the professional gambler, the limitation imposed under § 165(d) limiting wagering losses to wagering winnings overrides the deduction otherwise allowable under § 162(a) for ordinary business expenses. Whitten (P) apparently believed that *Kozma* stands for the proposition that all expenses related to a wagering activity are properly characterized as wagering losses, but the court did not glean any intention to eliminate the distinction between wagering losses, i.e., the amount of wagers or bets lost on wagering transactions, and expenses related thereto, e.g., expenses for transportation, meals, and lodging incurred to engage in wagering transactions.

■ CASE VOCABULARY

PRO SE: One who does not retain a lawyer and appears for himself in court.

Henderson v. Commissioner

(Office–Decorating Employer) v. *(Government)*
46 T.C.M. 566 (1983)

IT IS NOT ENOUGH THAT THERE MAY BE SOME REMOTE OR INCIDENTAL CONNECTION WITH THE TAXPAYER'S BUSINESS TO SUPPORT A DEDUCTION

■ **INSTANT FACTS** A woman brought suit after she was not allowed to deduct amounts she spent in purchasing a picture and a plant to decorate her office, and the rental of a parking space.

■ **BLACK LETTER RULE** Amounts paid for a framed print and live plant used to decorate an office, and amounts paid to rent a parking space are nondeductible personal expenses under section 262.

■ **PROCEDURAL BASIS**

Commissioner's (D) disallowing of the plaintiff's business expense deductions.

■ **FACTS**

As an employee of the State of South Carolina as an assistant attorney general, Henderson (P) was provided an office with furniture and furnishings that consisted of a desk, a desk chair, a work table, a telephone, a dictaphone, a bookcase, a filing cabinet, law books, and two chairs for visitors. She purchased a framed print for $35 and a live plant for $35 for the purpose of decorating her office [the nerve!]. In addition, she paid a total of $180 to rent a parking space located across the street from her office. Henderson (P) occasionally used her automobile for business purposes when a car from the pool of State vehicles was not available. In the statutory notice of deficiency, the Commissioner (D) disallowed the deduction for the framed print, live plant, and parking fees in their entirety.

■ **ISSUE**

Is a person entitled to a deduction under section 162(a) for amounts paid for a framed print and live plant used to decorate an office, and for amounts paid to rent a parking space?

■ **DECISION AND RATIONALE**

(Judge Not Stated) No. Henderson (P) contends that the expenses were all ordinary and necessary business expenses deductible under section 162(a). The Commissioner (D) counters that the expenses were not ordinary and necessary, and that the expenses are nondeductible personal expenses under section 262. We agree with the Commissioner. We find that the amounts paid for the framed print and live plant were expended to improve the appearance of Henderson's (P) office, a personal expense, and only tangentially, if at all, aided her in the performance of her duties as an employee of the State. Her employer had provided her with all the furnishings considered necessary to do her job. No evidence was presented to prove that the presence of the print and plant in her office were either necessary or helpful in performing her required services. It is not enough that there may be some remote or incidental connection with the taxpayer's business to support the deduction. Accordingly, we deny the deduction for these two expenditures.

Analysis:

Section 162(a) allows a deduction for all the ordinary and necessary expenses paid or incurred during the taxable year in carrying on any trade or business. However, even assuming an expense meets the requirements of section 162(a), it may still be disallowed if the amount was expended for a personal, living, or family expense. The essential inquiry in this case was whether a sufficient nexus existed between Henderson's (P) expenses and the "carrying on" of her trade or business, or whether they were in essence personal or living expenses and nondeductible. It seems that a picture on the wall and a plant in the corner would not help Henderson (P) carry on her business.

Rudolph v. United States

(*Business Travelers*) v. (*Government*)
370 U.S. 269, 82 S.Ct. 1277 (1962)

THE CRUCIAL QUESTION IN DETERMINING ALLOWABLE TRAVEL DEDUCTIONS IS WHETHER THE PURPOSE OF THE TRIP WAS RELATED PRIMARILY TO BUSINESS, OR WAS RATHER PRIMARILY PERSONAL IN NATURE

■ **INSTANT FACTS** An insurance salesman and his wife were awarded an expenses-paid company trip to New York City for business/pleasure, and the Commissioner assessed its value to them as taxable income.

■ **BLACK LETTER RULE** When the purpose of the trip is primarily personal in nature, rather than related primarily to business, expenses for transportation, meals, and lodging are not deductible as "ordinary and necessary" business expenses under section 162.

■ **PROCEDURAL BASIS**

Appeal from the Court of Appeals' affirmance of the District Court's decision against the plaintiff.

■ **FACTS**

Having sold a predetermined amount of insurance, Rudolph (P) qualified to attend his company's convention in New York City. It was also in line with company policy for wives to attend such events with their husbands. Rudolph (P) and his wife, together with 150 other employees and officers of the insurance company and 141 wives, traveled to and from New York City on special trains, and were housed in a single hotel during their two-and-one-half-day visit. One morning was devoted to a "business meeting" and group luncheon, while the rest of the time in New York City was for travel, sightseeing, entertainment, or free time. The entire trip lasted one week [that's quite a train ride!]. The insurance company paid all the expenses of the convention-trip, and Rudolph's (P) allocable share amounted to $560. The District Court held that the value of the trip was in the nature of a bonus, reward, and compensation for a job well done, and thus was income to Rudolph (P), but being primarily a pleasure trip in the nature of a vacation, the costs were personal and nondeductible. The Court of Appeals approved these findings, and this appeal followed.

■ **ISSUE**

Are expenses for transportation, meals, and lodging related to a business/pleasure trip deductible as an "ordinary and necessary" business expense?

■ **DECISION AND RATIONALE**

(Per Curiam) No. It appears that the tax consequences of the trip turn upon the dominant motive and purpose of the trip. In this regard, the District Court found that the trip was provided by the company for the primary purpose of affording a pleasure trip in the nature of a bonus reward for a job well done. The District Court also found that from the point of view of the Rudolphs (P) it was primarily a pleasure trip in the nature of a vacation. Such ultimate facts are subject to the "clearly erroneous" rule and, since the findings of the District Court can not be found to be clearly erroneous, the appeal must be dismissed.

■ **CONCURRENCE**

(Harlan, J.) Rudolph (P) placed great emphasis on the fact that he is an entrapped "organization man," required to attend such conventions, and that his future promotions depend on his presence. Suffice it to say that the District Court did not find any element of compulsion. To the contrary, it found that the Rudolphs (P) regarded the convention as a pleasure trip in the nature of a vacation.

■ DISSENT

(Douglas, J.) It could not, I think, be seriously contended that a professional man who attends a convention with all expenses paid has received "income." Income has the connotation of something other than the mere payment of expenses.

Analysis:

The Court held here that the trip was a reward or bonus for a job well done, and as such was income. But then the Court says that expenses related to the "earning" of this "income" are not deductible as related primarily to business, which seems contradictory. If a taxpayer is required to report an item as "income," should he be allowed to take deductions related to the expenses incurred as "related primarily to business"?

■ CASE VOCABULARY

PER CURIAM: By the court; a phrase used to distinguish an opinion of the whole court from an opinion written by an opinion written by any one judge.

Moss v. Commissioner

(Hungry Lawyer) v. *(Government)*

758 F.2d 211 (7th Cir.1985)

TO ALLOW A DEDUCTION FOR ALL BUSINESS–RELATED MEALS WOULD CONFER A WINDFALL ON PEOPLE WHO CAN ARRANGE THEIR WORK SCHEDULES SO THEY DO SOME OF THEIR WORK AT LUNCH

■ **INSTANT FACTS** The Commissioner (D) disallowed Moss' (P) federal income tax deductions representing his share of his law firm's daily lunch expense.

■ **BLACK LETTER RULE** Meals are deductible under section 162(a) when they are ordinary and necessary business expenses.

■ **PROCEDURAL BASIS**

Appeal from the Tax Court's decision disallowing the plaintiff's federal income tax deductions for lunch expense.

■ **FACTS**

Moss (P) was a partner in a small law firm. Each of the firm's lawyers spent most of every working day in court. The members of the firm met for lunch daily at a café near their office. At lunch, the lawyers would discuss their cases with the head of the firm, whose approval was required for most settlements, and they would decide which lawyer would meet which court call that afternoon or the next morning. Lunchtime was chosen for the daily meeting because the courts were in recess then. The alternatives were to meet at 7:00 a.m. or 6:00 p.m., and these were less convenient times [well we couldn't have *that*!]. There is no suggestion that the lawyers dawdled over lunch, or that the café is luxurious. The Tax Court disallowed Moss' (P) federal income tax deductions of a little more than $1,000 in each of two years, representing Moss' (P) share of the firm's lunch expense.

■ **ISSUE**

Are the plaintiff's daily lunch costs "ordinary and necessary" business expenses, thereby constituting allowable income tax deductions?

■ **DECISION AND RATIONALE**

(Posner, C.J.) No. The framework of statutes and regulations for deciding this case is simple, but not clear. Section 262 of the Internal Revenue Code disallows, "except as otherwise expressly provided in this chapter," the deduction of "personal, family, or living expenses." Section 119 excludes from income the value of meals provided by an employer to his employees for his convenience, but only if they are provided on the employer's premises. And section 162(a) allows the deduction of "all the ordinary and necessary expenses paid or incurred during the taxable year in carrying on any trade or business," including "traveling expenses (including amounts expended for meals) while away from home." Since Moss (P) was not an employee but a partner in a partnership not taxed as an entity, since the meals were not served on the employer's premises, and since he was not away from home (that is, on an overnight trip), neither section 119 nor 162(a) applies to this case. Although an argument can thus be made for disallowing any deduction for business meals on the theory that people have to eat whether they work or not, the result would be excessive taxation of people who spend more money on business meals because they are business meals than they would spend on their meals if they were not working. Thus, the IRS (D) concedes that meals can be necessary business expenses (provided the expense is substantiated with adequate records) even if they are not within the express provision and even though the expense of commuting to and from work, a traveling expense but not one incurred away from home, is not deductible. Because the law allows this generous deduction, which tempts people to have more (and costlier) business meals than are necessary, the IRS has every right to insist that the meal be shown to be a real business necessity. This condition is most easily satisfied when a client or customer or supplier or other outsider to the business is a guest. However, if a large firm had a monthly lunch to allow partners to get to know associates, the expense of the meal might well be necessary, and would be allowed by the IRS. But Moss' (P) firm never had more than eight lawyers (partners and associates), and did not need a daily lunch to cement relationships among them. It is all a matter of degree and circumstance, and particularly frequency. Daily—for a full year—is too often, perhaps even for entertainment of clients. We may assume it was necessary for Moss' (P) firm to meet daily to coordinate the work of the firm, and also, as the Tax Court found, that lunch was the most convenient time. But it does not follow that the expense of the lunch was a necessary business expense. The members of the firm had to eat somewhere, and the café was both convenient and not too expensive. They do not claim to have incurred a greater daily lunch expense than they would have incurred if there had been no lunch meetings. Although it saved time to combine lunch with work, the meal itself was not an organic part of the meeting, as where the business objective, to be fully achieved, required sharing a meal. Affirmed.

Analysis:

Read literally, § 162 would make irrelevant whether a business expense is also a personal expense. So long as it is ordinary and necessary in the taxpayer's business, an expense is (the statute seems to say) deductible from his income tax. But the statute has not been read literally. There is a reluctance, most clearly manifested in the regulation disallowing deduction of the expense of commuting, to lighten the tax burden of people who have the good fortune to interweave work with consumption. To allow a deduction for commuting would confer a windfall on people who live in the suburbs and commute to work in the cities; to allow a deduction for all business-related meals would confer a windfall on people who can arrange their work schedules so they do some of their work at lunch.

Danville Plywood Corporation v. United States

(Superbowl Trip Organizer) v. *(Government)*

899 F.2d 3 (Fed. Cir.1990)

TO BE DEDUCTIBLE, AN ENTERTAINMENT EXPENSE MUST MEET THE REQUIREMENTS OF BOTH SECTION 162 AND SECTION 274

NOW, LET ME SHOW YOU SOME OF OUR FINE MAPLE PRODUCTS!!

■ **INSTANT FACTS** A plywood company tried to deduct as a business expense the cost of taking 120 people away to New Orleans for the weekend to attend the Super Bowl.

■ **BLACK LETTER RULE** To qualify as an "ordinary and necessary" business expense under section 162(a), an expenditure must be both "common and accepted" in the taxpayer's community, as well as "appropriate" for the development of the taxpayer's business.

■ **PROCEDURAL BASIS**

Appeal from the Commissioner's disallowance of the deductions claimed by the plaintiff.

■ **FACTS**

Buchanan is the president of Danville Plywood (P), a closely held corporation which manufactures custom plywood for use in kitchen cabinets, store fixtures, furniture, and similar items. Danville (P) sells to wholesale distributors who in turn sell to architects, mill work houses, and cabinet shops. During the years at issue, Danville (P) claimed deductions totaling $103,444.51 in connection with a weekend trip for 120 people to the Super Bowl in New Orleans. Danville (P) looked at the current and potential income from each of its customers, sent two invitations to selected customers and instructed them to decide whom to send on the weekend trip. Buchanan asserts that Danville (P) asked the customer to send individuals with "decision making authority." The majority of the customers sent one individual who was accompanied by that individual's spouse. In making arrangements for the weekend, Danville (P) requested accommodations, Super Bowl tickets, banquet facilities, and a river cruise. Notably, Danville (P) did not indicate that the trip was in any way business related, and failed to request access to meeting rooms or other facilities appropriate for a business trip. In addition, in a letter sent by Danville (P) to the selected customers, there was no reference to business meetings or discussions of any kind. Shortly before the weekend, Buchanan distributed a memo to the Danville employees who would be going to New Orleans. In the memo, Buchanan told his employees they should promote Danville (P) and its products to the customers. Upon arrival at the hotel, Danville's (P) customers were met in the lobby by family members of Danville's (P) employees. Danville (P) also displayed some of its products in an area adjacent to the lobby. During the weekend, Danville's (P) employees met informally with customers. None of the customers placed orders during the weekend, although some promised to contact Danville's (P) employees in the future. During an audit of Danville's (P) returns, the Commissioner disallowed the deductions claimed by Danville (P) for the expenses incurred relating to Super Bowl weekend.

■ **ISSUE**

Are the expenses surrounding a company's taking of 120 people to the Super Bowl for the weekend deductible as business expense under section 162(a)?

■ DECISION AND RATIONALE

(Not Stated) No. The Claims Court held that the expenses surrounding the Super Bowl weekend were neither "ordinary and necessary" business expenses of Danville's (P) trade or business under section 162, nor "directly related to" or "associated with" the active conduct of Danville's (P) business under section 274. Danville (P) acknowledges that both of these findings are factual and must be sustained on appeal unless clearly erroneous. Three of Buchanan's children and two children of Danville's (P) customers as well as a shareholder of Danville (P) attended Super Bowl weekend at Danville's (P) expense. Danville (P) conceded that these expenses were not deductible and thus we need not address this class of attendees. Five spouses of Danville (P) employees also attended Super Bowl weekend. Treasury regulations provide that when a taxpayer's wife accompanies him on a business trip, her expenses are not deductible unless the taxpayer can adequately show that her presence has a bona fide business purpose. The wife's performance of an incidental service does not meet this requirement. Applying that regulation to this case, the Claims Court concluded that the wives of Danville's (P) employees performed at best a social function in greeting the guests, and thus their expenses were not deductible. The Claims Court also found that Danville (P) failed to carry its burden of proof to establish that the expenses for the customer representatives met these requirements. The Claims Court stated that the entertainment was the central focus of the excursion, with all other activities running a distant second in importance. We cannot say that this finding is clearly erroneous. What business discussions that occurred were incidental to the main event, i.e., entertainment for Danville's (P) customers. Similarly, expenses for the customers are not deductible under section 162. The treasury regulations provide that only traveling expenses which are reasonable and necessary to the conduct of the taxpayer's business which are directly attributable to it may be deducted. The court found that Danville (P) failed to establish that the expenses of its employees were attributable to its business, and that the trip was undertaken primarily for business purposes. Furthermore, the Claims Court described the agenda distributed to the employees as little more than a "bootstrapping afterthought." Thus, on the narrow facts of this case, we hold that the decision of the Claims Court that Danville (P) failed to satisfy its burden of proof that the Super Bowl expenses were "ordinary and necessary" business expenses under section 162(a) of the Code is clearly not erroneous. Affirmed.

Analysis:

Prior to 1961, § 162 was the sole statutory provision regulating the deduction of entertainment expenses. In response to what was perceived as widespread abuse of expense accounts and entertainment expenses, Congress enacted § 274. This provision is referred to as a "disallowance provision," and its effect is to disallow certain deductions for entertainment expenses that would otherwise be properly deductible under § 162. Under the stricter limitations of § 274, no deduction for business expenses allowable under § 162 will be allowed unless the taxpayer establishes that the item was "directly related to" or "associated with" the active conduct of the taxpayer's trade or business. Therefore, to be deductible, an entertainment expense must meet the requirements of both §§ 162 and 274.

■ CASE VOCABULARY

ACCRUAL METHOD OF ACCOUNTING: A method of keeping accounts which shows expenses incurred and income earned for a given period, although such expenses and income may not have been actually paid or received.

CLOSELY HELD CORPORATION: A corporation whose shares, or at least voting shares, are held by a single shareholder or closely-knit group of shareholders.

FISCAL YEAR: A period of twelve consecutive months chosen by a business as the accounting period for annual reports (not necessarily the calendar year).

Churchill Downs, Inc. v. Commissioner

(Taxpayer) v. *(Commissioner of Internal Revenue Service)*

307 F.3d 423 (6th Cir. 2002)

THE COSTS OF INVITATION–ONLY EVENTS USED TO PUBLICIZE THE KENTUCKY DERBY ARE ENTERTAINMENT EXPENSES

You see the glass as half taxable... but I see it as half deductible!

stus.com

■ **INSTANT FACTS** Churchill Downs, Inc. (P) sought to deduct the full amount of expenses related to race-related entertainment events.

■ **BLACK LETTER RULE** Deductions for activities "generally considered to be entertainment" are limited to fifty percent of the amount of the expense, unless they are objectively integral to the taxpayer's business or occupation.

■ **PROCEDURAL BASIS**

On appeal to review a Tax Court decision for the Commissioner.

■ **FACTS**

Churchill Downs, Inc. (P) operates a racetrack in Louisville, Kentucky, among others, where it earns revenue from wagering, admissions, concessions commissions, sponsorships, licensing rights, and broadcast fees of its horse races. Churchill Downs' (P) most prominent race is the Kentucky Derby. In connection with the Derby, Churchill Downs (P) hosts a "Sport of Kings" gala, a brunch, a hospitality tent for the press, and a winner's party. In 1994, Churchill Downs (P) also hosted another race, the Breeders' Cup, which involved a press reception cocktail party and dinner, a brunch, and a press breakfast. On its 1994 and 1995 tax returns, Churchill Downs (P) claimed the full cost of these race-related events as "ordinary and necessary business expenses" on its tax return. The Commissioner (D) rejected the deduction, concluding instead that the expenses constituted entertainment expenses for which Churchill Downs (P) was entitled to a fifty-percent deduction. The Tax Court agreed with the Commissioner (P).

■ **ISSUE**

Are expenses related to invitation-only events for purposes of publicizing or glamorizing a taxpayer's event subject to the fifty-percent entertainment deduction limitation?

■ **DECISION AND RATIONALE**

(Judge undisclosed.) Yes. Although taxpayers are entitled to deductions for "all the ordinary and necessary expenses paid ... in carrying on any trade or business," § 274(n)(1) limits certain deductions. Under the statute, a deduction for "any expense for food or beverage," as well as "any item with respect to an activity which is of a type generally considered to constitute entertainment, amusement, or recreation," is limited to fifty percent of the amount of the expense, if such expenses are directly related to the active conduct of the taxpayer's business. In connection with the statute, the Commissioner (P) has promulgated a regulation that establishes an objective test to determine whether an activity is of a type generally considered to constitute entertainment for purposes of the deduction. Under Reg. § 1.274–2(b)(1)(ii), activities "generally considered to be entertainment," are subject to the fifty-percent deduction limitation, even if they may be described otherwise, such as for advertising or public relations purposes. However, when such activities are objectively integral to the taxpayer's business or occupation, they do not qualify as entertainment expenses and are fully deductible. By illustration, the regulation provides, for example, that a fashion show conducted by a fashion designer to promote its products to store buyers would not constitute an entertainment expense. A fashion show conducted by an appliance distributor for its retailers' wives, however, would be subject to the fifty-percent limitation.

Here, both parties rely on the language of the illustration in support of their respective positions. Churchill Downs (P) argues that the gala and other invitation-only events showcased its entertainment product, exposing its races to the public just as the fashion designer does with its products and store buyers in the example. The Commissioner (D) counters that galas and luncheons are "generally considered entertainment," which cannot be saved from the limitation by calling them promotional.

Unlike the fashion shows in the regulation, the events at the Kentucky Derby and Breeders' Cup qualify as "entertainment." In the fashion show example, the guests in attendance are the taxpayer's customers, to whom his business is directed. Churchill Downs (P) does not contend that its attendees are its target audience, but rather that the events are used to attract public attention to its races to increase its business. The galas and luncheon do not make its product more available to the public, but rather increase the "aura of glamour" surrounding its product. Just as with the hypothetical appliance distributors' fashion show, the Kentucky Derby and Breeders' Cup events are best characterized as entertainment.

Nor are the events saved from the fifty-percent limitation by Churchill Downs' (P) argument that these events are themselves the product to be sold, as an essential component of the Kentucky Derby and Breeders' Cup races. However, Churchill Downs (P) did not generate any revenue from these events, and they are separable from the races in that the general public targeted by the races was not invited to attend the events.

Likewise, the events are not items made available to the general public nor are they sold or provided by Churchill Downs (P) in a bona fide transaction for adequate and full consideration. Unlike "comps" afforded by casinos to "high rollers," Churchill Downs (P) did not make its goods available to all who chose to partake in them, nor did it receive any consideration, such as ticket admission, for attendance at the events. The expense associated with the Kentucky Derby and Breeders' Cup events at issue are entertainment expenses subject to the fifty-percent limitation.

Analysis:

Although the court refers to the Commissioner's regulation as an "objective" test for determining when an activity involves an entertainment expense, there is potentially a high degree of subjectivity involved. With a purely objective test, all events would be treated equally for each taxpayer, allowing the Commissioner to explicitly list all entertainment activities. Because activities must be viewed in the context of the taxpayer's business objectives, however, the determination is often difficult.

Smith v. Commissioner

(Working Mother) v. *(Government)*

40 B.T.A. 1038 (1939), aff'd without opinion, 113 F.2d 114 (2d Cir.1940)

THE CARE OF CHILDREN IS NOTHING MORE THAN A PERSONAL CONCERN

■ **INSTANT FACTS** The plaintiffs claimed child-care expenses on their federal income taxes as business expenses, but the Commissioner disallowed the deduction.

■ **BLACK LETTER RULE** Nursemaids retained to care for infant children are expenses which are personal in nature and not deductible for federal income tax purposes.

■ **PROCEDURAL BASIS**

Appeal from the Commissioner's disallowance of the plaintiff's deduction for nursemaids.

■ **FACTS**

The Smiths (P) were disallowed a deduction claimed for sums spent by Mrs. Smith (P) in employing nursemaids to care for their young child, as they were both employed. The Smiths (P) here appeal the Commissioner's ruling of non-deductibility.

■ **ISSUE**

Are the expenses associated with retaining nursemaids to care for infant children business expenses deductible for federal income tax purposes?

■ **DECISION AND RATIONALE**

(Opper, J.) No. We are told that the working wife is a new phenomenon. This is relied on to account for the apparent inconsistency that the expenses in issue are now a commonplace, yet have not been the subject of legislation, ruling, or adjudicated controversy. But if that is true, it becomes all the more necessary to apply the accepted principles to the novel facts. We are not prepared to say that the care of children, like similar aspects of family and household life, is other than a personal concern. The wife's services as custodian of the home and protector of its children are ordinarily rendered without monetary compensation. There results no taxable income from the performance of this service and the correlative expenditure is personal and not susceptible of deduction. Here the wife has chosen to employ others to discharge her domestic function and the services she performs are rendered outside the home. They are a source of actual income and taxable as such. But that does not deprive the same work performed by others of its personal character. We therefore hold that nursemaids retained to care for infant children fall into the category of activities which, though they may in some indirect and tenuous degree relate to the circumstances of a profitable occupation, are nevertheless personal in their nature and are not deductible.

Analysis:

The Smiths (P) propose that but for the nurses, the wife could not leave her child. But for the freedom so secured, she could not pursue her gainful labors, and but for them, there would be no income and no tax. This thought evokes an array of interesting possibilities. The very house one lives in, which gives shelter and rest, and the food that provides energy, might all by extension of the same proposition be construed as necessary to the operation of business and to the creation of income. Yet these are the very essence of "personal" expenses, the deductibility of which is expressly denied. The court properly applied the principle and arrived at the correct result in this case.

Commissioner v. Flowers

(Government) v. *(Traveling Lawyer)*
326 U.S. 465, 66 S.Ct. 250 (1946)

TRAVEL EXPENSES BETWEEN TWO DIFFERENT OFFICES IN DIFFERENT CITIES MAY NOT BE DEDUCTIBLE

■ **INSTANT FACTS** A lawyer unsuccessfully attempted to deduct the traveling expenses associated with his commuting from his home in Jackson, Mississippi to his work in Mobile, Alabama.

■ **BLACK LETTER RULE** Travel expenses in pursuit of business within the meaning of section 162(a)(2) can arise only when the business forces the taxpayer to travel and to live temporarily at some place other than his home, thereby advancing the interests of the business.

■ **PROCEDURAL BASIS**

Appeal from the Court of Appeals' reversal of the Tax Court's judgment against the plaintiff.

■ **FACTS**

Flowers (P), a lawyer, has lived with his family in Jackson, Mississippi for nearly thirty years. He has been connected with several law firms in Jackson, one of which he formed and bears his name. Flowers (P) began to represent the predecessor of the gulf, Mobile & Ohio Railroad, his present employer, and later was elected general solicitor. After working as counsel in progressively higher positions for several years, he eventually was elected general counsel. The main office of his employer was located in Mobile, Alabama. When offered the position of general solicitor thirteen years earlier, Flowers was unwilling to accept it if it required him to move from Jackson to Mobile. As a result, an arrangement was made between him and the railroad whereby he could accept the position and continue to reside in Jackson on condition that he pay his traveling expenses between Mobile and Jackson and pay his living expenses in both places. The railroad company provided an office for Flowers (P) in Mobile but not in Jackson. When he worked in Jackson his law firm provided him with office space, although he no longer participated in the firm's business or shared in its profits. The railroad, however, furnished telephone service and a typewriter and desk for his secretary. It also paid the secretary's expenses while in Jackson. Flowers' (P) principal place of business was at the main office in Mobile, however he chose to spend most of his time in Jackson, making between 33 and 40 trips between the two cities during the years in question. The railroad paid all of his traveling expenses when he went on business trips to points other than Jackson or Mobile. But it paid none of his expenses in traveling between these two points or while he was at either of them. Flowers (P) deducted amounts from his income tax returns as traveling expenses incurred in making trips from Jackson to Mobile and as expenditures for meals and hotel accommodations while in Mobile. The Commissioner (D) disallowed the deductions, and the Court of Appeals reversed, holding the deduction was permissible.

■ **ISSUE**

May the plaintiff deduct traveling expenses incurred in making trips from his home to his place of business in a different city?

■ **DECISION AND RATIONALE**

(Murphy, J.) No. Three conditions must be satisfied before a traveling expense deduction may be made under section 162(a)(2). First, the expense must be a reasonable and necessary traveling expense.

Second, the expense must be incurred "while away from home." Third, the expense must be incurred in pursuit of business. This means that there must be a direct connection between the expenditure and the carrying on of the trade or business of the taxpayer or of his employer. Moreover, such an expenditure must be necessary or appropriate to the development and pursuit of the business or trade. Whether particular expenditures fulfill these three conditions so as to entitle a taxpayer to a deduction is purely a question of fact in most instances, and the Tax Court's inferences and conclusions should not be disturbed by an appellate court. The court below accepted the Tax Court's findings of fact but reversed its judgment on a basis that it had improperly construed the word "home" as used in the second condition precedent to a traveling expense deduction. The Tax Court, it was said, erroneously construed the word to mean the post, station or place of business where the taxpayer was employed—in this instance Mobile—and thus erred in concluding that the expenditures in issue were not incurred "while away from home." The Court of Appeals felt the word was to be given no such "unusual" meaning, but rather that it simply meant "that place where one in fact resides." Since Flowers (P) here admittedly had his home, as thus defined, in Jackson, and since the expenses were incurred while he was away from Jackson, the Court of Appeals held that the deduction was permissible. We deem it unnecessary here to enter into or to decide this conflict. The Tax Court's opinion, as we read it, was grounded neither solely nor primarily upon that agency's conception of the word "home." Its discussion was directed mainly toward the relation of the expenditures to the railroad's business, a relationship required by the third condition of the deduction. Turning our attention to the third condition, this case is disposed of quickly. It is readily apparent from the facts that its inferences were supported by evidence and that its conclusion that the expenditures in issue were non-deductible living and personal expenses was fully justified. The facts demonstrate clearly that the expenses were not incurred in the pursuit of the business of the taxpayer's employer, the railroad. The added costs in issue were as unnecessary and inappropriate to the development of the railroad's business as were his personal and living costs in Jackson. They were incurred solely as the result of Flowers' (P) desire to maintain a home in Jackson while working in Mobile, a factor irrelevant to the maintenance and prosecution of the railroad's legal business. Travel expenses in pursuit of business within the meaning of section 162(a)(2) could arise only when the railroad's business forced Flowers (P) to travel and live temporarily at some place other that Mobile, thereby advancing the interests of the railroad. Business trips are to be identified in relation to business demands and the traveler's business headquarters. The exigencies of business rather than the personal conveniences and necessities of the traveler must be the motivating factors. Such was not the case here. It follows that the court below erred in reversing the judgment of the Tax Court. Reversed.

■ DISSENT

(Rutledge, J.) I think the judgment of the Court of Appeals should be affirmed. When Congress used the word "home" in section 162 of the Code, I do not believe it meant "business headquarters." And in my opinion this case presents no other question.

Analysis:

Here, Jackson was Flowers' (P) regular home. Had his post of duty been in that city, the cost of maintaining his home there and of commuting to work would be non-deductible living and personal expenses lacking the necessary direct relation to the prosecution of the business. The character of such expenses is unaltered by the circumstance that his post of duty was in Mobile, thereby increasing the costs of transportation, food, and lodging. The railroad did not require Flowers (P) to travel on business from Jackson to Mobile, or to maintain living quarters in both cities. It simply asked him to be at his principal post in Mobile as business demanded and as his personal convenience was served, allowing him to divide his time as he saw fit. The fact that he traveled frequently between the two cities and incurred extra living expenses was occasioned solely by his personal propensities. The railroad gained nothing from this arrangement, except the personal satisfaction of Flowers (P).

■ CASE VOCABULARY

EXIGENCY: A pressing necessity.

Hantzis v. Commissioner

(Commuting Law Student) v. *(Government)*

638 F.2d 248 (1st Cir.), cert. denied, 452 U.S. 962, 101 S.Ct. 3112 (1981)

■ THE TEMPORARY EMPLOYMENT DOCTRINE DOES NOT PURPORT TO ELIMINATE ANY REQUIREMENT THAT CONTINUED MAINTENANCE OF A FIRST HOME HAVE A BUSINESS JUSTIFICATION

■ **INSTANT FACTS** A law student living and attending law school in Massachusetts got a summer job in New York and attempted to deduct her living and traveling expenses for temporarily residing in New York from her taxes.

■ **BLACK LETTER RULE** For a taxpayer to be "away from home in the pursuit of a trade or business," she must establish the existence of some sort of business relation both to the location she claims as "home" and to the location of her temporary employment sufficient to support a finding that her duplicative expenses are necessitated by business exigencies.

■ PROCEDURAL BASIS

Appeal from the Tax Court's decision in favor of the plaintiff.

■ FACTS

Hantzis (P), a second year law student at Harvard, obtained a summer job with a law firm in New York City. Her husband remained in their home in Boston while Hantzis (P) rented a small apartment in New York City. On their joint tax return, Hantzis (P) reported the earnings from her summer job, and deducted the cost of transportation between Boston and New York, the cost of her apartment in New York, and the cost of her meals in New York. The Commissioner (D) disallowed the deduction on the ground that her home for purposes of section 162(a)(2) was her place of employment, therefore the cost of travel to and living in New York was not incurred while "away from home." The Commissioner also argued that the expenses were not incurred "in the pursuit of a trade or business." Both positions were rejected by the Tax Court, which found that Boston was Hantzis' (P) home because her employment in New York was only temporary, and that her expenses in New York were "necessitated" by her employment there. The court thus held the expenses deductible, and the Commissioner (D) appealed.

■ ISSUE

Can a taxpayer deduct duplicative living expenses due to temporary employment in a different state?

■ DECISION AND RATIONALE

(Campbell, C.J.) No. The Commissioner (D) has directed his argument at the meaning of "in pursuit of a trade or business." He interprets this phrase as requiring that a deductible traveling expense be incurred under the demands of a trade or business which predates the expense, i.e., an "already" existing trade or business. The Commissioner's (D) proposed interpretation erects at the threshold of deductibility under section 162(a)(2) the requirement that a taxpayer be engaged in a trade or business before incurring a travel expense. Only if that requirement is satisfied would an inquiry into the deductibility of an expense proceed to ask whether the expense was a result of exigencies, incurred while away from home, and reasonable and necessary. Such a reading of the statute is semantically possible and would perhaps expedite the disposition of certain cases. Nevertheless, we reject it as unsupported by case law and inappropriate to the policies behind section 162(a)(2). *Flowers* construed section 162(a)(2) to mean that a traveling expense is deductible only if it is (1) reasonable and necessary, (2) incurred while away from home, and (3) necessitated by the exigencies of business. Because the Commissioner (D) does not suggest that Hantzis' (P) expenses were unreasonable or unnecessary, we may pass directly to the remaining requirements. Of these, we find dispositive the requirement that an expense be incurred while away from home. As we think Hantzis' (P) expenses were not so incurred, we hold the deduction to be improper. We begin by recognizing that the location of a person's home for purposes of section 162(a)(2) becomes problematic only when the person lives one place and works another. Where a taxpayer resides and works at a single location, he is always home, however defined; and where a taxpayer is constantly on the move due to his work, he is never "away" from home. However, in the present case, the need to determine "home" is plainly before us, since Hantzis (P) resided in Boston and worked, albeit briefly, in New York. We think the critical step in defining "home" in these situations is to recognize that the "while away from home" requirement has to be construed in light of the further requirement that the expense be the result of business exigencies. The traveling expense deduction obviously is not intended to exclude from taxation every expense incurred by a taxpayer who, in the course of business, maintains two homes. Section 162(a)(2) seeks rather to "mitigate the burden of the taxpayer who, because of the exigencies of his trade or business, *must* maintain two places of abode and thereby incur additional and duplicate living expenses." However, in this case, Hantzis' (P) trade or business did not require that she maintain a home in Boston as well as one in New York. The home in Boston was kept up for reasons involving Mr. Hantzis, but those reasons cannot substitute for a showing by Mrs. Hantzis (P) that the exigencies of *her* trade or business require *her* to maintain two homes. Mrs. Hantzis' (P) decision to keep two homes must be seen as a choice dictated by personal, albeit wholly reasonable, considerations and not a business or occupational necessity. We therefore hold that her home for purposes of Section 162(a)(2) was New York and that the expenses at issue in this case were not incurred "while away from home." We are not dissuaded from this conclusion by the temporary nature of Hantzis' (P) employment in New York. She argues that the brevity of her stay in New York excepts her from the business exigencies requirement of section 162(a)(2) under the temporary employment doctrine. At first glance, this doctrine may seem to find support in the court decisions holding that, when a taxpayer works for a limited time away from his usual home, section 162(a)(2) allows a deduction for the expense of maintaining a second home so long as the employment is "temporary" and not "indefinite" or "permanent." The temporary employment doctrine does not, however, purport to eliminate any requirement that continued maintenance of a first home have a business justification. We think the rule has no application where the taxpayer has no business connection with his usual place of residence. If no business exigency dictates the location of the taxpayer's usual residence, then the mere fact of his taking temporary employment elsewhere cannot supply a compelling business reason for continuing to maintain that residence. Only a taxpayer who lives one place, works another and has business ties to *both* is in the ambiguous situation that the temporary employment doctrine is designed to resolve. On this reasoning, the temporary nature of Hantzis' (P) employment in New York does not affect the outcome of her case. She had no business ties to Boston that would bring her within the temporary employment doctrine. Thus we hold that for a taxpayer to be "away from home in the pursuit of a trade or business," she must establish the existence of some sort of business relation both to the location she claims as "home" and to the location of her temporary employment sufficient to support a finding that her duplicative expenses are necessitated by business exigencies. Reversed.

■ CONCURRENCE

(Keeton, D.J.) Although I agree with the result reached in the Court's opinion, and with much of its underlying analysis, I write separately because I cannot join in the court's determination that New York was the taxpayer's home for purposes of section 162(a)(2).

Analysis:

When Congress enacted the travel expense deduction, it apparently was unsure whether, to be deductible, an expense must be incurred away from a person's residence or away from his principal place of business. This ambiguity persists, and courts, sometimes within a single circuit, are divided over the issue. The ultimate allowance or disallowance of a deduction is a function of the court's assessment of the reason for a taxpayer's maintenance of two homes. If the reason is perceived to be personal, the taxpayer's home will generally be held to be his place of employment, rather than his residence, and the deduction will be denied. If the reason is related to business exigencies, the person's home will usually be held to be his residence, and the deduction will be allowed.

Pevsner v. Commissioner

(Clothing Salesperson) v. *(Government)*
628 F.2d 467 (5th 1980).

AN OBJECTIVE TEST ALLOWS A TAXPAYER OR REVENUE AGENT TO LOOK ONLY TO OBJECTIVE FACTS IN DETERMINING WHETHER CLOTHING REQUIRED AS A CONDITION OF EMPLOYMENT IS ADAPTABLE TO GENERAL USE AS ORDINARY STREETWEAR

■ **INSTANT FACTS** A YSL salesperson deducted the cost of her YSL clothing and accessories, as well as the maintenance costs for the clothing, from her taxes as a business expense.

■ **BLACK LETTER RULE** The cost of clothing is deductible as a business expense only if the clothing is of a type specifically required as a condition of employment, is not adaptable to general usage as ordinary clothing, and is not so worn.

■ **PROCEDURAL BASIS**

Appeal from the Tax Court's judgment in favor of the plaintiff.

■ **FACTS**

Pevsner (P) was employed as a manager of a boutique which sells only women's clothes and accessories designed by Yves St. Laurent (YSL), one of the leading designers of women's apparel. Although the clothing is ready to wear, it is highly fashionable and expensively priced. As manager of the boutique, Pevsner (P) is expected by her employer to wear YSL clothes at work. Because the boutique sells YSL clothes exclusively, she must be able to project the image of an exclusive lifestyle, demonstrate to her customers she is aware of YSL trends, and say that her clothing is designed by YSL. In addition to wearing YSL clothing while at the boutique, she wears them while commuting to and from work, to fashion shows sponsored by the boutique, and to business luncheons at which she represents the boutique. Although the clothing and accessories purchased by Pevsner (P) were the type used for general purposes by the regular customers of the boutique, Pevsner (P) is not a normal purchaser of these clothes. She and her partially disabled husband lead a simple life and their social activities are very limited and informal. Although Pevsner's (P) employer has no objection to her wearing the apparel away from work, she stated that she does not wear the clothes during off-work hours because she felt that they were too expensive for her simple everyday lifestyle. Another reason she did not wear the YSL clothes apart from work was to make them last longer. The Tax Court allowed Pevsner (P) to deduct the cost of the apparel as well as the cost of maintaining the apparel on the grounds that the apparel was not suitable to the private lifestyle maintained by Pevsner (P). The Commissioner (D) appealed that ruling.

■ **ISSUE**

May a clothing salesperson properly deduct the cost of designer clothes and the costs to maintain the clothes from her income taxes?

■ **DECISION AND RATIONALE**

(Johnson, C.J.) No. The generally accepted rule governing the deductibility of clothing expenses is that the cost of clothing is deductible as a business expense only if the clothing is of a type specifically required as a condition of employment, is not adaptable to general usage as ordinary clothing, and is not so worn. The Circuits that have addressed the issue have taken an objective, rather than subjective, approach. Under an objective test, no reference is made to the individual taxpayer's lifestyle or personal taste. Instead, adaptability for personal or general use depends upon what is generally accepted for ordinary streetwear. The principal argument in support of an objective test is, of course, administrative necessity. As a practical matter, it is virtually impossible to determine at what point either price or style makes clothing inconsistent with or inappropriate to a taxpayer's lifestyle. Moreover, the price one pays and the styles one selects are inherently personal choices governed by taste, fashion, and other unmeasurable values. Indeed, the Tax Court has rejected the argument that a taxpayer's personal taste can dictate whether clothing is appropriate for general use. In addition to achieving a practical administrative result, an objective test also tends to promote substantial fairness among the greatest number of taxpayers. Thus, the decision of the tax court upholding the deduction for Pevsner's (P) purchase of YSL clothing is reversed. Consequently, the portion of the Tax Court's deduction for maintenance costs for the clothing is also reversed.

Analysis:

The Tax Court, in rejecting the Commissioner's (D) argument for an objective test, recognized that the test for deductibility was whether the clothing was "suitable for general or personal wear," but determined that the matter of suitability was to be judged subjectively, in light of Pevsner's (P) lifestyle. An objective test, although not perfect, provides a practical administrative approach that allows a taxpayer or revenue agent to look only to objective facts in determining whether clothing required as a condition of employment is adaptable to general use as ordinary streetwear. Reliance on subjective factors provides fewer concrete guidelines in determining the deductibility of clothing purchased as a condition of employment.

United States v. Gilmore

(*Government*) v. (*Fighting Divorcee*)
372 U.S. 39, 83 S.Ct. 623 (1963)

LEGAL EXPENSES DO NOT BECOME DEDUCTIBLE MERELY BECAUSE THEY ARE PAID FOR
SERVICES WHICH RELIEVE A TAXPAYER OF LIABILITY

■ **INSTANT FACTS** A man deducted over
$40,000 in legal expenses incurred in resisting
his wife's community property claims in divorce
proceedings from his income taxes.

■ **BLACK LETTER RULE** The only kind of expenses deductible under section 212(1) and (2)
are those that relate to a "business," or profit-
seeking, purpose.

■ **PROCEDURAL BASIS**

Appeal from the Tax Court's judgment in favor of the plaintiff.

■ **FACTS**

At the time of the divorce proceedings, instituted by the wife but in which the husband, Gilmore (P), also
cross-claimed for divorce, Gilmore's (P) property consisted primarily of controlling stock interests in
three corporations. As president of the three corporations, he received salaries from them aggregating
about $66,800 annually, and in recent years his total annual dividends had averaged about $83,000. His
income from other sources was negligible. Gilmore's (P) primary concern in the divorce litigation was to
protect these assets against the claims of his wife under the community property laws. The end result of
this bitterly fought divorce case was a complete victory for Gilmore (P). He, not the wife, was granted a
divorce on his cross-claim, the wife's community property claims were denied in their entirety, and she
was held entitled to no alimony. Gilmore's (P) legal expenses in connection with this litigation amounted
to a total of $40,611.36. The Commissioner found all of these expenditures "personal" or "family"
expenses and as such none of them deductible. In the ensuing refund suit, however, the Court of
Claims held that 80% of such expense was attributable to Gilmore's (P) defense against his wife's
community property claims respecting his stockholdings and hence deductible under section 212(2) as
an expense "incurred for the conservation of property held for the production of income."

■ **ISSUE**

Are the legal expenses incurred in divorce proceedings deductible for federal income tax purposes?

■ **DECISION AND RATIONALE**

(Harlan, J.) No. Prior to 1942, the Code allowed deductions only for expenses incurred "in carrying on
any trade or business," the deduction presently authorized by section 162(a). The Revenue Act of 1942,
by adding what is now section 212(1) and (2), sought to remedy the inequity inherent in the
disallowance of expense deductions in respect of such profit-seeking activities, the income from which
was nonetheless taxable. A basic restriction upon the availability of a section 162(a) deduction is that
the expense item involved must be one that has a business origin. That restriction not only inheres in
the language of section 162(a) itself, confining such deductions to "expenses incurred in carrying on
any trade or business," but also follows from section 262, expressly rendering nondeductible in any
case "personal, living, or family expenses." It is clear that the personal or family expenses restriction of

section 262 must impose the same limitation upon the reach of section 212(1) and (2)—in other words that the only kind of expenses deductible under section 212(1) and (2) are those that relate to a "business," i.e., profit-seeking, purpose. The pivotal issue in this case then becomes: was this part of Gilmore's (P) litigation cost a "business" rather than a "personal" or "family" expense? The characterization as "business" or "personal" of the litigation costs of resisting a claim depends on whether or not the claim *arises in connection with* the taxpayer's profit-seeking activities. It does not depend on the *consequences* that might result to a taxpayer's income-producing property from a failure to defeat the claim. In classifying Gilmore's (P) legal expenses, the court below did not distinguish between those relating to the claims of the wife with respect to the *existence* of community property and those involving the *division* of any such property. Nor is such a break-down necessary for a disposition of the present case. It is enough to say that in both aspects the wife's claims stemmed entirely from the marital relationship, and that, under any tenable view of things, from income-producing activity. The same conclusion is no less true respecting the claim relating to the existence of community property. For no such property could have existed but for the marriage relationship. Thus, none of Gilmore's (P) expenditures in resisting these claims can be deemed "business" expenses, and they are therefore not deductible under section 212(2).

■ DISSENT

(Justice Not Stated) Justice Black and Justice Douglas believe that the Court reverses this case because of an unjustifiably narrow interpretation of the 1942 amendment to the Internal Revenue Code and would accordingly affirm the judgment of the Court of Claims.

Analysis:

The Commissioner's (D) sole contention here is that the court below misconceived the test governing section 212(1) and (2) deductions, in that the deductibility of these expenses turns not upon the *consequences* to Gilmore (P) of a failure to defeat his wife's community property claims, but upon the *origin* and *nature* of the claims themselves. For income tax purposes, Congress regards an individual as having two personalities: one as a seeker of profit who can deduct the expenses incurred in that search, and the other as a creature satisfying his needs as a human and those of his family but who cannot deduct such consumption and related expenditures. The Court regards § 212(1) and (2) as embodying a category of expenses embraced in the first of these roles. Legal expenses do not become deductible merely because they are paid for services that relieve a taxpayer of liability. That would mean that the expense of defending almost any claim would be deductible by a taxpayer on the ground that such defense helped him keep clear of liens on whatever income-producing property he might have.

■ CASE VOCABULARY

COMMUNITY PROPERTY: Property owned in common by husband and wife each having an undivided one-half interest by reason of their marital status.

IN PARI MATERIA: Upon the same matter or subject.

PRO TANTO: As far as it goes.

Carroll v. Commissioner

(School–Going Cop) v. *(Government)*

418 F.2d 91 (7th Cir.1969)

ALTHOUGH A COLLEGE EDUCATION IMPROVES THE JOB SKILLS OF ALL WHO AVAIL THEMSELVES OF IT, THIS RELATIONSHIP IS INSUFFICIENT TO REMOVE THE EXPENSE OF SUCH EDUCATION FROM THE REALM OF PERSONAL EXPENSES WHICH ARE DISALLOWED UNDER SECTION 262

■ **INSTANT FACTS** A police officer deducted the cost of attending college classes in preparation of attending law school as a business expense.

■ **BLACK LETTER RULE** The cost of education may be deducted as a business expense if there is a sufficient relationship between such an education and the particular job skills required.

■ **PROCEDURAL BASIS**

Appeal from the Tax Court's judgment against the plaintiff.

■ **FACTS**

Carroll (P) was employed by the police department as a detective. He enrolled in college courses in order to prepare for entrance to law school. He deducted the cost of the classes as an expense "relative to improving job skills to maintain his position as a detective." The Commissioner (D) disallowed the deduction, and the Tax Court affirmed that decision. This appeal followed.

■ **ISSUE**

Are the costs of attending college tax-deductible?

■ **DECISION AND RATIONALE**

(Castle, C.J.) No. Carroll (P) must, in this case, justify his deduction as maintaining or improving skills required by him in his employment. While the Commissioner (D) concedes that a general college education holds out the potential for improved performance as a policeman, he argues that Gilmore (P) has failed to demonstrate a sufficient relationship between such an education and the particular job skills required by a policeman. Thus, although a college education improves the job skills of all who avail themselves of it, this relationship is insufficient to remove the expense of such education from the realm of personal expenses which are disallowed under section 262. While tax incentives might be employed as an effective tool to encourage such valuable public servants as policemen, as well as others, to acquire a college education so as to improve their general competence, we feel that such a decision should be made by Congress rather than the courts. To allow as a deduction the cost of a general college education would surely go beyond the original intention of Congress in its enactment of the Internal Revenue Code of 1954. Accordingly, we affirm the judgment of the Tax Court.

Analysis:

Not all college courses are nondeductible. The cost of a course in industrial psychology would be properly deducted from the income of an industrial psychologist, even though it leads to an advanced degree and new job opportunities. Similarly, a housing administrator was allowed to deduct the cost of courses in housing administration, and a professional musician has been allowed to deduct the cost of music lessons. The difference between those cases and the instant case is that Carroll's (P) courses were general and basically unrelated to his duties as a police officer. If he were to take courses that related directly to the duties of his employment, along with other, more general, courses, their cost, or that part of the tuition representing their cost, would be deductible under § 162(a).

CHAPTER SIX

Deductions for the Costs of Earning Income

Encyclopaedia Britannica v. Commissioner

Instant Facts: A publisher is held to have made a capital expenditure, after hiring an outside publishing company to prepare a manuscript for a dictionary, despite a Tax Court ruling that the expenditures were for services, rather than for the acquisition of an asset.

Black Letter Rule: Expenditures that can be unambiguously identified with specific capital assets are not immediately deductible.

Midland Empire Packing Co. v. Commissioner

Instant Facts: A meat packing company is adjudged to have made a deductible repair after lining the basement walls of its plant with concrete, in order to keep out oil from a nearby factory.

Black Letter Rule: Repairs to property made during the taxable year are deductible as an ordinary and necessary business expense.

Norwest Corporation and Subsidiaries v. Commissioner

Instant Facts: A corporation removed asbestos from a building that it owned at the same time that it remodeled the building.

Black Letter Rule: Expenses incurred in connection with a plan of rehabilitation or improvement must be capitalized, even if the same expenses would have been deductible business expenses had they been incurred separately.

Starr's Estate v. Commissioner

Instant Facts: The Commissioner disallowed a taxpayer a deduction for payments made on a sprinkler system he obtained through an agreement termed as a "lease," but which was, in reality, a sale.

Black Letter Rule: Where the foreordained practical effect of the rent is to produce title eventually, the rental agreement can be treated as a sale.

Welch v. Helvering

Instant Facts: The owner of a grain purchasing business sought to deduct from his income payments he made and that were directed to the creditors of a grain company for which he had served as secretary and which had all its debts legally discharged in bankruptcy.

Black Letter Rule: An "ordinary" expense is not one that is habitual, but rather one that is common in the taxpayer's particular industry or business.

Gilliam v. Commissioner

Instant Facts: A noted artist and lecturer of art attacked an airplane passenger while traveling to a lecture and claims the right to deduct the costs of his legal defense and damages paid.

Black Letter Rule: Ordinary business expenses are those arising out of activities that constitute an integral part of, or are directly in the conduct of a taxpayer's trade or business.

Stephens v. Commissioner

Instant Facts: Stephens (P), after being fined and ordered to pay restitution for wire fraud, seeks to deduct the fines and restitution.

Black Letter Rule: Deductions for losses will not be allowed if it will frustrate sharply defined national or state policies proscribing particular types of conduct.

Knetsch v. United States

Instant Facts: Knetsch (P) entered into an annuity purchase from Houston Life which cost him more than he received but provided interest deductions.

Black Letter Rule: Deductions for amounts paid on indebtedness incurred to purchase or carry single-premium annuities will be denied when a transaction creates no true obligation to pay interest.

Estate of Franklin v. Commissioner

Instant Facts: A limited partnership is denied deductions for interest and depreciation losses related to the purchase of a motel and other related property, after it was found that the purchase did not constitute a true investment, nor any real debt liability.

Black Letter Rule: A taxpayer is not entitled to interest or depreciation expenses for property, where the purchase price paid does not yield equity, constitute an investment, nor create any real obligation to pay debt.

Winn–Dixie Stores, Inc. v. Commissioner

Instant Facts: Winn–Dixie Stores, Inc. (TP), pursuant to a company-owned life insurance (COLI) program, purchased life insurance policies on almost all of its full-time employees, named itself as the sole beneficiary on those policies, and then borrowed against those policies' account values.

Black Letter Rule: A COLI program that is set up and operated as a tax shelter, and that cannot generate a pre-tax profit, lacks sufficient economic substance to be treated as a tax shelter.

Klaassen v. Commissioner

Instant Facts: The Klaassens (TP), who were parents of ten dependent children, completed and submitted their federal income tax return without providing any computations for alternative minimum tax (AMT) liability.

Black Letter Rule: The alternative minimum tax (AMT) provisions do not apply exclusively to wealthy taxpayers.

Prosman v. Commissioner

Instant Facts: A computer consultant and spouse are determined to be subject to AMT, and are disallowed deductions for taxes paid and for job expenses and other miscellaneous deductions, despite the fact that a "per diem allowance" amount for employee business expenses were identified as wages.

Black Letter Rule: The alternative minimum tax will apply to low income taxpayers, whose business expenses are identified as wages.

Encyclopaedia Britannica v. Commissioner

(Publishing Company) v. *(IRS)*
685 F.2d 212 (7th Cir.1982)

EXPENSES ATTRIBUTABLE TO PRODUCING OR ACQUIRING SPECIFIC CAPITAL ASSETS MUST BE CAPITALIZED

■ **INSTANT FACTS** A publisher is held to have made a capital expenditure, after hiring an outside publishing company to prepare a manuscript for a dictionary, despite a Tax Court ruling that the expenditures were for services, rather than for the acquisition of an asset.

■ **BLACK LETTER RULE** Expenditures that can be unambiguously identified with specific capital assets are not immediately deductible.

■ **PROCEDURAL BASIS**

Appeal to the 7th Circuit Court of Appeals, of a judgment by the Tax Court, which allowed an immediate deduction for expenses related to the outside, rather than in-house creation of a manuscript.

■ **FACTS**

Encyclopaedia Britannica (Britannica) (P), who normally prepares its books in-house but was temporarily shorthanded, hired David–Stewart Publishing Company (David–Stewart) to research, prepare, edit and arrange the manuscript and all illustrative and other material for a book to be called The Dictionary of Natural Science (The Dictionary). Although under the contract David–Stewart agreed to work closely with Britannica's (P) editorial board, it was contemplated that David–Stewart would turn over a complete manuscript that Britannica (P) would copyright, publish, and sell. In exchange, David–Stewart would receive advances against royalties that Britannica (P) expected to earn from the book. Britannica (P) treated these advances as ordinary and necessary business expenses deductible in the years when they were paid, though it had not yet obtained any royalties. The Internal Revenue Service (IRS) (D) disallowed the deductions and assessed deficiencies. Britannica (P) petitioned the Tax Court for a redetermination of its tax liability and prevailed. The Tax Court reasoned that the agreement provided for substantial editorial supervision by Britannica (P), and that David–Stewart was just the vehicle selected to assist with the editorial phase of The Dictionary. Therefore, since Britannica (P) was the owner of The Dictionary at all stages of completion and the dominating force associated with The Dictionary, the expenditures were for a "service," rather than for the acquisition of an asset, and thus were deductible immediately rather than being, as the IRS had ruled, capital expenditures. The IRS appeals.

■ **ISSUE**

May expenses related to the hiring of an outside publishing company, to produce a manuscript for a specific book, be deducted as a necessary and ordinary expense?

■ **DECISION AND RATIONALE**

(Posner, J.) No. Expenditures that can be unambiguously identified with specific capital assets are not immediately deductible. Although, section 162(a) of the Internal Revenue Code (The Code) allows the deduction of all ordinary and necessary expenses paid or incurred during the taxable year in carrying on any trade or business, § 263(a) forbids the immediate deduction of "capital expenditures" even if they are ordinary and necessary business expenditures. We have no doubts that the payments to Davis–Stewart were capital expenditures regardless of who was the "dominating force" in the creation of The Dictionary. Where income is generated over a period of years, the expenditures should be classified as capital. Just as the expenditures in putting a building into shape to be rented must be capitalized, so should expenditures used to create a book, since a book is just another rental property from the publisher's standpoint. It makes no difference whether Britannica (P) hired David–Stewart as a mere consultant or bought the right to a book that David–Stewart had already published. If you hire a carpenter to build a tree house that you plan to rent out, his wage is a capital expenditure to you. We are not impressed by Britannica's (P) efforts to conjure up practical difficulties in matching expenditures on a book to income from it, by asking what the result would be if it had scrapped a portion of the manuscript it received. If there was loss or breakage in the construction of our hypothetical tree house, the effect would be to increase the costs of construction, which are deductible over the useful life of the asset. If the scrapped portion of the manuscript was replaced, the analogy would be perfect. If not replaced, the tax consequence would increase or decrease the publisher's taxable income from the published book. However, we must consider a series of decisions where authors of books have been allowed to treat expenses incurred in the creation of their books, immediately deductible as ordinary and necessary business expenses. In analyzing the leading case, *Faura v. Commissioner* [where an author's office and travel expenses, normal and recurrent in operating a business, happened to produce capital assets], we can think of a practical reason for allowing authors, as well as publishers, to deduct their expenses immediately. For those in the business of producing a series of assets that will yield income over a period of years, it may be very difficult to identify particular expenditures with particular books, since the expenditures tend to be joint among several books. Furthermore, allocating these expenditures among different books is not always necessary to produce the temporal matching of income and expenditures that the Code desires, because taxable income of the author or publisher who's output is neither increasing or decreasing, will be at least approximately the same whether his costs are expensed or capitalized. Under these conditions the benefits of capitalization are unlikely to exceed the accounting and other administrative costs entailed in capitalization. Yet, we hesitate to endorse the *Faura* line of cases not only in light of *Idaho Power* [where expenditures were made on transportation equipment used in constructing capital facilities that Idaho Power employed in its business of producing and distributing electricity], in which the Supreme Court of Idaho treated expenses as capitalized if they are incurred in creating a capital asset, but also because *Faura* line of cases fail to articulate a persuasive rationale for their result. While *Faura* relied on cases holding that the normal expenses of authors are deductible business expenses rather that nondeductible personal expenses, most of these cases in question only consider whether the author's expenditures are deductible at all, and not whether, if deductible, the expenditures must first be capitalized. *Faura's* principle only comes into play when the taxpayer is in the business of producing a series of assets that yield the taxpayer income over a period of years, so that a complex allocation would be necessary if the taxpayer had to capitalize all his expenses of producing them. This is not such a case. The expenditures are specifically identified with The Dictionary, and we need not consider the proper tax treatment of any other expenses. Just like *Idaho Power*, where expenditures were unambiguously identified with specific capital assets, Britannica's payment to Davis–Stewart for the manuscript was unambiguously identified with a specific capital asset. Moreover, the commissioning of the manuscript was somewhat out of the ordinary for Britannica. According to § 162 of The Code, the word ordinary is used: 1) to prevent the deduction of certain expenses that are not normally incurred in the type of business in which the taxpayer is engaged, and 2) to clarify the distinction between expenses that are immediately deductible and expenses that must first be capitalized. Most "ordinary" or recurring expenses of a business are noncapital in nature, and most of its capital expenditures are extraordinary or nonrecurring. In *Idaho Power*, Idaho Power's business was the production and distribution of electricity, and not the construction of buildings. Accordingly here, Britannica (P) stepped out of its normal method of doing business, by operating like a conventional publisher, which obtains a complete manuscript from an author or in this case a compiler. Although a conventional publisher may make a considerable contribution to the work both at the ideas stage and at the editorial stage, the deal is for the manuscript, not for services in assisting the publisher to prepare the manuscript itself. Finally, if the concept of capital expenditures is taken literally as anything that yields income, actual or imputed, beyond the period (conventionally one year) in which the expenditure is made, the result will be to force the capitalization of virtually every business expense. Therefore, the distinction between recurring and nonrecurring business expenses provides a very crude but perhaps serviceable demarcation between those capital expenditures that can feasibly be capitalized and those that cannot. Whether Britannica's (P) entire business is the production of capital assets, so that it is literally true that all of its business expenses are capital in nature, is not a question we have to decide here, for it is clear that Britannica's (P) payments to David–Stewart were of a nonnormal, nonrecurrent nature. In light of all we have said, the contention that David–Stewart was hired to render consulting services to Britannica (P), no different from the services of a consultant whom Britannica (P) might have hired on one of its in-house projects, is of doubtful relevance. What Britannica (P) was buying in the completed manuscript, was indeed a product, remote from what is ordinarily understood by editorial consultation. Although some creators or buyers of capital goods may deduct as current expenses what realistically are capital expenditures, they may not do so when the expense is tied to producing or acquiring a specific capital asset. Britannica's (P) alternative ground for sustaining the Tax Court decision was that the payments to David–Stewart were immediately deductible as research and experimental expenditures under § 174. Since this was not considered by the Tax Court, it would be premature for us to consider it without benefit of that court's review. Reversed and remanded.

Analysis:

This case illustrates the inconsistencies inherent in the rules governing capitalization. The court states that allocating expenditures among different books may prove difficult, and that the in-house costs of producing a manuscript, as opposed to the purchase of a completed manuscript from an unrelated company, would be currently deductible, since an in-house employee may spend time on many different projects. However, the allocation of costs may be vital to making sound business judgments, since it allows a business person to decide whether a project will be or has been profitable. Furthermore, the court states that the taxable income of the author or publisher in a steady state would be the same whether expenses where expensed or capitalized. Although this may be true in the long run, imagine if an author with income from other sources were allowed to deduct expenses this year for writing a series of books that he or she will receive royalties for next year, and continues this practice until retirement. That author will have the advantage of a premature deduction of expense attributable to the next year's income in every year until retirement. In response to these inconsistencies, and in recognizing that revenue needs outweigh administrative concerns in this area, Congress adopted § 263A, the uniform capitalization rules (UNICAP), which require the capitalization of all costs directly and indirectly related to the production of self-created assets, such as the in-house production of a manuscript.

■ CASE VOCABULARY

CAPITAL EXPENDITURE: An expense incurred in the creation, acquisition, or improvement of a long-term asset.

Midland Empire Packing Co. v. Commissioner

(*Meat Packers*) v. (*The IRS*)

14 T.C. 635 (1950)

EXPENDITURES MADE FOR THE PURPOSE OF KEEPING PROPERTY IN A NORMAL OPERATING CONDITION ARE DEDUCTIBLE

■ **INSTANT FACTS** A meat packing company is adjudged to have made a deductible repair after lining the basement walls of its plant with concrete, in order to keep out oil from a nearby factory.

■ **BLACK LETTER RULE** Repairs to property made during the taxable year are deductible as an ordinary and necessary business expense.

■ **PROCEDURAL BASIS**

Judgment by the Tax Court concerning expenditures made to repair a meat packing plant.

■ **FACTS**

For some 25 years prior to the taxable year, Midland Empire Packing Co. (Midland) (P) had used the basement rooms of its plant as a place for the curing of hams and bacon and for the storage of meat and hides. Although at times water would seep into this room, the basement had been entirely satisfactory for this purpose. However, in the taxable year, it was found that oil, created by a neighboring refinery, was also seeping through the concrete walls of the basement and could not be drained out. For this reason, a thick scum of oil was left on the basement floor which gave off a strong odor, permeated the air of the entire plant, and created a fire hazard with its fumes [to say nothing about how it affected the taste of the hams]. Furthermore, the oil had also made its way into the water wells which served to furnish water for Midland's (P) plant. As a result, the Federal meat inspectors advised Midland (P) that it must discontinue the use of the water and oil-proof the basement, or else shut down its plant. In response, Midland (P) undertook steps to oil proof its basement, by adding a concrete lining to the walls from the floor to a height of about four feet, and also added concrete to the floor of the basement. Midland (P) argues that the expenditure of $4868.81 for the concrete lining should be deductible as an ordinary and necessary expense under § 162(a) of the Internal Revenue Code, on the theory that it was an expenditure for repair. Alternatively, Midland (P) argues that the expenditure may be treated as the measure of loss sustained during the taxable year and not compensated for by insurance or otherwise within the meaning of § 165(a). The Commissioner (D) argues that the expenditure is for a capital improvement that should be recovered through depreciation charges, and not through deductions as an ordinary and necessary business expense or loss.

■ **ISSUE**

Are expenditures made for the purpose of keeping property in an ordinarily efficient operating condition, deductible as ordinary and necessary business expense?

■ **DECISION AND RATIONALE**

(Arundell, J.) Yes. Repairs to property made during the taxable year are deductible as an ordinary and necessary business expense. A repair is an expenditure made for the purpose of restoring property to a sound state, or for keeping the property in an ordinarily efficient operating condition. It does not add to the value of the property, nor appreciably prolong its life. On the other hand, expenditures for replacements, alterations, improvements, or additions connotes substitution, which prolong the life of property, increase its value, or make it adaptable to a different use. The basement was not enlarged by this work, nor did the oil-proofing serve to make the basement more desirable for its present purposes. Furthermore, the expenditure did not add to the value or prolong the expected life of the property beyond what it was before the event occurred. Although seepage of water was also stopped after the work, the presence of water had never been found objectionable. While it is conceded that the that the expenditure was "necessary," the Commissioner (D) contends that it was not an "ordinary" expense in petitioner's particular business. However, the fact that Midland (P) has not previously made a similar expenditure to prevent damage and disaster to its property does not remove that expense from the classification of "ordinary." Ordinary does not mean that expenses must be habitual or normal in the sense that the same taxpayer will have to make them often. It is enough that the situation is unique in the life of the taxpayer affected, but not in the life of the group or community which he is a part. Protecting a business building from the seepage of oil caused by a nearby factory, would seem to be a normal thing to do. We have previously allowed deduction for extensive expenditures made to prevent disaster, even when the repairs were of a type which had never been needed before and were unlikely to recur, on the ground that they were ordinary and necessary expenses. In *American Bemberg Corporation* [where a taxpayer hired engineers to inject grout into cavities beneath its manufacturing plant to prevent a cave-in], we found that the purpose of the expenses was not to improve or prolong the life of the original plant, but instead to enable the taxpayer to continue the plant in operation on the same scale and as efficiently as it had operated before. Therefore, in our opinion, the expenditure for lining Midland's (P) basement walls and floor was essentially a repair, deductible as an ordinary and necessary business expense. This holding makes it unnecessary to consider Midland's (P) alternative contention.

Analysis:

In order to deduct for repairs, the expenses must be made for the purpose of keeping the property in an ordinarily efficient operating condition, rather than for improving, increasing the value of, or prolonging the life of the property. Although this case seemed straightforward, there may at times be a fine line between repair and capital improvement. For example, in the instant case, Midland (P) did not need to protect against the seepage of water in order operate its business. Furthermore, the concrete lining may not have significantly added to the value of the investment. The outcome of this case may have been different if the water had been a significant burden that needed to be dealt with, in order for the basement to be used for its originally intended purpose. Here, it could have been determined the concrete lining was a forseeable part of the process of completing Midland's (P) initial investment, and therefore needed to be capitalized.

■ CASE VOCABULARY

REPAIRS: An expenditure made for the purpose of keeping or restoring property to its ordinarily efficient operating condition.

CAPITAL IMPROVEMENT: An expenditure made for the purpose of prolonging the life of property, increasing its value, or making it adaptable to a different use.

Norwest Corporation and Subsidiaries v. Commissioner

(Subsidiary Bank) v. *(IRS)*

108 T.C. 265 (1997)

COST INCURRED FOR REPAIR, ALTHOUGH NORMALLY DEDUCTIBLE, MUST BE CAPITALIZED WHEN MADE IN CONNECTION WITH IMPROVEMENTS

■ **INSTANT FACTS** A corporation removed asbestos from a building that it owned at the same time that it remodeled the building.

■ **BLACK LETTER RULE** Expenses incurred in connection with a plan of rehabilitation or improvement must be capitalized, even if the same expenses would have been deductible business expenses had they been incurred separately.

■ **PROCEDURAL BASIS**

Judgment by the Tax Court concerning repairs made in connection with a capital improvement.

■ **FACTS**

One of Norwest Corporation's subsidiaries, Norwest Bank Nebraska (Norwest Nebraska) (P), undertook to rehabilitate its Douglas Street building, which was built in 1969 in Omaha, Nebraska, for a cost of $4,883,232. Because the building was constructed before the health dangers of asbestos were widely known, asbestos-containing materials were used as the buildings main fire-retardant material, and was sprayed on all columns, steel I-bearns, the decking between floors, and the top part of the ventilation system's air plenum, which is used to remove existing air from a room. As the asbestos-containing fireproofing began to delaminate, the decking, suspended ceiling tiles, and light fixtures became contaminated throughout the building. By the 1970's research had confirmed that asbestos-containing material can release fibers that cause serious diseases when inhaled, and the Environmental Protection Agency (EPA) designated asbestos a hazardous substance. However, since the danger of asbestos arises only when asbestos-containing material is disturbed, thereby releasing fibers into the air, relevant laws and regulation did not require its removal from buildings if they could be controlled in place. In 1985 and 1986, Norwest Nebraska (P) undertook to determine the most efficient means for providing more space to accommodate additional operations personnel within the building. Although testing by Norwest Nebraska's (P) liability insurer revealed that airborne asbestos fiber concentration in the building did not exceed EPA and other relevant standards, Norwest Nebraska (P) decided to remove the asbestos-containing materials in coordination with the complete remodeling of the building. Given the extent of the remodeling, Norwest Nebraska (P) concluded that it would be impossible not to disturb the asbestos, and that it would be more cost efficient than conducting the removal and renovations as two separate projects. Subsequently, although there was no original intention to remove the asbestos from the parking garage, Norwest Nebraska (P) also decided that it would be financially advantageous to conduct this removal in connection with the garage renovation, since the garage tiles would eventually deteriorate. The asbestos removal and remodeling were performed in 13 phases. Each phase involved first the removal of the asbestos, then the remodeling. By 1989, the removal of the asbestos-containing material was substantially completed, but did not extend the buildings useful life. Norwest Nebraska (P) argues that the $902,206 expense made to remove the asbestos containing material should be deducted as an ordinary and necessary business expense. The Commissioner (D) argues that the cost should be capitalized because the asbestos removal was part of a general plan of rehabilitation and renovation that improved the Douglas Street building.

■ **ISSUE**

Are repair costs, incurred in connection with a plan of rehabilitation or improvement, deductible as an ordinary and necessary business expense?

■ **DECISION AND RATIONALE**

(Jacobs, J.) No. Expenses incurred in connection with a plan of rehabilitation or improvement must be capitalized. Section 263 requires taxpayers to capitalize costs incurred for improvements, betterments, restorations, and expenditures that add value or substantially prolong the life of the property or adapt such property to a new or different use. In contrast, § 162 permits taxpayers to currently deduct the costs of ordinary and necessary expenses that neither materially add to the value, nor appreciably prolong the life of property, but keep the property in an ordinarily efficient operating condition. Whether an expense is deductible or must be capitalized is a factual determination, requiring a practical case-by-case approach in applying the principles of capitalization and deductibility. According to the Court in *Plainfield–Union Water Co. v. Commissioner* it is necessary when determining whether an expenditure is capital, to compare the value, use, life expectancy, strength, or capacity of the property after the expenditure, with the status of the property before the condition necessitating the expenditure arose. Moreover, the Internal Revenue Code's capitalization provision envisions consideration of the duration and extent of the benefits realized by the taxpayer. According to the general plan of rehabilitation doctrine, expenses incurred as part of a plan of rehabilitation or improvement must be capitalized even if the same expenses would have been deductible as business expenses had they been incurred separately. The parties disagree as to whether the *Plainfield–Union* test is appropriate for determining whether Norwest Nebraska's (P) asbestos removal expenditures are capital. Norwest Nebraska (P) argues that it is the appropriate test, because the physical presence of the asbestos had no effect on the building's value until after the danger was discovered. Thus, the contamination could only affect the building's operation and reduce its value after the danger was perceived according to Revenue Ruling 94–38 [where the costs of remediating soil and treating groundwater that a taxpayer had contaminated with hazardous waste, was held currently deductible]. The Commissioner (D) on the other hand, argues that the discovery that the building contained hazardous material is not relevant, and that the Plainfield–Union test does not apply because a comparison cannot be made between the status of the building before it contained asbestos and after the asbestos was removed. In cases where this test has been applied, the condition necessitating the repair resulted from a physical change in the property's condition. In this case, no change occurred to the buildings physical condition that necessitated the removal. The only change was Norwest Nebraska's (P) awareness. Moreover, the Commissioner (D) argues that Revenue Ruling 94–38 does not apply, because the building always contained asbestos, and thus the expenditures did not return the property to the same state that existed when the property was constructed. Rather, this improved the property beyond its original, unsafe condition. The extent of asbestos-containing materials or the concentration of airborne asbestos fibers were not discovered until remodeling had been approved. The remodeling would disturb the asbestos fireproofing, and its removal in connection with the remodeling was more cost effective, since removing the asbestos on a later date, would have damaged remodeling work and created additional costs. Although the parties have stipulated that the asbestos removal did not increase the useful life of the building, it did increase the value of the building from what it was originally. However, we do not find that the expenditures for asbestos removal materially increased the value of the building as to require them to be capitalized. On the other hand, we do find that the asbestos would have remained in place and would not have been removed until a later date, had it not been for the remodeling. The purpose for removing the asbestos was primarily to effectuate the remodeling and renovation of the building, and secondarily to create a safer and healthier environment for the buildings employees and to avoid or minimize its potential liability for damages from injuries resulting from asbestos exposure. Since the asbestos removal and remodeling were part of one intertwined project, entailing a full-blown general plan of rehabilitation, we hold that the costs of removing the asbestos-containing material must be capitalized.

Analysis:

This case raises awareness of the fact that expenditures that are normally deductible as ordinary and necessary expenses may require capitalization when made in connection with improvement. More importantly, it provides a good example of how tax burdens could affect economic behavior, since the timing of the deduction is money in the bank. In this case, it would have been more costly to do each project separately. However, deductions taken over a period of years may adversely affect the rate of return on the original investment. Therefore, in the long run, depending on the overall tax consequences, it may turn out to be more profitable to separate the projects and take an immediate deduction for the removal of asbestos, even if the costs of a subsequent renovation project would increase.

■ **CASE VOCABULARY**

GENERAL PLAN OF REHABILITATION: A doctrine which requires the capitalization of expenses incurred pursuant to a plan of rehabilitation, even if they would have been deductible business expenses if incurred in isolation.

Starr's Estate v. Commissioner

(Taxpayer's Estate) v. *(Commissioner of Internal Revenue)*

274 F.2d 294 (9th Cir. 1959)

A TAXPAYER MAY NOT SEEK BUSINESS DEDUCTIONS FOR NECESSARY RENTAL PAYMENTS IF THE RENTAL OR LEASE AGREEMENT IS, IN SUBSTANCE, A SALE

■ **INSTANT FACTS** The Commissioner disallowed a taxpayer a deduction for payments made on a sprinkler system he obtained through an agreement termed as a "lease," but which was, in reality, a sale.

■ **BLACK LETTER RULE** Where the foreordained practical effect of the rent is to produce title eventually, the rental agreement can be treated as a sale.

■ **PROCEDURAL BASIS**

Appeal to the Ninth Circuit, challenging the decision of the Tax Court sustaining the Commissioner's disallowance of deductions taken on monthly payments pursuant to an installment contract.

■ **FACTS**

Delano Starr (P), owner of the Gross Manufacturing Company, entered into an agreement with Automatic Sprinkler of the Pacific, Inc. (Automatic) for the installation of a sprinkler system in Gross Manufacturing's plant. The agreement was entitled a "Lease Form of Contract," providing for annual rentals of $1,240 for five years, with the option to renew for an additional five years at a rental of $32.00 per year. The agreement gave Automatic the right to remove the sprinkler system, which was custom made, if Starr (P) did not renew. No provisions addressed the status of the system in the eleventh year. The Tax Court held that the five payments of $1,240 were a capital expense and not deductible rental, but it did allow for a annual depreciation deduction of $269.60.

■ **ISSUE**

Are payments made under a lease contract that has the effect of a sale deductible as necessary rental payments?

■ **DECISION AND RATIONALE**

(Chambers, Cir. J.) No. Where the foreordained practical effect of the rent is to produce title eventually, the rental agreement can be treated as a sale. It is true that the agreement in question did not by its terms pass title to Mr. Starr (P), but the internal revenue service is not always bound by form and can often recast a contract according to the practical realities. The sprinkler system in question was tailor made for Gross Manufacturing. There was never any real threat that Automatic would remove the system, for its salvage value thereafter would be negligible. It is obvious that the rental payments after five years of $32.00 were only a maintenance fee. The Commissioner (D) was entitled to recast the "lease" as a sale, disallowing rental payment deductions taken there on. However, we do find it necessary for the Tax Court to consider interest paid on the contract as a deductible item. The normal selling price of the system was $4,960, while the total rental payments amounted to $6,200. The difference could be regarded as interest for the five years on an amortized basis. In any event, after an allowance has been made for depreciation and interest, the attack this lease seems to be a zero sum game. Reversed and remanded.

Analysis:

This case provides a good introduction to the relationship between deductions for necessary rental payments and capitalization of an asset. Section 162(a)(3) provides: "There shall be allowed as a deduction all the ordinary and necessary expenses paid or incurred during the taxable year in carrying on any trade or business, including—rentals or other payments required to be made as a condition to the continued use or possession, for purposes of the trade or business, of property to which the taxpayer has not taken or is not taking title or in which he has no equity." Parties often choose to rent or lease equipment solely for the purpose of taking the deductions provided under § 162(a)(3). The court here thought that the payments made were an installment purchase, even though title did not pass. In the court's view, the fact that Starr would likely possess the sprinkler forever was enough to treat the agreement as a sale. Even as a sale, the contract provides Starr (P) with some tax benefits, specifically depreciation and interest deductions.

Welch v. Helvering

(Taxpayer) v. *(Commissioner of Internal Revenue)*
290 U.S. 111, 54 S.Ct. 8 (1933)

BUSINESS EXPENSES ARE DEDUCTIBLE AS ORDINARY AND NECESSARY EXPENSES IF THEY ARE COMMON AND ACCEPTED, AND APPROPRIATE AND HELPFUL

■ **INSTANT FACTS** The owner of a grain purchasing business sought to deduct from his income payments he made and that were directed to the creditors of a grain company for which he had served as secretary and which had all its debts legally discharged in bankruptcy.

■ **BLACK LETTER RULE** An "ordinary" expense is not one that is habitual, but rather one that is common in the taxpayer's particular industry or business.

■ **PROCEDURAL BASIS**

Appeal to the United State Supreme Court from the decision of the Board of Tax Appeals, sustaining the Commissioner's ruling that payments made to establish credit are not deductible.

■ **FACTS**

Mr. Welch (P) served as secretary of the E.L. Welch Company, a corporation engaged in the grain business. The E.L. Welch Company was adjudged an involuntary bankrupt, and had all its debts discharged. Thereafter, Mr. Welch (P) contracted with the Kellogg Company to purchase grain on commission. In order to reestablish his relations with customers, Mr. Welch decided to pay the debts of the E.L. Welch Company. From 1923 to 1928 Mr. Welch (P) paid debts totaling nearly $50,000, all of which were deducted in the year they were made. The Commissioner ruled that these payments were not deductible as ordinary and necessary expenses because they were in the nature of capital expenditures for reputation and goodwill. The Board of Tax Appeals sustained the ruling.

■ **ISSUE**

Are payments by a taxpayer, who is in business as a commission agent, ordinary and necessary if made to the creditors of a bankrupt corporation in an endeavor to strengthen his own credit standing?

■ **DECISION AND RATIONALE**

(Cardozo, J.) No. We can assume that the payments made to the creditors of the E.L. Welch Company were necessary in the sense that they were appropriate and helpful. But we are also required to determine if the payments were "ordinary." An "ordinary" expense is not one that his habitual, but rather one that is common in the particular industry or business. The norms of the particular business or community make this inquiry objective. It is true that at time people pay the debts of others, but they do not do so ordinarily. We could even say that the payments made here were "extraordinary." The issue of ordinary is one of degree, not kind. There is no bright-line rule. Life itself must supply the answer. The Commissioner's ruling carries with it a presumption of correctness, and Mr. Welch has the burden of proving otherwise. He has failed to do so. Nothing in the record permits us to say that these expenses were ordinary and necessary according to the prevailing norms of business. In fact, reputation is akin to a capital asset, much like goodwill. The money spent in acquiring it is not an ordinary expense in the operation of a business. Affirmed.

Analysis:

Section 162 of the Internal Revenue Code allows a deduction for all the *ordinary and necessary* expenses paid or incurred during the taxable year in carrying on any trade or business. It is the statutory meaning of ordinary and necessary that the Court here attempts to address. The Court defines necessary as "appropriate and helpful," citing Justice Marshal's definition of the word as used in the Necessary and Proper Clause of the Constitution. This broad definition makes the "necessary" requirement easy to satisfy, since businesses rarely make expenditures that are not appropriate and helpful. The real issue, however, was the extent of the "ordinary" requirement. The Court eschews a restrictive definition that would require the payments to be habitual. Instead, Justice Cardozo adopts a factual inquiry that focuses on accepted business practices and norms. The thrust of the decision is that those payments that are common and accepted within a particular industry will be held "ordinary" within the meaning of the Code.

Gilliam v. Commissioner

(*Crazy Artist*) v. (*IRS*)

51 T.C.M. 515 (1986)

EXPENSES INCURRED FROM EXTRAORDINARY ACTIVITIES ARE NOT DEDUCTIBLE BUSINESS EXPENSES

■ **INSTANT FACTS** A noted artist and lecturer of art attacked an airplane passenger while traveling to a lecture and claims the right to deduct the costs of his legal defense and damages paid.

■ **BLACK LETTER RULE** Ordinary business expenses are those arising out of activities that constitute an integral part of, or are directly in the conduct of a taxpayer's trade or business.

■ **PROCEDURAL BASIS**

Judgment by the Tax Court concerning a taxpayer's attempt to deduct expenses incurred from extraordinary behavior while traveling.

■ **FACTS**

Sam Gilliam, Jr. (Gilliam) (P), was at all material periods, a noted artists and teacher of art, having works exhibited in numerous art galleries throughout the United States and Europe, and having taught at various institutions. Gilliam (P) had a history of mental and emotional disturbances, which required hospitalization in 1963, 1965, 1966, and 1970. Although in 1973, while visiting at a number of universities in California, he found it necessary to consult an airport physician, Gilliam (P) did not require hospitalization until he returned to his home in Washington, D.C. On Sunday, February 23, 1975, Gilliam (P) flew to Memphis Tennessee, after accepting an invitation to lecture and teach for a week at the Memphis Academy of Arts. On the night before this trip, Gilliam (P) felt anxious and unable to rest. The next morning, he contacted Ranville Clark, a doctor Gilliam (P) had been consulting over the years, who arranged for Gilliam (P) to pick up Dalmane, a prescription drug Gilliam (P) had never taken before, on the way to the airport. Gilliam (P) took the Dalmane shortly after boarding the plane to Memphis. After about one and one-half hours, Gilliam (P) began to act irrationally. He talked about bizarre events, and felt trapped, anxious, disoriented, and very agitated. Feeling that the plane was going to crash, and after attempting to exit the plane from three different doors, Gilliam (P) then struck passenger Seiji Nakamura (Nakamura), who was seated near one of the exits, several times with a telephone receiver, and also threatened the navigator. As a result, Nakamura sustained a one-inch laceration above his left eyebrow, and suffered ecchymosis of the left arm and pains in his left wrist. Upon arriving at Memphis, Gilliam (P) was arrested by Federal officials, and subsequently criminally indicted on March 10, 1975. Gilliam (P) pleaded not guilty, and the district court granted his motion for a judgment of acquittal by reason of temporary insanity. Gilliam (P) paid $9,250 and $9,600 for legal fees in 1975 and 1976 respectively, in connection with both the criminal trial and Nakamura's civil claim. He also paid $3,900 to Nakamura in settlement of a civil claim. Deductions for the amounts paid in 1975 and 1976, were claimed on the appropriate individual tax returns. However, the Commissioner (D) disallowed the amounts claimed in both years, attributable to the incident on the airplane.

■ **ISSUE**

Are expenses arising out of activity that is not an integral part of or directly in the conduct of a taxpayer's trade or business "ordinary"?

■ **DECISION AND RATIONALE**

(Justice Not Named) No. Ordinary expenses are those arising out of activities that constitute an integral part of, or are directly in the conduct of a taxpayer's trade or business. Gilliam (P) contends that he is entitled to the deductions under § 162 [which allows immediate deduction for all ordinary and necessary business expenses], and maintains that this case is directly controlled by *Dancer v. Missioner* and *Clark v. Commissioner* [which both held that expenses for litigation arising out of an accident occurring during a business trip are deductible as ordinary and necessary business expenses]. The Commissioner (D) argues that the expenses in issue are not deductible, and maintain that *Dancer* and *Clark* are distinguishable, because the criminal charges were not directly connected with Gilliam's (P) trade or business, and because the legal fees were not paid for the production of income. The Commissioner (D) further argues that the criminal charges could hardly be deemed "ordinary" given the nature of Gilliam's (P) profession, and that settlement of the civil claim, resulting from an intentional tort, constituted a nondeductible personal expense. In order for an expense to be deductible under § 162, it must be ordinary and necessary, and it must be an expense of carrying on a taxpayer's trade or business. The Supreme Court set forth a guide for application of the requirement of "ordinary" in *Deputy v. du Pont* [where a taxpayer claimed a deduction for certain expenditures arising from his sale in the du Pont Corporation to a group of young executives, for the purpose of giving these executives financial interest in the corporation, to the end that his beneficial stock ownership might be conserved and enhanced]. According to the Supreme Court, ordinary has the connotation of normal, usual, or customary. Although an expense may be ordinary if it happens but once in the taxpayer's lifetime, the transaction which gives rise to it must be of common or frequent occurrence in the type of business involved. The Supreme Court went on to hold in *du Pont*, that there is no evidence that investors in furtherance of enhancing and conserving their estates, ordinarily lend such assistance to employee stock purchase plans of their corporations. It is undoubtedly ordinary for people in Gilliam's (P) trade to travel in the course of business. However, we do not believe it is ordinary for people in such trades to be involved in altercations of the sort here involved. It is obvious that neither the altercation nor the expenses were undertaken to further Gilliam's (P) trade or business. Furthermore, the travel itself was not the conduct of Gilliam's (P) trade, nor were the expenses here strictly a cost of his transportation. In *Dancer*, the taxpayer was driving an automobile when he caused an accident which resulted in injuries to a child. Although *Dancer* involved an expenditure that did not further petitioner's business in any economic sense, there was a direct relationship between the expenditure and the taxpayer's business. Automobile travel was an integral part of his business, and lapses by drivers seem to be an inseparable incident of driving a car. In *Clark* [where a taxpayer who was responsible for hiring people to solicit magazines, was charged with assault and battery which allegedly occurred during an interview in an applicant's home], the Tax Court allowed deductions for legal settlement expenses on the ground that expenditures incurred by a taxpayer to protect his business reputation have been regarded as deductible. While the expenses in the instant case are similar, the taxpayer's activities in *Clark* that gave rise to the prosecution and civil claim, were activities directly in the conduct of Clark's trade or business. Gilliam's (P) activities on the other hand merely occurred in the course of transportation connected with his trades or businesses. Gilliam (P) also relied on *Commissioner v. Tellier* [where a taxpayer was allowed to deduct the cost of an unsuccessful criminal defense to securities fraud]. However, in that case, the activities that gave rise to the criminal prosecution were, like *Clark*, directly in the conduct of Tellier's trade. Thus, while these cases all have similarities to the instant case, they are distinguishable in important respects. The expenses are not deductible under § 162(a).

Analysis:

Generally speaking, expenses will be deductible if they are closely or causally related to attempts to produce income, or if they are common or frequent to the taxpayer's industry. Thus, the outcome may have been different in the instant case had Gilliam (P) injured a student after having an anxiety attack when lecturing in a classroom. Although, injuring a student is surely not a common activity of Gilliam's (P) business, it is definitely an activity directly in the conduct of Gilliam's (P) trade or business.

■ CASE VOCABULARY

NECESSARY EXPENSES: Expenses incurred from any appropriate and helpful activity, while in pursuit of a trade, business, or profit seeking venture.

ORDINARY EXPENSES: Expenses incurred from activities common to, essential to, or directly in the conduct of a taxpayer's trade or business.

Stephens v. Commissioner

(*Convicted Criminal*) v. (*IRS*)

905 F.2d 667 (2d Cir. 1990)

DEDUCTIONS THAT SEVERELY AND IMMEDIATELY FRUSTRATE PUBLIC POLICY ARE NOT ALLOWED

■ **INSTANT FACTS** Stephens (P), after being fined and ordered to pay restitution for wire fraud, seeks to deduct the fines and restitution.

■ **BLACK LETTER RULE** Deductions for losses will not be allowed if it will frustrate sharply defined national or state policies proscribing particular types of conduct.

■ **PROCEDURAL BASIS**

Appeal to the United States Court of Appeals, of a decision by the IRS to deny deductions for a loss sustained pursuant to a criminal conviction.

■ **FACTS**

On December of 1982, Stephens (P) was convicted of four counts of wire fraud, one count of transportation of the proceeds of fraud in interstate commerce, and one count of conspiracy, after participating in a scheme to defraud Raytheon, a Delaware corporation doing business in the United States and in foreign countries. Upon the recommendation of the U.S. Attorney, the sentencing judge agreed that restitution was required along with the periods of imprisonment, since Stephens (P) was among the most culpable. On each count of wire fraud, Stephens (P) was sentenced to a concurrent five year prison term and a $1,000 fine. Stephens (P) was also sentenced to a prison term of 5 years and $10,000 fine for the conspiracy count, and a $5,000 fine on the count of interstate transportation of the proceeds of fraud. Stephens (P) was then placed on five years of probation on the condition that he make restitution to Raytheon in the amount of $1,000,000, $530,000 of which represented the amount which was initially embezzled from Raytheon, while the rest represented the interest. Stephens (P) was taxed upon his receipt of the $530,000 in 1976. In 1984, Stephens (P) turned over to Raytheon the $530,000 fund, and executed a $470,000 promissory note, representing interest, as part of a settlement agreement with Raytheon in connection with two civil actions. Stephens (P) claimed as a deduction the $530,000 restitution payment.

■ **ISSUE**

Are deductions for losses allowable if they would frustrate sharply defined national or state policies proscribing particular types of conduct?

■ **DECISION AND RATIONALE**

(Justice Not Named) Section 165(c)(2) of the Tax Code permits deductions for uncompensated losses sustained during the taxable year, incurred in any transaction entered into for profit, even if not connected with a trade or business. However, as stated in *Commissioner v. Tellier*, deductions will not be allowed if it will frustrate sharply defined national or state policies proscribing particular types of conduct. The test of nondeductibility is always the severity and immediacy of the frustration resulting from allowance of the deduction. For instance in *Tellier,* the Supreme Court allowed a tax deduction for the successful defense of a criminal prosecution, emphasizing that the policies frustrated must be national or state policies evidenced by some governmental declaration of them, and concluding that no public policy is offended when a man faced with serious criminal charges employs a lawyer to help his defenses. Although that case was decided pursuant to Tax Code provisions relating to business expenses, the test enunciated in those opinions is applicable to loss deductions under § 165. Thus, the issue before us is whether a deduction for Stephen's (P) restitution payment of embezzled funds so sharply and immediately frustrates a governmentally declared public policy, that the deduction should be disallowed. Taxpayers who repay embezzled funds are generally entitled to a deduction in the year in which the funds are repaid. Although clearly, no public policy would be frustrated if restitution payments unrelated to a criminal prosecution were at issue, the Commissioner (D) argues that because Stephens (P) made the restitution payment in lieu of punishment, the deduction should be disallowed. The Commissioner (D) contends that allowing Stephens (P) a deduction would take "the sting" out of Stephen's (P) punishment, thereby sharply and immediately frustrating public policy. However, because Stephens (P) has already paid taxes on the embezzled funds, disallowing the deduction for repaying the funds would in effect result in a "double sting." The sentencing judge made no reference to these tax consequences, and Stephens (P) received a stem sentence of five years in prison and a total of $16,000 in fines. We believe that allowing a deduction for Stephen's (P) restitution payments would not severely and immediately frustrate public policy. However, having reviewed the cases that have sought to elucidate the meaning and scope of the public policy exception under § 165, and finding them insufficiently decisive, we turn next to § 162, the Tax Code provision on deductibility of business expenses, as an aid in applying § 165. In 1969, Congress codified the public policy doctrine and limited exceptions to: 1) illegal bribes, kickbacks, and other illegal payments, fines or similar penalties paid to a government for the violation of any law (§ 162(f)), and 2) a portion of treble damage payments under the anti-trust laws (§ 162(g)). Congress intended these provisions to be all inclusive, stating that public policy in other circumstances, were generally insufficiently clearly defined to justify the disallowance of deductions. The public policy exception to deductibility under § 165 was not explicitly affected by the amendments to § 162. The Internal Revenue Service summarized its view on the impact of the amendments in a Revenue Ruling, by stating that a disallowance of deduction under 165, was not limited to amounts of a type for which deduction would be disallowed under § 162(c), (f), and (g) and the regulations thereunder. However, the Tax Court announced a different view, by questioning whether the public policy doctrine retained any vitality since the enactment of § 162(f). Although Congress, in amending § 162, did not explicitly amend § 165, we believe that the public policy considerations embodied in § 162(f) are highly relevant in determining whether the payment to Raytheon was deductible under § 165. It can hardly be considered that Congress intended to create a scheme where a payment would pass muster under § 162(f), but not under § 165. Reference to § 162(f) supports our conclusion that allowing Stephens (P) a deduction for his restitution payment would not severely and immediately frustrate public policy. Stephen's (P) restitution payment is primarily a remedial measure to compensate another party, and not a fine or similar penalty, even though Stephens (P) repaid the embezzled funds as a condition of his probation. Moreover, payment was made to Raytheon and not to the government. We hold that neither the public policy exception to § 165, nor the codification of the public policy exception to deductibility of expenses pursuant to § 162, bars deduction of Stephen's (P) restitution payment. Reversed and remanded.

Analysis:

Before 1970, the laws concerning deductions that frustrated public policy were uncertain and controversial. However, in 1969, Congress responded to the complaints about this area of law and added three new subsections to § 162. Pertinent to this case was § 162(f), which flatly prohibits deductions of "any fine or similar penalty paid to a government in violation of any law." Congress intended for these amendments to be all-inclusive. In other words, frustration of public policy in other circumstances should not be regarded as a sufficient justification for disallowing deductions. The only question that remains is whether Congress intended for these amendments to modify allowable deductions under § 165. This court takes somewhat of a middle ground, believing that the public policy considerations in § 162 are highly relevant in determining whether a payment is deductible under § 165. However, the court does not decide whether these considerations are all-inclusive under § 165, as they are under § 162.

■ CASE VOCABULARY

PUBLIC POLICY DOCTRINE: The rule that deductions for business expenses or losses will be disallowed, only if it would frustrate sharply defined national or state policies proscribing particular types of conduct.

Knetsch v. United States

(Tax Shelter) v. *(Congress)*
364 U.S 361, 81 S.Ct. 132 (1960)

AMOUNTS PAID ON INDEBTEDNESS INCURRED TO PURCHASE ANNUITIES WILL BE DENIED DEDUCTIONS WHEN INTENDED TO PROTECT SHAM TRANSACTIONS

■ **INSTANT FACTS** Knetsch (P) entered into an annuity purchase from Houston Life which cost him more than he received but provided interest deductions.

■ **BLACK LETTER RULE** Deductions for amounts paid on indebtedness incurred to purchase or carry single-premium annuities will be denied when a transaction creates no true obligation to pay interest.

■ **PROCEDURAL BASIS**

Certification to the United States Supreme Court, of the trial court's denial of deductions for amounts paid on indebtedness for annuities.

■ **FACTS**

On December 11, 1953, Sam Houston Life Insurance Company (Houston Life) sold Karl F. Knetsch (Knetsch) (P) ten 30–year maturity deferred annuity bonds, each in the face amount of $400,000 and bearing interest at two and one-half percent compounded annually, at a purchase price of $4,004,000. After giving Houston Life a check for $4,000, Knetsch (P) signed $4,000,000 of nonrecourse annuity loan notes for the balance, which bore a three and one-half percent interest and were secured by annuity bonds. The interest was payable in advance and Knetsch (P) on the same day prepaid the first year's interest, which was $140,000. Although, by December 11, 1954, the end of the first contract year, their cash or loan value was to be $4,100,000, the contract terms permitted Knetsch (P) to borrow any excess of this value above his indebtedness without waiting until that date. Knetsch (P) took advantage of this provision only five days after the purchase, and received from the company $99,000 of the $100,000 excess, for which he gave his notes. The interest on these notes was also payable in advance and on the same day he prepaid the first year's interest of $3,465. In their joint return for 1953, Knetsch (P) and Houston Life deducted the sum of the interest payments, $143,465, as "interest paid within the taxable year on indebtedness." When the second contract year began on December 11, 1954, interest in advance $143,465 was payable to Knetsch (P) on his aggregate indebtedness of $4,099,000. Knetsch (P) paid this amount on December 27, and three days later, received cash from the company in the amount of $104,000, the difference less $1,000 between his then $4,099,000 indebtedness and the cash or loan value of the bonds of $4,204,000. Knetsch (P) gave the company appropriate notes and prepaid the interest thereon of $3,640. In their joint return for the taxable year of 1954, Knetsch (P) and Houston Life deducted the sum of the two interest payments totaling $147,105. This was roughly repeated in December 1955. Knetsch (P) terminated the contract on December 27, 1956 with a total indebtedness of $4,307,000. The cash value of the bonds was $4,308,000. Knetsch (P) surrendered the bonds and his indebtedness was canceled. He received the difference of $1000 in cash. The contract called for a monthly annuity of $90,171 at maturity, or for such smaller amount as would be produced by the cash or loan value after deduction of the then existing indebtedness. If Knetsch (P) had held the bonds to maturity and continued annually to borrow the net cash value less $1,000, the sum available for the annuity at maturity would have provided only $43.00 per month. The trial court held that this transaction had no commercial substance, that it was not intended that Knetsch (D) become indebted to Houston Life, that no indebtedness was created by any of the transactions, and that no economic gain could be achieved from the purchase of the bonds without regard to the tax consequences. The court's conclusion of law was that, because there was no real obligation to pay interest, the transaction was a sham. Knetsch (D) appeals.

■ ISSUE

Does section 264(a)(2) only deny deductions for amounts paid on indebtedness incurred to purchase single-premium annuities, on contracts purchased after its enactment?

■ DECISION AND RATIONALE

(Brennan, J.) No. Deductions for amounts paid on indebtedness incurred to purchase or carry single-premium annuities will be denied when a transaction creates no true obligation to pay interest. First, it is necessary to determine whether the transaction created an indebtedness, putting aside the District Court's findings that Knetsch's (P) sole motive for purchasing these 10 bonds was an attempt to secure an interest deduction, and also putting aside Knetsch's (P) argument that his motive in taking out the annuities could not have been tax avoidance, since he had suffered a net loss even if the deductions are allowed. The legal right of a taxpayer to decrease or avoid an amount that would otherwise be his taxes, by means which the law permits, cannot be doubted. However, the question is whether what was done, apart from the tax motive, was the thing which the statute intended. Here, Knetsch (P) paid $294,540 to Houston Life during the two taxable years involved, and received $203,00 back in the form of loans. In form, for the out-of-pocket difference of $91,570, Knetsch (P) had an annuity contract which would produce a monthly annuity payments of $90,171, or substantial life insurance proceeds. This however was a fiction, since each year Knetsch (P) annual borrowings kept the net cash value, on which any annuity or insurance payment would depend, at the relative pittance of $1,000. Thus, what was really lent back was only the rebate of a substantial part of the so-called "interest" payments. The $91,570 difference retained by Houston Life was its fee for providing the disguised loans whereby Knetsch (P) and Houston Life sought to reduce their 1953 and 1954 taxes in the sum of $233,298, or about 80 percent of the "interest deduction." Knetsch (P) and Houston Life argue that while § 264(a)(2) denies a deduction for amounts paid on indebtedness incurred to purchase or carry a single-premium annuity contract, it only applies to contracts purchased after March 1, 1954, when the provision was enacted. Knetsch (P) argues that there is a congressional purpose for allowing the deduction of pre–1954 payments under transactions of the kind carried on here, without regard to whether the transaction created a true obligation to pay interest. However, the 1954 provision is extending Congress's 1942 denial of deductions for amounts paid on indebtedness incurred to purchase single-premium life insurance and endowment contracts, in order to close a loophole in respect of interest allocable to partially exempt income. Furthermore, the provision itself negates any suggestion that sham transactions were the congressional concern, for the deduction denied is of certain interest payments on actual "indebtedness." We see nothing to suggest that Congress is exempting pre–1954 annuities intended to protect sham transactions. Affirmed.

■ DISSENT

(Douglas, J.) It is true that Knetsch (P) was bound to lose, and never intended to come out ahead apart from his income tax deduction. However, as long as the transaction itself is not hocuspocus, the interest seems to be deductible as made prior to March 1, 1954, the date Congress selected for terminating this class of deductions. Houston Life existed, operating under Texas law, and was authorized to issue these policies and to make these annuity loans. Although tax avoidance is a dominating motive behind scores of transactions as the one here, will the Service that calls this transaction a "sham" today, not press for collection of taxes arising out of the surrender of the annuity contract? It is the legislative job to particularize the evils or abuses.

Analysis:

This case introduces the problem of tax shelters. In this form of tax shelter, an individual would borrow a certain amount at, say, ten percent, in order to buy a deferred annuity that provided a lower return of nine percent. Although, apart from the taxes, this would seem to be a loss, the interest would be currently deductible, while the appreciation would not be taxed until payments on the annuity began. This court denied the interest deduction on the ground that the transaction was a "sham," despite the fact that, as the dissent notes, the transaction was legal and legitimate. Because of the difficulty in determining the theory on which the court based its determination, the United States court of appeals in *Goldstein v. Commissioner* refused to follow *Knetsch* by considering whether the transaction had a purpose or utility apart from its anticipated tax consequences, rather than characterizing the transaction as a sham.

■ **CASE VOCABULARY**

DEFERRED ANNUITY: A fixed sum payable periodically, which does not begin until some specified date in the future.

NONRECOURSE LOAN: A secured loan which limits a borrower's liability to collateral, as opposed personal assets, in case of default.

Estate of Franklin v. Commissioner

(*Motel Purchaser*) v. (*IRS*)

544 F.2d 1045 (9th Cir.1976)

A PURCHASE TRANSACTION FOR PROPERTY IS FOUND TO HAVE NO SUBSTANCE DUE TO THE OVERVALUATION OF THE ASSET

■ **INSTANT FACTS** A limited partnership is denied deductions for interest and depreciation losses related to the purchase of a motel and other related property, after it was found that the purchase did not constitute a true investment, nor any real debt liability.

■ **BLACK LETTER RULE** A taxpayer is not entitled to interest or depreciation expenses for property, where the purchase price paid does not yield equity, constitute an investment, nor create any real obligation to pay debt.

■ **PROCEDURAL BASIS**

Appeal to the United States Court of Appeals, of a judgment by the Tax Court, disallowing deductions claimed with respect to purchased property.

■ **FACTS**

On November 15, 1968, Twenty–Fourth Property Associates (Associates), a California limited partnership of which Charles T. Franklin and seven other doctors were the limited partners, purchased the Arizona motel, Thunderbird Inn, from Wayne L. Romney and Joan E. Romney (the Romneys). After attempting to deduct interest and depreciation with respect to the acquisition of this and other related property, the Commissioner (P) disallowed the deductions for each of the taxpayer's distributive share, on the ground that either the acquisition was a sham, or that the entire acquisition transaction was in substance the purchase by Associates of an option to acquire the motel and related property on January 15, 1979. After finding that the transaction constituted an option exercisable in 1979, the Tax Court disallowed the taxpayer's deductions. Estate of Charles T. Franklin (P) appeals.

■ **ISSUE**

Is an investor entitled to interest and depreciation deductions for property, where the purchase price paid does not yield equity, constitute an investment, nor create any real obligation to pay debt?

■ **DECISION AND RATIONALE**

(Sneed, J.) No. A taxpayer is not entitled to interest or depreciation expenses for property, where the purchase price paid does not yield equity, constitute an investment, nor create any real obligation to pay debt. Under the "Sales Agreement" the Romneys agreed to "sell" the Thunderbird Inn to Associates for $1,224,000, which was to be paid over a period of ten years, with interest of seven and one-half percent annum. "Prepaid interest" in the amount of $75,000 was payable immediately. The monthly principal and interest installments of $9,045.36 or $108,544 per year would be paid for approximately the first ten years, with Associates required to make a balloon payment at the end of the ten years of the difference between the remaining purchase price, and any mortgages then outstanding against the property. This was a nonrecourse payment obligation, with the remedy for default being forfeiture of the partnership's interest. The sales agreement was recorded in the local county and a warranty was placed in an escrow along with a quitclaim deed from Associates to the Romneys. Both documents were to be delivered to Associates upon full payment, or the Romneys in the event of default. Accordingly, in coming to its conclusion, the Tax Court emphasized that the sale was combined with a leaseback of the property by Associates to the Romneys, and thus Associates never took physical possession, nor was a deed ever recorded. Moreover, the lease payments were designed to approximate closely the principal interest. Thus, except for the $75,000 prepaid interest payment, no cash would cross between Associates and the Romneys until the balloon payment. Since the lease was on a net basis, the Romneys were responsible for all of the typical expenses of owning the motel property, and for the first and second mortgage until the final purchase installment was made. Also, the Romneys were allowed to propose new capital improvements which Associates would be required to either build or allow the Romneys to construct with compensating modifications in rent or purchase price. Finally, the nature of the purchase money debt was nonrecourse, and there was a nice balance between the rental and purchase money payment. We believe, however that the characteristics set out above can exist in a situation in which the transaction imposes upon the purchaser a genuine indebtedness. In *Hudspeth v. Commissioner* [where parents entered into sale-leaseback transactions with their children], the children paid for the property by executing nonnegotiable notes and mortgages equal to the fair market value of the property. Although, payments were offset in part by rental payments, with the difference met by gifts from the parents, this court held that there was a bona fide indebtedness on which the children, to the extent of the rental payments, could base interest deductions. In none of these cases, however, did the taxpayer fail to demonstrate that the purchase price was at least equivalent to the fair market value. The Tax Court found that Associates had not shown that the sales price had any relationship to the actual market value. Although Associates spent a substantial amount of time at trial attempting to establish that they acted in the good-faith belief that the market value of the property was equal to the selling price, this evidence only goes to the issue of sham, and will not supply substance to the transaction. Since Associates had the burden and a fair opportunity to present evidence that the purchase price did not exceed the fair market value, we see no reason to remand this case. If the Association acquired the property at a price approximately equal to the fair market value of the property, this would quickly yield an equity in the property which the purchaser could not prudently abandon. However, this will not occur when the purchase price exceeds a reasonable estimate of the fair market value. Payments on the principal of the purchase price yield no equity so long as the unpaid balance of the purchase price exceeds the then existing fair market value. Here, a purchaser who abandons the transaction can lose nothing more than a mere chance to acquire an equity in the future, should the value of the acquired property increase. Thus, the transaction in this case fails to supply the substance necessary to justify treating the transaction as a sale from the start. Courts have held that depreciation is not predicated upon ownership or property, but rather upon an investment in the property. No such investment exists when payments of the purchase price yield no equity. Thus, depreciation was properly disallowed. As for the interest deductions, it has long been recognized that the absence of personal liability for the purchase money debt secured by a mortgage on the acquired property, does not deprive the debt of its character as a bona fide debt obligation able to support an interest deduction. However, this is no longer true when it appears that the debt has economic significance only if the property substantially appreciates in value prior to the date at which a very large portion of the purchase price is to be discharged. Under these circumstances the purchaser has not secured the use or forbearance of money, nor has the seller advanced money or forborne its use. Prior to the date at which the balloon payment on the purchase price is required, and assuming no substantial increase in the fair market value of the property, the absence of personal liability on the debt reduces the transaction to a mere chance that a debt obligation may arise. To justify the deduction the debt must exist. For debt to exist the purchaser, in the absence of personal liability, must confront a situation in which it is presently reasonable from an economic point of view, for him to make a capital investment in the amount of the unpaid purchase price. We do not intend to hold that a sale is not a sale if the purchaser pays too much. Rather, our holding and explanation should be understood as limited to transactions substantially similar to that now before us. Affirmed.

Analysis:

This case illustrates why overvaluation of assets and the use of nonrecourse debts are so important to many tax shelters. Imagine if a taxpayer invests in overvalued property, paying the actual value of the property in cash, and securing the overvalued portion with non-recourse promissory notes payable out of the proceeds of its exploitation. The investor could recover his actual investment from depreciation or amortization deductions on an asset with a claimed basis that is higher than its actual or fair market value. Although, eventually, the investor would default on the note and recognize gain from the discharge of indebtedness, the value of deferral would have made the transaction advantageous. Thus, in response to the problem of overvaluation, in 1976 Congress enacted § 465, which disallows deductions for losses on an investment in excess of the amount that the taxpayer had at risk in that investment.

■ **CASE VOCABULARY**

NONRECOURSE LOAN: A secured loan which limits a borrower's liability to collateral, as opposed to personal assets, in case of default.

Winn–Dixie Stores, Inc. v. Commissioner

(Grocery Store Chain–Taxpayer) v. *(Internal Revenue Service)*

254 F.3d 1313 (11th Cir. 2001), *cert. denied*, 535 U.S. 986, 122 S.Ct. 1537 (2002)

LOAN TRANSACTIONS THAT GENERATED ONLY POST–TAX BENEFITS WERE A SUBSTANTIVE SHAM

■ **INSTANT FACTS** Winn–Dixie Stores, Inc. (TP), pursuant to a company-owned life insurance (COLI) program, purchased life insurance policies on almost all of its full-time employees, named itself as the sole beneficiary on those policies, and then borrowed against those policies' account values.

■ **BLACK LETTER RULE** A COLI program that is set up and operated as a tax shelter, and that cannot generate a pre-tax profit, lacks sufficient economic substance to be treated as a tax shelter.

■ PROCEDURAL BASIS

Appeal from a tax court decision affirming a determination by the IRS that Winn–Dixie's (TP) COLI program was a sham and that interest and administrative fees that Winn–Dixie (TP) incurred pursuant to that program were not deductible.

■ FACTS

Winn–Dixie Stores, Inc. (TP) entered into a company-owned life insurance (COLI) program whereby it purchased whole-life insurance policies on almost all of its full-time employees. Winn–Dixie (TP) was the sole beneficiary of the policies and it borrowed against the policies. Because the high interest rates and the administrative fees outweighed the net cash surrender value and benefits, Winn–Dixie (TP) lost money on the COLI program on a pre-tax basis. However, because of the deductibility of the interest and fees post tax, the COLI program created a significant post-tax financial benefit. When tax laws jeopardized the post-tax benefits of this program, Winn–Dixie (TP) got out of the program. The IRS determined that the interest and administrative fees that Winn–Dixie (TP) paid were not deductible and determined a deficiency. Winn–Dixie (TP) challenged the determination in tax court. The tax court held that Winn–Dixie's (TP) loans against the policies were substantive shams and upheld the determination by the IRS.

■ ISSUE

Are the interest and administrative fees that Winn–Dixie (TP) paid, pursuant to the loans it took out under its COLI program, deductible?

■ DECISION AND RATIONALE

(Ruwe, J.) No. Winn–Dixie (TP) was not entitled to deduct the interest and administrative fees it paid because the loans that it took under its COLI program were sham transactions. Under the sham-transaction doctrine, a transaction is a sham and, therefore, not entitled to tax respect, if it lacks economic substance (other than the generation of tax benefits) or if the transaction serves no business purpose. There was no evidence that the COLI program served any business need of Winn–Dixie (TP) (e.g., indemnifying it for the loss of key employees), and it wasn't an employee benefit because Winn–Dixie (TP) was the policy beneficiary. Furthermore, the COLI program not only failed to generate a pre-tax profit, it resulted in a pre-tax loss. The only benefit of the COLI program was the deductibility of interest and administrative fees on the loans that Winn–Dixie (TP) took out. That Winn–Dixie (TP) set up the program solely for it post-tax benefits is further supported by the fact that Winn–Dixie (TP) withdrew from the program when changes to the tax law threatened the post-tax benefits it was receiving. The decision of the tax court is affirmed.

Analysis:

Winn–Dixie Stores clarifies that a transaction whose sole function is to produce tax benefits is a substantive sham and is not entitled to legal recognition. Conversely, it also suggests that if a transaction is capable of generating a pre-tax profit, the transaction will be considered to have economic substance and the sham-transaction doctrine will not apply.

■ CASE VOCABULARY

TAX SHELTER: A financial operation or investment strategy that is created primarily for the purpose of reducing or deferring income tax payments.

SHAM TRANSACTION: An agreement or exchange that has no independent economic benefit or business purpose and is entered into solely to create a tax advantage (such as a deduction for business loss). The Internal Revenue Service is entitled to ignore the purported tax benefits of a sham transaction.

Klaassen v. Commissioner

(Parents–Taxpayers) v. *(Internal Revenue Service)*
182 F.3d 932 (10th Cir. 1999) (unpublished opinion)

A FAMILY OF TWELVE WITH MODERATE INCOME WAS SUBECT TO THE ALTERNATIVE MINIMUM TAX

THE 12 PERSONAL EXEMPTIONS

■ **INSTANT FACTS** The Klaassens (TP), who were parents of ten dependent children, completed and submitted their federal income tax return without providing any computations for alternative minimum tax (AMT) liability.

■ **BLACK LETTER RULE** The alternative minimum tax (AMT) provisions do not apply exclusively to wealthy taxpayers.

■ **PROCEDURAL BASIS**

Appeal from a tax court decision affirming a determination by the IRS that the Klaassens (TP) were liable for alternative minimum tax (AMT).

■ **FACTS**

The Klaassens (TP) were parents of ten dependent children. During the tax year in question, they had an adjusted gross income of approximately $83,000 and claimed deductions and personal exemptions of approximately $49,000. They did not provide any computations for alternative minimum tax (AMT) liability. Following an audit, the IRS determined that the Klaassens (TP) were subject to the AMT and, after recalculating the Klaassens' (TP) federal tax return, issued them a notice of deficiency. The Klaassens (TP) filed a petition for redetermination with the Tax Court, claiming that the AMT provisions did not apply to them, or, in the alternative, that the application of the AMT provisions to them violated their First and Fifth Amendment rights. Tax Court upheld the determination by the IRS.

■ **ISSUE**

Are the alternative minimum tax provisions applicable only to wealthy taxpayers?

■ **DECISION AND RATIONALE**

(Anderson, J.) No. Congress created the AMT provisions with a high degree of specificity for determining when deductions or advantages in computing "regular tax" deductions are disallowed and the AMT computations must be used. If Congress had intended to apply the AMT only to taxpayers whose incomes reached certain thresholds or only to taxpayers with I.R.C. § 57 tax preferences, it could have drafted the statute to achieve this result. Furthermore, the uniform application of the AMT provisions does not violate any of the Klaassens' (TP) constitutional rights because the AMT provisions further a compelling government interest. The decision of the tax court is affirmed.

■ **CONCURRENCE**

(Kelly, J.) The court's decision that the AMT provisions applied to the Klaassens (TP) was correct because the law must be applied as it is written. However, the increasing number of moderate-income taxpayers that have been subject to the AMT suggests that steps should be taken to ensure that the AMT is more fairly applied, including (1) eliminating itemized deductions and personal exemptions as adjustments to regular taxable income in arriving at AMT income, (2) exempting low-and moderate-income taxpayers from the AMT, or (3) raising and indexing the AMT exemption amount.

Analysis:

The decision in *Klaassen* clearly points out that the AMT provisions, as written, have a much broader application than originally intended. That the Klaassens, whose extensive deductions stemmed solely from having a large family, could be subject to the AMT indicates a need to revise those provisions so that they once again serve the purpose they were intended to serve.

■ CASE VOCABULARY

ALTERNATIVE MINIMUM TAX: A flat tax potentially imposed on corporations and higher-income individuals to ensure that those taxpayers do not avoid all income tax liability by using exclusions, deductions, and credits.

EXEMPTION: An amount allowed as a deduction from adjusted gross income, used to determine taxable income.

Prosman v. Commissioner

(Low–Bracket Taxpayer Who Was Subject to Alternative Minimum Tax) v. *(IRS)*

77 T.C.M. 1580

EMPLOYEE BUSINESSES EXPENSES CAN BE IDENTIFIED AS TAX PREFERENCES BY THE ALTERNATIVE MINIMUM TAX

■ **INSTANT FACTS** A computer consultant and spouse are determined to be subject to AMT, and are disallowed deductions for taxes paid and for job expenses and other miscellaneous deductions, despite the fact that a "per diem allowance" amount for employee business expenses were identified as wages.

■ **BLACK LETTER RULE** The alternative minimum tax will apply to low income taxpayers, whose business expenses are identified as wages.

■ **PROCEDURAL BASIS**

Decision by Tax Court

■ **FACTS**

Prosman (P) was a computer consultant for Command Systems, Inc. (Command Systems). Comman Systems would bid on different projects using a formula which included both a standard hourly base rate and a "per diem allowance" amount. Since most of Prosman's (P) projects were out of town, the "per diem allowance" amount was included in the bid, because Prosman (P) incurred substantial meal and lodging expense while away from home. Although Prosman (P) requested that Command Systems separate the "per diem allowance" amount, which he used to pay for employee expenses, Command Systems refused and included both amounts as wages on Prosman's (P) 1995 Form W–2. On their Federal income tax return for 1995, the Prosmans (P) reported an adjusted gross income (AGI) in the amount of $83,143. On Schedule A of their 1995 return, they claimed, among other deductions, "taxes paid" in the amount of $8,824 and "job expenses and other miscellaneous deductions" of $28,589.63, totaling $37,414.45. For 1995, petitioners reported income prior to the deduction for exemptions of $37,843, taxable income of $32,843, and total tax of $4,924. The Commissioner (D), after determining that the Prosmans (P) were subject to the alternative minimum tax (AMT) for 1995, computed an AMT amount of $7,612 and determined a deficiency in the amount of $2,688.

■ **ISSUE**

Does the alternative minimum tax apply to low income taxpayers, whose business expenses are identified as wages?

■ **DECISION AND RATIONALE**

(Justice Not Named) Yes. The alternative minimum tax will apply to low income taxpayers, whose business expenses are identified as wages. Section 55(a) imposes a tax equal to the excess of the tentative minimum tax over the regular tax. For noncorporate taxpayers, the tentative minimum tax is equal to 26 percent of the amount that does not exceed $175,000, by which the alternative minimum taxable income (AMTI) exceeds the exemption amount, plus 28 percent of such taxable excess as exceeds $175,000. For married couples filing a joint tax return, the exemption amount is $45,000. AMTI equals the taxpayer's taxable income for the year with the adjustments provided in §§ 57 and 58 and increased by the amount of tax preference items described in § 57. No deduction is allowed for miscellaneous itemized deductions and State and local taxes paid, unless such amounts are deductible in determining AGI. Furthermore, no deductions for personal exemptions under § 151 are allowed. In the computation for the Prosman's (P) AMTI, which complies with provisions of § 55 and 56, the Commissioner (D) disallowed deductions for "taxes paid" and for "job expenses and other miscellaneous itemized deductions." The Prosman's (P) argue that the application of § 55 is inequitable, since AMT was intended to apply to high income earners rather than to lower income taxpayers such as themselves. However, they are still subject to the AMT under the plain meaning of the statute. The Prosman's (P) further argue that if Command Systems (P2) had separated Prosman's (P) "per diem allowance" for his base rate, Prosman (P) would not have been subject to the AMT. However, although Prosman (P) may be correct in asserting that the AMT would not apply if Command Systems had designated certain amounts paid to Prosman (P) as reimbursed employee business expenses rather than wages, Prosman (P) negotiated the best contract that he could and his remuneration must be taxed based on the manner in which it was received.

Analysis:

Since its creation, the AMT has expanded to the point where many consider it to be a second concept of taxable income. Because of its expansion, the AMT may be defeating the purpose or objectives served by preferences. The AMT can have a disparate effect among taxpayers, giving those with higher incomes taxable under the regular tax a greater benefit from a given tax preference. Absent legislative change, the AMT will apply to an increasing number of taxpayers, mainly because its exemption amount is not indexed for inflation, and thus has been losing value in real terms. As illustrated in the instant case, some items designated by the AMT as tax preferences, such as Prosman's (P) "per diem allowance," do not really deserve this label. As this case also depicts, the AMT can apply to individuals who are not the wealthiest of tax avoiders. However, in 1997 and 1999, legislation cut back the scope of the AMT in various respects, by narrowing or eliminating its application to certain items, such as accelerated depreciation.

■ CASE VOCABULARY

ALTERNATIVE MINIMUM TAX: Tax imposed at a reduced rate on a broader scale, generally achieved by taking taxable income, adding to it the amount of the preferences, and imposing a reduced-rate tax to this amount, payable only to the extent that it exceeds the normal tax amount.

PER DIEM ALLOWANCE: A day by day financial allowance used to cover expenses.

CHAPTER SEVEN

The Splitting of Income

Lucas v. Earl

Instant Facts: The IRS (P) sought to tax all of Mr. Earl's (D) salary despite the fact that Mr. Earl (D) and his wife had previously agreed that all their earnings would be owned by both of them as joint tenants.

Black Letter Rule: Income is taxable to the person who earned it.

Poe v. Seaborn

Instant Facts: The IRS (P) sought to tax all of Mr. Seaborn's (D) salary despite the fact that the Seaborns lived in a community property state and one half of Mr. Seaborn's (D) income was Mrs. Seaborn's community property.

Black Letter Rule: In a community property state, one half a married couple's income is taxable to each spouse.

Armantrout v. Commissioner

Instant Facts: The Commissioner (P) claimed that an employer's benefit plan providing college tuition for key employees' children was taxable income.

Black Letter Rule: An employment benefit plan that pays the education expenses of employees' children is taxable income to the employees.

Blair v. Commissioner

Instant Facts: The government sought to tax the owner of an income interest in a trust for life on portions of all his future income that were assigned to his children.

Black Letter Rule: The assignee of an unconditional assignment of a beneficial interest in a trust is taxable upon the income he receives as owner of the beneficial interest.

Helvering v. Horst

Instant Facts: After the owner of negotiable bonds gave to his son negotiable interest coupons detached from the bonds shortly before their due date, the government sought to tax the father for the interest payments.

Black Letter Rule: An assignment of the right to receive income from property is an economic benefit to the owner of the property, and is income realized and taxable to the owner of property.

Helvering v. Eubank

Instant Facts: Eubank (TP), a life insurance agent, gratuitously assigned to others the renewal commissions on life insurance policies he had written and serviced.

Black Letter Rule: The power to dispose of income is the equivalent of ownership of that income, such that one who chooses to dispose of income by assigning it to another retains the ownership, and thus the tax liability, for the income assigned.

Heim v. Fitzpatrick

Instant Facts: An inventor assigned his contract rights, including the right to receive royalties from his inventions, to his wife and children and argued that the royalty income was taxable to them rather than to him.

Black Letter Rule: If an inventor assigns an ownership interest in patents, and not just the right to collect royalties, the royalties are taxable to the assignees.

Brooke v. United States

Instant Facts: A doctor granted real estate to his children, collected the rents on their behalf, including rent for his own medical offices, and used the rents for the children's insurance, health, and education.

Black Letter Rule: After a gift and leaseback transaction, the transfer of a sufficient property interest justifies the taxation of the donees and the deduction of the rental payments by the donor.

Foglesong v. Commissioner

Instant Facts: A salesman created a corporation to collect his commissions, and transferred a portion of his commissions to his children through corporate dividends.

Black Letter Rule: Income of a personal service corporation may be taxable to the person who performs the services.

United States v. Basye

Instant Facts: Kaiser and a medical partnership entered into an agreement whereby the partnership would perform medical services for Kaiser members in exchange for a base payment and contributions by Kaiser to a partnership retirement fund. The Government sought to tax each partner for their distributive share of the retirement fund contributions.

Black Letter Rule: Contributions to a partnership retirement fund are taxable to the partners.

Lucas v. Earl

(Commissioner of Internal Revenue Service) v. *(Taxpayer)*
281 U.S. 111, 50 S.Ct. 241 (1930)

GIVING INCOME TO A SPOUSE DOESN'T EXCUSE PAYING INCOME TAX

■ **INSTANT FACTS** The IRS (P) sought to tax all of Mr. Earl's (D) salary despite the fact that Mr. Earl (D) and his wife had previously agreed that all their earnings would be owned by both of them as joint tenants.

■ **BLACK LETTER RULE** Income is taxable to the person who earned it.

■ **PROCEDURAL BASIS**

Certification of Board of Tax Appeals decision.

■ **FACTS**

In 1901, Mr. Earl (D) and his wife entered into a contract whereby they agreed that all the property they acquired during their marriage, including earnings, gifts, inheritances, and profits, would be owned by both of them as joint tenants. The IRS (P) determined that Mr. Earl (D) could be taxed for all the salary and attorney's fees he earned in 1920 and 1921. Mr. Earl (D) argued he could be taxed for only half because the other half belonged to his wife. The Circuit Court of Appeals held for Mr. Earl (D).

■ **ISSUE**

Is income taxable to the person who earns it, even if that person previously agreed to give the income to someone else?

■ **DECISION AND RATIONALE**

(Holmes, J.) Yes. The Revenue Act of 1918 imposes a tax upon the net income of every individual. A good argument can be made that the Act taxes only income beneficially received and that the instant Mr. Earl (D) received the income it became his and his wife's joint property. However, Mr. Earl (D) was the only party to the contracts by which the income was earned. In any event, this case does not turn on such technicalities. There is no doubt that the Act taxes salaries to those who earned them. This tax may not be escaped by anticipatory arrangements, even if they prevent the salary from vesting even for a second in the person who earned it. Mr. Earl's (D) motive for entering into the contract whereby "the fruits are attributed to a different tree from that on which they grew" is irrelevant. Reversed.

Analysis:

This case arose at a time when husbands and wives were considered separate taxpayers, and joint returns were not available. Thus, there was an advantage to shifting income from one spouse to another. Before joint tax returns were allowed, a husband who earned $10,000 would pay more income tax than a couple where each spouse earned $5000. Clearly, if Mr. Earl (D) had attempted to assign half his income to Mrs. Earl on the eve of his payday, the doctrine of "constructive receipt" would hold that Mr. Earl would be taxed because he actually received the income and gave half to his wife. Here, however, the Earls' agreement was made years before the tax question arose, and was likely not entered into for the purpose of evading taxes. Nonetheless, Justice Holmes held that Mr. Earl (D) had earned the income and that the tax law intended to tax income to the taxpayer who earned it. This case was decided before California changed its community property laws to provide that a wife is entitled to half of her husband's salary. The next case in this chapter, *Poe v. Seaborn*, holds that, in a community property state, each spouse could report one half of the couple's income, regardless of who earned it. *Lucas v. Earl* includes Justice Holmes's famous fruit and tree metaphor whereby Justice Holmes decrees that fruit (income) may not be attributed to a tree (taxpayer) different from that on which it grew.

Poe v. Seaborn

(Commissioner of Internal Revenue) v. *(Taxpayer)*
282 U.S. 101, 51 S.Ct. 58 (1930)

IN COMMUNITY PROPERTY STATE, EACH SPOUSE IS TAXED FOR ONE HALF OF THE COUPLE'S INCOME

■ **INSTANT FACTS** The IRS (P) sought to tax all of Mr. Seaborn's (D) salary despite the fact that the Seaborns lived in a community property state and one half of Mr. Seaborn's (D) income was Mrs. Seaborn's community property.

■ **BLACK LETTER RULE** In a community property state, one half a married couple's income is taxable to each spouse.

■ **PROCEDURAL BASIS**

Appeal to the U.S. Supreme Court challenging the lower court's decision on income tax issue.

■ **FACTS**

Mr. Seaborn (D) and his wife reside in Washington, a community property state. In 1927, only Mr. Seaborn (D) earned income, but the Seaborns filed separate tax returns, each declaring one half of Mr. Seaborn's (D) income and each deducting one half of the couple's expenses. The Commissioner of Internal Revenue ("Commissioner") (P) sued, arguing that Mr. Seaborn (D) should have declared all of the income. The district court held for Seaborn (D).

■ **ISSUE**

In a community property state, is income taxable to the spouse who earns it?

■ **DECISION AND RATIONALE**

(Roberts, J.) No. Sections 210(a) and 211(a) of the Revenue Act of 1926 provide that a tax shall be imposed on the net income of every individual. The word "of" denotes ownership of the income. Washington law provides that all property acquired after marriage by either spouse, except property acquired by gift, bequest, devise, or inheritance, is community property. It is true that a husband has the right to manage and control the community property, but a wife has certain rights too. A wife may borrow for community purposes, bind the community property, sue alone to enjoin collection of the husband's separate debt out of community property, and prevent the husband from making substantial gifts out of the community property. Clearly, in Washington, a wife has a vested property right in the community property, equal to the husband's. The Commissioner (P) argues that because a husband has such broad powers with respect to community property, i.e., he can do anything with it short of defrauding his wife, he "owns" the community property and should be taxed on it. We disagree. The law gives the husband broad powers with respect to community property because the community has to act through someone [and it might as well be the husband?]. This discourages lawsuits between spouses, and assures third parties dealing with the husband that the wife will not be permitted to nullify his transactions. However, the fact that husbands have such broad powers does not negate their wives' interests as co-owners. The cases cited by the Commissioner (P) are distinguishable. In *United States v. Robbins*, California law gave the wife only an expectancy in the community property and the husband's rights were so complete that he was the owner. In *Corliss v. Bowers*, a donor who retains the power to keep a gift of money still owns the money. And in *Lucas v. Earl*, Mr. Earl assigned one half of his income to his wife. The fact that Mr. Earl had to assign the income showed that the income was in fact his own property. Here, the husband never had ownership. Affirmed.

Analysis:

Under community property law, income earned by service rendered by either spouse during the course of the marriage is regarded as owned equally by each spouse. Therefore, for tax purposes, half the income is reportable by the husband and half is reportable by the wife, regardless of who earned the income. Therefore, at the time of this decision, spouses in community property states paid less tax than spouses in common law property states. As a result of *Poe*, many common law property states enacted systems that would allow their citizens to pay the same tax as citizens of community property states. In 1948, Congress enacted legislation allowing joint tax returns and new rates to remove the disparate tax treatment of married couples in community property and common law states. Married couples in all states were given the right to split their income. Single taxpayers paid higher taxes at equal income levels. In 1969, Congress changed the rate schedule for single persons, thereby reducing (but keeping) the tax disparity between single persons and married couples. However, in recent years, in some income ranges and proportions, a married couple, where each has income, pays more tax than an unmarried couple with identical incomes. The soundness of this "marriage penalty" has recently been a hot topic in the political arena.

■ CASE VOCABULARY

COMMUNITY PROPERTY: All property acquired during a marriage and before separation, other than by gift or inheritance, is presumed to be owned jointly by the spouses.

Armantrout v. Commissioner

(*Taxpayer*) v. (*Commissioner of Internal Revenue*)

67 T.C. 996 (1977), *aff'd per curiam*, 570 F.2d 210 (7th Cir. 1978)

EDUCATION BENEFIT TO CHILDREN IS TAXABLE INCOME TO PARENT

■ **INSTANT FACTS** The Commissioner (P) claimed that an employer's benefit plan providing college tuition for key employees' children was taxable income.

■ **BLACK LETTER RULE** An employment benefit plan that pays the education expenses of employees' children is taxable income to the employees.

■ PROCEDURAL BASIS

Tax Court decision regarding taxability of employment benefits.

■ FACTS

Hamlin, Inc. ("Hamlin") contracted with Educo, Inc. ("Educo") to implement a college education benefit plan. Under the plan, Hamlin contributed funds to a trust company and Educo provided the children of Hamlin's key employees with certain defined sums to defray their college expenses. Under the plan, the employees whose children participated in the Educo plan had no right or claim to the benefits or to any unused portion of the funds not expended by their children. Employees had the right to designate which of their children would participate in the plan. Hamlin did not increase the salary of employees without children to match the education benefit. Armantrout (D) was Hamlin's vice president in charge of marketing. The Commissioner (P) determined that the amounts distributed for Armantrout's (D) children's education were part of his compensation and were directly related to Armantrout's (D) relationship with Hamlin. Therefore, the Commissioner (P) determined that the money was includable in Armantrout's (D) gross income. Armantrout (D) argued that the Educo trust funds were not part of his gross income because he did not beneficially receive the funds, did not have the right to receive them, and did not have an ownership interest in them.

■ ISSUE

Is an employment benefit plan that pays the education expenses of employees' children taxable income to the employees?

■ DECISION AND RATIONALE

(Not stated) Yes. We start with some basic principles. First, income must be taxed to the person who earns it. Second, income must be attributed to the tree upon which it grew [*Lucas v. Earl*-income is taxable to the person who earned it, even if that person assigned it to someone else]. Third, the substance of a transaction governs its consequences. While we agree with Armantrout (D) that "familial" satisfaction is not sufficient to occasion a tax, this benefit was received in an employment setting in connection with the performance of services and is compensatory in nature. Other factors supporting our holding that the benefits are like compensation include that Hamlin incurred an identifiable cost for their benefit, eligible employees were selected based on their value to the company, only education expenses incurred during employees' employment with Hamlin were covered, Hamlin used the plan as an incentive to recruit and retain employees, and the plan enabled Hamlin to compete with employers that paid higher salaries. In substance, Armantrout (D) allowed a portion of his income to be shifted to his children. However, Armantrout (D) argues that the holding in *Lucas v. Earl*, that income is taxable to the person who earns it and that taxability cannot be shifted, is not applicable here. Armantrout (D) bases this argument on the fact that, unlike Mr. Earl, he never had a right to receive the income in question. This current situation is distinguishable from those in *Commissioner v. First Security Bank of Utah* and *Paul A. Teschner*, where the taxpayers did not have a right to receive the income at issue because it was illegal (*First Security Bank of Utah*) or contest rules prevented it (*Teschner*). First, Armantrout (D) was acting at arm's length with Hamlin and could have negotiated for a higher salary instead of participation in the Educo plan. In addition, Armantrout (D) had the power to designate which of his children would be enrolled in the Educo plan. This gave Armantrout (D) the power to influence how his compensation would be paid. In other words, Armantrout (D) consented to participating in the Educo plan. This is like an ''anticipatory arrangement'' to shift income which was prohibited in *Lucas v. Earl*. Our decision is supported by Section 83 [if in connection with performance of services, property is transferred to any person other than the person for whom the services were performed, the property is included in the gross income of the person who performed the services].

Analysis:

The assignment of income theory of *Lucas v. Earl* makes sense here. The Educo plan was basically a cash benefit to Armantrout (D) and the other Hamlin employees. The plan reduced the amount of cash the employees would have to pay for their children's education. So, basically, it was a cash benefit earmarked for a specific purpose. The opinion is in line with Justice Holmes's ''fruit and tree'' analogy in *Lucas v. Earl*. The deferred compensation (the fruit) was held to be taxable to the employee who earned it (the tree). Opinions vary as to when an employer, e.g., Hamlin, would be able to deduct the amount it contributes to the trust fund. One court held that the employer could deduct contributions to the fund only when the fund actually paid an employee's child's tuition and the benefits became taxable to the employee. Another court held that the employer could take the deduction as soon as it paid the money into the fund.

Blair v. Commissioner

(*Taxpayer*) v. (*Commissioner of Internal Revenue*)
300 U.S. 5, 57 S.Ct. 330 (1937)

A TAXPAYER MAY SUCCESSFULLY ASSIGN INCOME FROM PROPERTY IF THE TAXPAYER DOES NOT OWN THE PROPERTY FROM WHICH THE INCOME IS DERIVED

■ **INSTANT FACTS** The government sought to tax the owner of an income interest in a trust for life on portions of all his future income that were assigned to his children.

■ **BLACK LETTER RULE** The assignee of an unconditional assignment of a beneficial interest in a trust is taxable upon the income he receives as owner of the beneficial interest.

■ **PROCEDURAL BASIS**

Appeal to the United States Supreme Court, challenging the judgment of the Circuit Court of Appeals reversing the decision of the Board of Tax Appeals.

■ **FACTS**

Mr. Blair was the owner of an income interest in a trust for life. He assigned a portion of all of his future income from the trust to his children. The Supreme Court concluded the assignment was valid under state law.

■ **ISSUE**

Is the assignor of an income interest in a trust taxable upon the income paid to the assignees?

■ **DECISION AND RATIONALE**

(Hughes, C.J.) No. The assignee of an unconditional assignment of a beneficial interest in a trust is taxable upon the income he receives as owner of the beneficial interest. Unlike our cases dealing with the assignment of income earned by the assignor, this case concerns a tax upon income as to which the tax liability attaches to ownership. It is true that the beneficiary of trust is liable for the tax upon the income distributable to the beneficiary. But this does not preclude a valid assignment of the beneficial interest. The one who receives the income as the owner of the beneficial interest is to pay the tax. If there has been a valid, unconditional assignment of the beneficial interest, the assignee becomes the beneficiary. The assignee is then taxable for the income he receives. It matters not in this case that Mr. Blair (P) assigned only the "right to receive income." Mr. Blair (P) owned only a right to receive income from the trust, and a portion of that right is exactly what he assigned. Because the assignments were valid, the assignees became the owners of the specified beneficial interest in the income. The assignees, not Mr. Blair (P), were taxable on the income received from the trust.

Analysis:

This case demonstrates the difficulty in employing the fruit-tree metaphor in every case. In this case, the proceeds from the trust would normally be considered the fruit, while the trust would be the tree. In such a situation, the interest in the trust would be unassignable. However, in this case the interest in the trust becomes the underlying property—the tree—in Mr. Blair's (P) hands because that is all he owns and has control over. So when Mr. Blair assigned a portion of his interest in the trust, he assigned a portion of *his* tree, which just happened to be the fruit of another tree.

Helvering v. Horst

(Commissioner of Internal Revenue) v. *(Taxpayer)*

311 U.S. 112, 61 S.Ct. 144 (1940)

A TAXPAYER MAY NOT AVOID TAXATION BY ASSIGNING INCOME DERIVED FROM PROPERTY, UNLESS THE PROPERTY IS ALSO ASSIGNED

■ **INSTANT FACTS** After the owner of negotiable bonds gave to his son negotiable interest coupons detached from the bonds shortly before their due date, the government sought to tax the father for the interest payments.

■ **BLACK LETTER RULE** An assignment of the right to receive income from property is an economic benefit to the owner of the property, and is income realized and taxable to the owner of property.

■ **PROCEDURAL BASIS**

Appeal to the United States Supreme Court, challenging the decision of the Court of Appeals, which reversed the order of the Board of Tax Appeals sustaining the tax on the donor of the interest coupons.

■ **FACTS**

Mr. Horst (P), the owner of negotiable bonds, detached and gave to his son the interest coupons from the bonds. The Commissioner (P) ruled that the interest payments were taxable to Mr. Horst (P) as donor. The Board of Tax Appeals agreed, but the Court of Appeals reversed.

■ **ISSUE**

Is the owner of interest bearing property liable for interest paid on the property if those payments are assigned to a third party?

■ **DECISION AND RATIONALE**

(Stone, J.) Yes. An assignment of the right to receive income from property is an economic benefit to the owner of the property, and is income realized and taxable to the owner of property. The disposition of income to procure its payment to another is the enjoyment, and hence the realization, of the income by he who disposes of it. The holder of a coupon bond is the owner of two independent rights. One is the right to demand and receive at maturity the principal amount. The other is the right to receive interim interest payments. A taxpayer need not directly receive income in order to have realized it. Income may be realized if its disposition is controlled by the person who has the right to receive it. The rationale is that the assignor has diverted the payment from himself to others as the means of satisfying his wants. In other words, he has enjoyed the fruits of his labor or investment, just as one who uses the income to purchase goods. Mr. Horst (P) precluded any possibility of collecting the interest payments when he gave the coupons to his son. But this disposition of his right to receive income is, nonetheless, enjoyment of the income, no different than had he used the coupons to purchase goods, pay debts, or donated them to charity. Reversed.

Analysis:

For tax purposes, an assignment of income from property is invalid unless the property itself is also assigned. The fruit-tree metaphor used in *Lucas v. Earl* is useful in analyzing this case. There are two

---

aspects of property relevant for tax purposes: (1) the property itself (the tree), and (2) the income produced or derived from the property (the fruit). In this case, the tree was represented by the negotiable bonds, while the interest coupons represented the fruit. It was the latter that was held not to be assignable for tax purposes. In the Court's view, assigning the income from property is no different than assigning salary. Mr. Horst (P) "used" the interest to make a gift. He derived money's worth from the disposition of the coupons. The only other method of receiving this benefit would have been to give his son money, which would have obviously been taxable.

Helvering v. Eubank

(Internal Revenue Service) v. *(Life Insurance Agent–Taxpayer)*

311 U.S. 122, 61 S.Ct. 149 (1940)

COMMISSIONS COLLECTED BY ASSIGNEES WERE TAXABLE TO THE INSURANCE AGENT WHO EARNED THEM

■ **INSTANT FACTS** Eubank (TP), a life insurance agent, gratuitously assigned to others the renewal commissions on life insurance policies he had written and serviced.

■ **BLACK LETTER RULE** The power to dispose of income is the equivalent of ownership of that income, such that one who chooses to dispose of income by assigning it to another retains the ownership, and thus the tax liability, for the income assigned.

■ **PROCEDURAL BASIS**

Appeal from a tax court decision affirming a determination by the IRS that the commissions that Eubank (TP) assigned were taxable to Eubank (TP).

■ **FACTS**

After Eubanks (TP) terminated his agency contracts and services as a life insurance agent, he gratuitously assigned the renewal commissions to assignees. The renewal commissions had become payable to him as a result of life insurance policies that he had written and serviced. In the taxable year in which the assignees collected the renewal commissions that had been assigned to them, the IRS determined that those commissions were includable in Eubank's (TP) taxable income. The Board of Tax Appeals affirmed the determination by the IRS. The Court of Appeals then reversed the order of the Board of Tax Appeals.

■ **ISSUE**

Are the uncollected renewal commissions that were earned by Eubanks (TP), and that he assigned to the assignees, includable in his taxable income in the taxable year that the assignees collected those commissions?

■ **DECISION AND RATIONALE**

(Stone, J.) Yes. The uncollected renewal commissions that Eubanks (TP) had earned and later transferred to the assignees were includable in his taxable income in the taxable year in which the assignees collected those commissions because the assignments were voluntary transfers of the right to collect the commissions. The decision of the Court of Appeals is reversed.

■ **DISSENT**

(McReynolds, J.) When Eubanks (TP) assigned his right to the commissions, the right to collect them became the absolute property of the assignee and Eubanks (TP) had no control over when they would be collected. The mere right to collect future payments, for services already performed, is not presently taxable as "income derived" from those services. It is, instead, a property that may be assigned. Only if Eubanks (TP) had received consideration for the assignment would he realize any taxable income, and that taxable income would the consideration he received, not the amount of the renewal commissions.

Analysis:

As the court noted in the companion case to *Eubank*, *Helvering v. Horst*, 311 U.S. 112 (1940), the power to dispose of income is the equivalent of ownership of it. Exercising that power by assigning that income (in the case of *Eubanks*, assigning the renewal commissions that he had earned) is the enjoyment of that income. Therefore, the realization of income when that income is collected by the assignee is the responsibility of the assignor.

■ **CASE VOCABULARY**

ASSIGNOR: One who transfers property rights or power to another.

ASSIGNEE: One to whom property rights or powers are transferred by another.

COMMISSION: A fee paid to an agent or employee for a particular transaction; a percentage of the money received from the transaction.

Heim v. Fitzpatrick

(Taxpayer) v. *(Commissioner of Internal Revenue)*
262 F.2d 887 (2d Cir.1959)

ASSIGNING RIGHT TO CONTROL PROPERTY MAKES INCOME FROM THAT PROPERTY TAXABLE TO ASSIGNEES

■ **INSTANT FACTS** An inventor assigned his contract rights, including the right to receive royalties from his inventions, to his wife and children and argued that the royalty income was taxable to them rather than to him.

■ **BLACK LETTER RULE** If an inventor assigns an ownership interest in patents, and not just the right to collect royalties, the royalties are taxable to the assignees.

■ **PROCEDURAL BASIS**

Appeal of denial of motion for summary judgment in tax case.

■ **FACTS**

Heim (P) invented a new type of rod end and spherical bearing, and applied for a patent. He assigned the invention and the patents to The Heim Company (the "Company") which was owned by himself (1%), his wife (41%), his children (27% each), and their spouses (2% each). When the patent was granted, in July 1943, Heim (P) and the Company agreed that the Company would pay specified royalties on the bearings after a certain date and that the parties would negotiate a royalty payment on any new types of bearings. They also agreed that if the royalties for any two consecutive months fell below a certain amount, Heim (P) could cancel the agreement and retain ownership of the patents. In August 1943, Heim (P) assigned to his wife and children a portion of the rights in the July 1943 agreement with the Company. The Commissioner (D) claimed that Heim's (P) taxable income should be increased by the royalty payments his wife and children received. Heim (P) moved for summary judgment, arguing that the assignments transferred to his wife and children were income-producing property, and therefore the royalty payments were taxable to them. The district court ruled that Heim (P) owned a right to a portion of the income that the patents produced and assigned this right to his wife and children. Therefore, the court held that pursuant to *Helvering v. Horst* [assignment of right to receive income from property is taxable to owner of property] and *Helvering v. Eubank* [assignment of right to receive commissions is taxable to assignor] the royalty payments were taxable to Heim (P).

■ **ISSUE**

If an assignor assigns an ownership interest in patents, and not just the right to collect royalties, is the income taxable to the assignees?

■ **DECISION AND RATIONALE**

(Swan, J.) Yes. Heim (P) assigned more than the bare right to receive royalties. He assigned all his rights in the contract with the Company, including his right to bargain for additional royalties on new types of bearings and his right to cancel the agreement if the royalties fell below a certain amount. Thus, Heim (P) assigned income-producing property to his wife and children. The Commissioner (D) argues that Heim (P) retained control over the invention and thus should be treated as its owner for tax purposes. The Commissioner (D) argues that Heim (P) maintained control because Heim's (P) wife and daughter together owned 68% of the Company's stock and would follow Heim's (P) advice. We hold that the record does not support a finding that Heim (P) controlled the Company or that his daughter would follow Heim's (P) advice rather than her husband's or brother's. Reversed.

Analysis:

If a donor gives property to a donee and that property generates income in the donee's hands, the income generated is taxable to the donee. In other words, income from property is taxed to the owner of the property. Thus, income earned by the property while the donor owned it is taxed to him, and income earned after the donee owns the property is taxable to the donee. The question is what is the "property." Here, the court decided that Heim (P) assigned enough of his patent rights that he assigned an ownership interest in them, not just the right to receive the royalty payments. Specifically, he assigned the right to negotiate another royalty on new bearings (which was exercised) and the right to cancel the agreement (which was not exercised). If the court had ruled that Heim (P) assigned only the right to receive income from the patents, this case would have been like *Helvering v. Horst*, and the income most likely would have been taxable to Heim (P).

Brooke v. United States

(Taxpayer) v. *(Government)*
468 F.2d 1155 (9th Cir. 1972)

GIFT AND LEASEBACK TRANSACTION IS VALID IF DONOR GIVES UP SUBSTANTIAL CONTROL

■ **INSTANT FACTS** A doctor granted real estate to his children, collected the rents on their behalf, including rent for his own medical offices, and used the rents for the children's insurance, health, and education.

■ **BLACK LETTER RULE** After a gift and lease-back transaction, the transfer of a sufficient property interest justifies the taxation of the donees and the deduction of the rental payments by the donor.

■ **PROCEDURAL BASIS**

Appeal of district court ruling regarding the validity of a gift for tax purposes.

■ **FACTS**

Brooke (P) is a physician who granted to his children real estate, including a pharmacy, an apartment, and Brooke's (P) medical offices. The probate court appointed Brooke (P) as the children's guardian. As guardian, Brooke (P) collected rents from the apartment, pharmacy, and his own medical offices (for which there was no written lease). Brook (P) used the rents for the children's insurance, health, and education, including private school tuition, music lessons, public speaking lessons, and a car. Brooke (P) deducted his rental payments as ordinary and necessary business expenses. The Government (D) argued that the gift was not valid and was a sham to shift taxes. District court ruled for Brooke (P).

■ **ISSUE**

After a gift and leaseback transaction, are the donees taxed and may the donor deduct rental payments?

■ **DECISION AND RATIONALE**

(Not stated.) Yes, so long as the donee transferred sufficient control to the donees. We look at the following factors: (1) the duration of the transfer; (2) the controls retained by the donor; (3) the use of the gift property for the donor's benefit; and (4) the trustee's independence. Here, the transfer was absolute and irrevocable. Brooke (P) retained few controls over the property. His medical office was required to and did pay reasonable rent. The fact that there was no written lease indicates that the guardianship could terminate the month to month lease at any time. Also, Brooke (P) could be terminated as guardian at any time. The rental proceeds were used solely for the children's benefit. As a court-appointed guardian, Brooke (P) was sufficiently independent. If Brooke (P) breaches his fiduciary duty in the future, the Government (D) may renew its challenge to the validity of the gift. The transfer here is not a sham or a fraud. Brooke's (P) non-tax motives for the transfer include providing for his children, avoiding friction with his medical partners, removing his assets from the threat of malpractice suits, and diminishing the conflict between owning a medical practice and an adjoining pharmacy. The Government (D) argues that Brooke (P) should not be permitted to deduct the rental payments because he was obligated to support his children in any event. Under Montana law, Brooke (P) was obligated only to provide "support and education suitable to his circumstances." The district court held that

Brooke (P) was not required to make the type of expenditures he made here with the rental payments. Finally, we hold that a court-administered guardianship constitutes a trust for the purposes of taxation under § 677(b) [grantor not taxed on income that might be used to support children in discretion of another person]. Affirmed.

■ **DISSENT**

(Ely, J.) I dissent for two reasons. First, we previously held that gift and leaseback transactions are examined under the "business purpose" test. Here, the district court held that the transaction did not serve any substantial business purpose. Therefore, I would reverse. If a gift and leaseback are looked at as an integrated transaction, rather than independently, it is obvious that allowing rental deductions requires that the gift aspect of the transaction satisfy the business purpose test, not just the leaseback. Second, I dissent because the majority opinion creates a new legal standard that omits the requirement that the gift and leaseback transaction have "economic reality." In reality, Brooke (P) retained control over the property; he set the amount of the rent, determined the terms of the lease, and decided when they would be paid. His only impediment was that the court had to approve his actions. I find it hard to believe that Brooke (P) acted independently merely because of some speculative level of court supervision. If a transaction is grounded on economic reality and business purpose, then the fiduciary's independence may be minimal. However, if more leeway is given by requiring only economic reality, then more independence is required. Here, neither test works to Brooke's (P) advantage.

Analysis:

If a taxpayer transfers income-producing property in trust and retains so much control over the property that he is basically still its owner, he is taxed on the income of the trust even if he does not receive it. This rule stems from *Helvering v. Clifford*, where a husband established a five-year irrevocable trust for his wife's benefit. The trust would terminate on the death of the husband or the wife, whichever was earlier. On termination, the trust corpus would return to the grantor, but any undistributed income was to go to the wife. The husband was the trustee and had absolute discretion in deciding whether to pay income to his wife or keep it in the trust. The U.S. Supreme Court held that the grantor should be taxed because he retained many incidents of ownership. The Court looked at the trust's short duration, the husband's retention of control, and the fact that his wife was the beneficiary. In response to *Clifford*, the IRS passed regulations regarding when trust income is taxable to the grantor. These regulations have become statutes (IRC §§ 671–677). The four-prong test the court applied in *Brooke* is a variation of these statutes.

■ **CASE VOCABULARY**

GIFT AND LEASEBACK: A transaction in which a donor gives property and then leases it back from the donee.

Foglesong v. Commissioner

(Taxpayer) v. *(Commissioner of Internal Revenue)*

621 F.2d 865 (7th Cir. 1980)

INCOME OF PERSONAL SERVICE CORPORATION MAY BE TAXABLE TO PERSON RENDERING THE SERVICES

■ **INSTANT FACTS** A salesman created a corporation to collect his commissions, and transferred a portion of his commissions to his children through corporate dividends.

■ **BLACK LETTER RULE** Income of a personal service corporation may be taxable to the person who performs the services.

■ **PROCEDURAL BASIS**

Appeal from United States Tax Court decision.

■ **FACTS**

Foglesong (D) was a successful salesman of cold drawn steel tubing for the Plymouth Tube division of the Van Pelt Corporation (Plymouth Tube) and the Pittsburgh Tube Company (Pittsburgh Tube). On August 30, 1966, Foglesong (D) formed a corporation called "Frederick H. Foglesong Company, Inc." (the Corporation). Foglesong (D) owned 98 of the 100 shares and his wife and accountant each held 1 share. The Corporation paid no dividends on its common stock from 1966–1969. The Corporation issued preferred stock to Foglesong's (D) four minor children. They received dividends of $32,000 from 1966–1969. The Corporation entered agreements with Plymouth Tube and Pittsburgh Tube granting exclusive territorial rights. The commissions Foglesong (D) earned from Plymouth Tube and Pittsburgh Tube were paid to the Corporation. In January 1967, the Corporation began making monthly salary payments to Foglesong (D). Foglesong (D) did not report any personal income from any business as a sole proprietor. The Corporation reported the commissions it received and deducted the compensation it paid to Foglesong (D). Ninety-eight percent of the commissions were from Foglesong's (D) personal sales efforts, and 2% were from sales made within the Corporation's exclusive sales territories. Foglesong (D) testified that he incorporated in order to obtain limited liability protection and to expand into several new business ventures. However, he had no documentation of these expansion efforts. From 1966–1969, Foglesong (D) was an employee only of the Corporation, and not of Plymouth Tube or Pittsburgh Tube. The Tax Court held that, although the Corporation was a viable, taxable entity, 98% of its income was taxable to Foglesong (D) rather than to the Corporation. It based its decision on IRC § 61 [gross income means all income from any source] and *Lucas v. Earl* [income is taxable to the person who earned it].

■ **ISSUE**

Is income of a personal services corporation taxable to the person who performs the services?

■ **DECISION AND RATIONALE**

(Cudahy, J.) Yes. Generally (the court remanded the case and never answered this question). There is a tension between the *Lucas v. Earl* rule about not splitting income and the recognition of corporations as taxable entities. Here, the following facts are relevant: (1) the Corporation is the party to the contracts under which services are performed; (2) the Corporation is viable and not a mere sham; (3) while tax avoidance is a major motive, non-tax business purposes are present; (4) the Corporation was not formed to take advantage of a separate business's losses; (5) Foglesong (D) has honored the corporate form; (6) Foglesong (D) is not an employee of any entity other than the Corporation; (7) the law does not require that Foglesong's (D) services be performed by an individual; (8) Foglesong (D) does not control Plymouth Tube or Pittsburgh Tube; and (9) other legal bases exist for attacking tax avoidance than disregarding the corporate form through application of the assignment of income theory. It is inappropriate here to weigh "business purpose" against "tax avoidance motives." This case is distinguishable from *Lucas v. Earl* because Foglesong (D) assigned not just income to the Corporation, but the service contracts as well. Here, Foglesong (D) transferred the fruit and the tree, like in *Fox v. Commissioner* [cartoonist assigned copyrights and contracts to corporation; court held assignment was of property and income was taxable to corporation]. Also, as in *Fox*, and unlike *Rubin v. Commissioner* [Tax Court held income taxable to personal services corporation where taxpayer controlled corporation and company for which services performed], Foglesong (D) had no control over the companies for which he performed services. *Rubin* was later reversed on appeal by Judge Friendly who believed that IRC § 482 [providing for reallocation of gross income of commonly controlled organizations, trades or business] should apply. This case is also distinguishable from *Roubik v. Commissioner* [income of professional corporation taxable to shareholders], where the corporate form was repeatedly flouted and a covenant not to compete had no realistic effect. Here, while there is no covenant not to compete, Foglesong (D) worked exclusively for the Corporation. A test that attempts to strike a balance between tax avoidance motives and legitimate business purposes is inappropriate here because such an approach places too low a value on the recognition of corporations as economic actors and essentially disregards the corporate form. Instead, we think IRC § 482 should be applied to allocate the income and deductions to prevent evasion of taxes and to clearly reflect each party's income. Therefore, we remand this case to the Tax Court for consideration of § 482. Reversed and remanded.

■ DISSENT

(Wood, J.) I agree with the Tax Court's opinion. In the alternative, I think § 482 should apply. The Corporation is nothing more than a few papers in a desk drawer. Foglesong (D) conducted his business as he always did and was able to divert income to his children.

Analysis:

Often, the IRS is more tolerant of shifting income through a corporation, rather than directly, because the players face double taxation. The corporation must pay taxes on its income and the shareholders must pay individual taxes on the dividends. However, where, like here, the corporation is set up primarily to evade taxes, the IRS is less tolerant. Determining a taxpayer's motive is difficult. It is possible that an objective determination, where the court looks at whether there is a rational business basis for the transaction, may be more appropriate. The aftermath of this case is worth noting. On remand, the Tax Court applied § 482 and again found that Foglesong (D) was taxable on 98% of the corporation's income. The court of appeals reversed and remanded again, holding that § 482 was applicable only when the profits of one business are used to offset the losses of another. The Tax Court later reaffirmed its view that § 482 applied to one-person personal service corporations.

■ CASE VOCABULARY

PERSONAL SERVICE CORPORATION: A corporation whose principal activity is the performance of personal services that are substantially performed by owner-employees.

United States v. Basye

(*Government*) v. (*Partner in Medical Partnership*)

410 U.S. 441, 93 S.Ct. 1080 (1973)

PARTNERS ARE TAXED ON CONTRIBUTIONS TO PARTNERSHIP RETIREMENT FUND

■ **INSTANT FACTS** Kaiser and a medical partnership entered into an agreement whereby the partnership would perform medical services for Kaiser members in exchange for a base payment and contributions by Kaiser to a partnership retirement fund. The Government sought to tax each partner for their distributive share of the retirement fund contributions.

■ **BLACK LETTER RULE** Contributions to a partnership retirement fund are taxable to the partners.

■ PROCEDURAL BASIS

Certification to U.S. Supreme Court of Court of Appeals decision granting a refund of a tax assessment.

■ FACTS

Basye (P) and the other plaintiffs (collectively "Basye") were physicians and partners in a limited partnership called the Permanente Medical Group ("Permanente"). In 1959, Permanente entered into an agreement with Kaiser Foundation Health Plan, Inc. ("Kaiser") whereby Permanente agreed to provide medical services to Kaiser members in the San Francisco Bay area. Kaiser agreed to pay Permanente a base compensation composed of two elements: a monthly fee based on the number of members enrolled in Kaiser and a retirement benefit trust fund, which is at issue here. To receive the retirement benefits, Permanente physicians had to complete a certain number of years of service, reach a certain age, and work only for Permanente or Kaiser even after retirement. None of the doctors had a vested interest in the trust until they retired. Under no circumstances could Kaiser recoup its payments to the fund. The retirement plan was designed to create an incentive for physicians to remain with Permanente and minimize turnover for Kaiser. Until 1963 when the plan was discontinued, Permanente did not report these payments as income in its partnership returns and Basye (P) did not include these payments in his taxable income. The Commissioner (D) argued that Kaiser's payments to the fund were compensation, and assessed deficiencies against each partner for their share of the fund. Basye (P) paid the assessment under protest and sued for a refund. The district court and the Court of Appeal held that the payments to the fund were not income to the partnership because the partnership did not actually receive them and did not have a right to receive them. They held that the partnership should be disregarded and that no presently taxable income should be attributed to Basye (P), a cash basis taxpayer, because the payments were contingent and forfeitable.

■ ISSUE

Are contributions to a partnership retirement fund taxable income to the partners?

■ DECISION AND RATIONALE

(Powell, J.) Yes. Basye (P) was properly taxed on the partnership's retirement fund income because income is taxed to the party who earns it. Basye (P) was taxable on his distributive share of partnership income irrespective of whether it was distributed to him. Under IRC § 703(a), partnerships must report the income they generate in the same way that individuals do. However, once a partnership's income is ascertained, its existence is disregarded and each partner pays a tax on the partner's portion of the partnership's income. We first look at Permanente's gross income. There is no question that Kaiser's payments to the retirement trust were compensation for Permanente's services, and, therefore, were includable in Permanente's gross income. The payments were integral to the employment arrangement. Kaiser's payments to Permanente were not forfeitable or contingent. The fact that Kaiser paid the money to a trust rather than directly to Permanente is irrelevant. It is a basic rule that income is taxable to the person who earns it. As held in *Lucas v. Earl* [income is taxable to the person who earned it], tax liability may not be avoided by "anticipatory assignments of income." Here Permanente earned the income as a result of arm's-length bargaining with Kaiser. The Court of Appeal held that Permanente could not have received that income except in the form in which it was received. This seems to be based on the idea that the Government (D) must prove that Permanente agreed to accept less direct compensation from Kaiser in exchange for the retirement plan payments. We know of no authority imposing this burden on the Government (D). Kaiser's motives are irrelevant. The Government (D) does not have to prove that Basye (P) had the power to designate how his income would be received. Since Permanente should have reported the retirement fund payments as income, Basye (P) should have included his share of that income in his individual return. It is axiomatic that each partner must pay taxes on his distributive share of the partnership's income whether or not it is distributed to him. The contingent and unascertainable nature of each partner's share of the retirement trust is irrelevant when computing each partner's distributive share. The sole consideration is that the income had been received by the partnership and, therefore, must be taxed to the partners. Reversed.

■ DISSENT

(Douglas, J.) Not provided in casebook.

Analysis:

The Supreme Court here adopts the "entity" view of partnerships, whereas the district court and the court of appeals seem to have applied the "aggregate" view of partnerships. Under the lower courts' view, a partnership has no separate identity, but is merely an agreement among partners to act collectively. Under this view, the partnership does not have any income, but keeps track of the partners' income. Thus, the court of appeals held that the retirement funds were not yet income to the partners because they had not actually received it. It is interesting to note that under the Supreme Court's holding, Basye (P) and the other partners are taxed on all of Kaiser's contributions to the retirement fund, even those that would ultimately go to doctors who are not Permanente partners, but are Permanente employees.

■ CASE VOCABULARY

CASH BASIS TAXPAYERS: Taxpayers whose income is taxable when they actually or constructively receive it. The mere right to income does not require that amount to be included in the taxpayer's gross income.

VEST: To pass into possession or ownership and no longer be subject to forfeiture.

CHAPTER EIGHT

Capital Gains and Losses

Bielfeldt v. Commissioner

Instant Facts: Bielfeldt (TP), who claimed to be dealer in securities, sought to offset immense trading losses that he had incurred against his ordinary income.

Black Letter Rule: An individual taxpayer can only deduct a maximum of $3000 in capital losses from his ordinary income for a particular year.

Biedenharn Realty Co. v. United States

Instant Facts: Biedenharn (P) bought property for an investment and then, a number of years later, sold off individual lots for homes.

Black Letter Rule: Where there has been a subdivision of property that was originally purchased as an investment by a taxpayer and substantial and frequent sales of the subdivision property over an extended period of time, such activity can negate the original investment intent of the taxpayer and result in the characterization of any gain from the sale as ordinary income rather than capital gain.

Corn Products Refining Co. v. Commissioner

Instant Facts: A manufacturer of corn products, which had bought corn future contracts to ensure a ready supply of raw materials and then later sold some of the contracts, appealed an IRS determination that the gains and losses constituted ordinary income.

Black Letter Rule: Gains and losses arising from the sale of future contracts bought to ensure a ready supply of raw materials for a manufacturer's everyday business operations are ordinary income and losses and not capital gains and losses.

Arkansas Best Corp. v. Commissioner

Instant Facts: Taxpayer acquired stock in a bank for business purposes and then claimed an ordinary loss when that stock was sold for less than it was purchased.

Black Letter Rule: Stock held by a business is a capital asset, regardless of whether it was purchased for business or investment purposes.

Hort v. Commissioner

Instant Facts: Taxpayer, a landlord, agreed to accept a sum certain in exchange for cancellation of a long-term lease and then claimed the foregone rent payments as a loss and the sum certain paid as a capital gain.

Black Letter Rule: Amounts accepted in exchange for cancellation of a lease constitute ordinary income to the landlord, from which the foregone rent payments cannot be offset as a loss.

Womack v. Commissioner

Instant Facts: Womack (P) sold his rights to his future annual lottery-winnings payments and claimed that the sale proceeds were entitled to capital-assets treatment, but the tax court deemed the proceeds to be ordinary income; Womack (P) appealed.

Black Letter Rule: Under the substitute-for-ordinary-income doctrine, when a party receives a lump-sum payment essentially as a substitute for what otherwise would have been received, at a future time, as ordinary income, that lump sum payment is taxable as ordinary income as well.

McAllister v. Commissioner

Instant Facts: A taxpayer appealed an IRS holding disallowing capital loss treatment for the sale of her life estate and requiring the amounts received from the sale to be treated as ordinary income.

Black Letter Rule: A life estate is a capital asset.

Commissioner v. P.G. Lake, Inc.

Instant Facts: The taxpayer accepted three years' worth of proceeds from the sale of oil and gas in exchange for cancellation of a debt.

Black Letter Rule: The assignment of a portion of a payment right to the proceeds of future sales of oil and gas from a working interest in an oil and gas lease, in return for the cancellation of a debt owed to the assignee, results in the assignor having realized ordinary income rather than capital gain.

Commissioner v. Brown

Instant Facts: A group of taxpayers transferred their stock in a lumber company to a tax-exempt entity in return for a sum of money payable out of the future earnings of the lumber company which would be managed by the taxpayers under a leaseback arrangement.

Black Letter Rule: Property may be sold or exchanged within the meaning of the capital gains provisions of the Internal Revenue Code, even if the purchase price for the transferred property is payable out of the property's own future earnings.

Baker v. Commissioner

Instant Facts: Baker (TP), a retired insurance agent, reported the termination payment he received from the insurance company, for which he had worked as an independent contractor, as a long-term capital gain.

Black Letter Rule: A termination payment made to an independent contractor-insurance agent, and that is conditioned on the return of assets of the business to the insurance company, is not a capital gain if the assets of the business belong to the insurance company.

Commissioner v. Ferrer

Instant Facts: A taxpayer sold the exclusive rights to the production of a play in return for a percentage of the profits from a film to be made based on the play.

Black Letter Rule: The release of an equitable property interest in the copyright of a play can constitute the sale or exchange of a capital asset within the meaning of the Internal Revenue Code.

Miller v. Commissioner

Instant Facts: The wife of a deceased entertainer who had sold the exclusive right to her husband's story to a movie company appealed a U.S. Tax Court judgment that the sums received under the contract constituted ordinary income.

Black Letter Rule: Beneficiaries of the estate of a deceased entertainer do not receive a capitalizable "property interest" in the name, reputation, right of publicity, or public image of the deceased for purposes of the capital gains provisions of the Internal Revenue Code.

Gregory v. Helvering

Instant Facts: A taxpayer transferred stock from a corporation she owned to a newly formed corporation and then dissolved the new corporation to receive the stock.

Black Letter Rule: Although meeting the literal requirements for a tax-free corporate reorganization, a proposed reorganization will not be recognized as tax-exempt if it lacks a business purpose other than tax avoidance.

Williams v. McGowan

Instant Facts: A taxpayer sued the IRS to recover taxes which he felt should not have been paid.

Black Letter Rule: When a going business is sold, it should be comminuted into fragments that are matched against the definition in § 117(a)(1) to determine whether gains or losses realized upon sale are to be characterized as capital or ordinary.

Merchants National Bank v. Commissioner

Instant Facts: A taxpayer bank that had charged off notes it held as worthless and deducted their value as ordinary income in a prior tax year appealed an IRS ruling that amounts received from the sale of those notes in a subsequent tax year should be treated as ordinary income rather than capital gain.

Black Letter Rule: When a deduction for income tax purposes is taken and allowed for debts deemed worthless, a recovery on the debts in a later year constitutes taxable income for that year, to the extent that a tax benefit was received from the prior year deduction.

Arrowsmith v. Commissioner

Instant Facts: A former shareholder of a liquidated corporation was personally required to pay a judgment issued against his old corporation in a tax year subsequent to the liquidation. He appealed an IRS holding that the payment in the subsequent year was a capital loss rather than an ordinary loss.

Black Letter Rule: A transaction that is related to a transaction in a prior tax year must take its character as ordinary or capital on the basis of the tax benefit claimed by the taxpayer in the earlier year.

Bielfeldt v. Commissioner

(Trader–Taxpayer) v. *(Internal Revenue Service)*

231 F.3d 1035 (7th Cir. 2000)

WHEN THE TAXPAYER IS NOT A SECURITIES DEALER, STOCK TRADING LOSSES ARE CAPITAL LOSSES

■ **INSTANT FACTS** Bielfeldt (TP), who claimed to be dealer in securities, sought to offset immense trading losses that he had incurred against his ordinary income.

■ **BLACK LETTER RULE** An individual taxpayer can only deduct a maximum of $3000 in capital losses from his ordinary income for a particular year.

■ **PROCEDURAL BASIS**

Appeal from a tax court decision affirming a determination by the IRS that Bielfeldt's (TP) trading losses were capital losses.

■ **FACTS**

Bielfeldt (TP) made his living trading in Treasury securities that were auctioned off by the Treasury. His trading income depended upon changes in the market value of his securities between the time he acquired them and the time he sold them. Bielfeldt (TP) incurred immense trading losses and sought to use them to offset his ordinary income. The IRS determined he was a trader, not a dealer, and, therefore, found that his losses were capital losses. Pursuant to I.R.C. § 1211(b), only a maximum of $3000 of capital losses could be used TO offset ordinary income. Biefeldt (TP) filed a petition for redetermination in the tax court. The tax court upheld the determination by the IRS.

■ **ISSUE**

Do Bielfeldt's (TP) trading activities qualify him as dealer and, therefore, qualify his trading losses as ordinary, rather than capital, losses that can be fully offset against ordinary income?

■ **DECISION AND RATIONALE**

(Posner, J.) No. Bielfeldt's (TP) trading activities qualify him as a trader, not a dealer. Therefore, his trading losses are capital losses and he may only deduct a maximum of $3000 in capital losses against ordinary income in any particular year. The distinction between a dealer and a trader is generally that a dealer's income is based on the service he provides in the chain of distribution of the goods he buys and resells. The trader's income, on the other hand, is based on the fluctuations in the market value of the securities or other assets that he trades in. Bielfeldt (TP) was not paid for his trading services. Rather, his trading income depended on changes in the market value of securities between the time he acquired them and the time he resold them. Both floor specialists and primary dealers qualify as dealers, even though their compensation comes from their purchase and sales, but their business activities are distinguishable from Bielfeldt's (TP) activities because Bielfeldt (TP) (1) did not maintain an inventory in specified stock in order to maintain liquidity; (2) was not a registered or primary dealer; and (3) only participated in a small percentage of the Treasury auctions that were held and, as a result, was out of the market up to 200 days per year. The court also dismissed Bielfeldt's (TP) argument that Treasury securities are notes receivable acquired in the ordinary course of trade or business and, therefore, are not capital assets because that characterization would imply that no bonds are capital assets. The decision of the tax court is affirmed.

Analysis:

Although the court distinguished the activities of a dealer from the activities of a trader, for purposes of determining whether their trading losses qualified as a capital loss or an ordinary loss, it side-stepped the issue of whether a trader, who structured his operation to resemble that of a floor specialist, should be recognized by the IRS as a dealer. That omission leaves unanswered questions and a lack of guidance for others who make their income—or sustain their losses—by trading in the stock market.

■ CASE VOCABULARY

CAPITAL LOSS: The loss realized in selling or exchanging a capital asset.

ORDINARY LOSS: A loss incurred from the sale or exchange of an item that is used in a trade or business.

SECURITY: An instrument that evidences the holder's ownership rights in a firm (e.g., a stock), the holder's creditor relationship with a firm or government (e.g., a bond), or the holder's other rights (e.g., an option).

Biedenharn Realty Co. v. United States

(Taxpayer) v. *(Federal Government)*
526 F.2d 409 (5th Cir.1976)

FEDERAL APPEALS COURT HOLDS THAT TAXPAYER'S ORIGINAL INVESTMENT INTENT DID NOT CONTROL IN DECIDING CHARACTER OF GAIN RECEIVED FROM SALE OF SUBDIVISION PROPERTIES

■ **INSTANT FACTS** Biedenharn (P) bought property for an investment and then, a number of years later, sold off individual lots for homes.

■ **BLACK LETTER RULE** Where there has been a subdivision of property that was originally purchased as an investment by a taxpayer and substantial and frequent sales of the subdivision property over an extended period of time, such activity can negate the original investment intent of the taxpayer and result in the characterization of any gain from the sale as ordinary income rather than capital gain.

■ **PROCEDURAL BASIS**

Appeal of a U.S. District Court judgment granting a refund of income tax paid by a taxpayer.

■ **FACTS**

Biedenharn Realty Co. ("Biedenharn") (P), a real estate holding company, owned a "Hardtimes," a Louisiana plantation it bought in 1935 for farming and as an investment. It was farmed for a few years and then leased for farming. From 1939 through 1966, Biedenharn (P) carved three residential subdivisions covering 185 acres from the plantation. It sold 208 lots in 158 separate sales at an $800,000 profit. Biedenharn (P) made improvements in the subdivisions, including adding streets, drainage, water, sewers, and electricity. Under a settlement with the IRS for tax years prior to 1964, Biedenharn (P) reported its gain from the sale of the lots in those years by treating 60% of its gain as ordinary income and 40% of its gain as capital gain. On its tax returns for the 1964 through 1966 tax years, Biedenharn (P) reported its gains in those years under the same method it had used for prior years. The IRS asserted a deficiency, arguing that all the 1964 through 1966 gains were ordinary income. Biedenharn (P) then filed a refund claim asserting that all the gains for those years were capital. After the IRS rejected the refund claim, Biedenharn (P) filed suit for a refund in federal district court. The district court found that the plantation had been originally bought as an investment, that the intent to subdivide arose later, that the property sales largely resulted from unsolicited bids by individuals, but that from 1964 through 1966, 75% of the sales were induced by independent brokers hired by Biedenharn (P). The district court ruled for Biedenharn (P) that the gains at issue were capital gains and the United States (D) appealed, arguing that the lots sold from 1964 through 1966 constituted property held primarily for sale to customers in the ordinary course of business and were non-capital assets under the Internal Revenue Code ("the Code").

■ **ISSUE**

Where there has been a subdivision of property and substantial and frequent sales over an extended period of time, can such activity result in the characterization of any gain as ordinary income rather than capital gain?

■ **DECISION AND RATIONALE**

(Goldberg, J.) Yes. To determine whether the property sold here was held as an investment or as a property held primarily for sale to customers in the ordinary course of business, we judge the facts here in light of several factors: substantiality and frequency of sales; improvements; solicitation and advertising efforts, and broker's activities. When dispositions of subdivided property extend over a long period of time and are especially numerous, the likelihood of capital gains is slight. Here, Biedenharn (P) cannot claim "isolated" sales or passive and gradual liquidation. There were numerous sales over an extended period of time. In addition, Biedenharn (P) vigorously improved its subdivisions, adding streets, drainage, sewers, and utilities in an effort to increase sales. While Biedenharn (P) contends that it avoided direct advertising or other solicitation of customers, we find that, even one clearly in the real estate business need not engage in promotion of properties where there is a favorable sales market. As in this case, the sale of a few lots and construction of the first homes, as well as the addition of improvements, constitute a highly visible form of advertising. Moreover, Biedenharn (P) hired brokers who, using media and on-site advertising, worked vigorously on Biedenharn's (P) behalf. Their activities should be attributed to Biedenharn (P). Biedenharn (P) argues that by hiring independent contractor brokers, who were clearly in the real estate business, it should not be held to have entered that business. In this case, however, Biedenharn (P) determined the prices and general credit policy for the sales and did not make all of its sales through the brokers. We find that Biedenharn's (P) brokers did not so completely take charge of the sales as to permit Biedenharn (P) to wall itself off legally from their activities. Biedenharn (P) argues that its original investment intent when it acquired the property ought to control the outcome of this case. The district court agreed, finding that Biedenharn (P) was merely liquidating its original investment over a long period of time in the most advantageous way possible. The United States (D) argues that original investment purpose is always irrelevant. We reject the sweeping view that prior investment intent is always irrelevant. We would find it relevant where the change from investment holding to sales activity results from unanticipated, externally induced factors, such as condemnation or new zoning regulations, which make impossible the continued preexisting use of the property. Here, however, Biedenharn's (P) change of purpose was entirely voluntary. Moreover, its original investment intent is so overwhelmed by the substantiality and frequency of sales, the improvements it made, and its broker's activities, that original investment intent cannot have decisive effect. We find that Biedenharn's (P) real property sales activities compel an ordinary income conclusion. Reversed.

Analysis:

This case involves a determination of whether the property sold was held primarily for sale in the ordinary course of business. Biedenharn (P) argued that the property at issue had been bought as an investment and not with the purpose to subdivide and sell as inventory. The subdivision plan only arose as the best way to dispose of the investment. In its view, the original investment intent should have controlled the character of the gain it realized on the sale of the property, making the gain from the sale capital gain, taxed at a lower rate than ordinary income. The United States (D), on the other hand, argued that the original investment intent is always irrelevant. While not going as far as the government wanted and finding original intent not to matter, the court does conclude that a change of intent can and did occur in this instance. Focusing on the large number and frequency of Biedenharn's (P) sales, which occurred over a long period of time, as well as the improvements made to the properties in order to increase sales, the court finds that Biedenharn (P) held the property at issue primarily for sale to customers in the ordinary course of its business, and rules that the resulting gain from the sales constitutes ordinary income.

■ CASE VOCABULARY

IMPROVEMENTS: Additions made to real property that increase its value. Examples include paved roads, sidewalks, sewers, utilities, and landscaping.

INDEPENDENT CONTRACTOR: A person who contracts with another to perform a service, but is not controlled or subject to control by that person in the performance of that service, except as to being required to achieve the end result desired by the person paying for the service.

SUBDIVISION: The division of a parcel of land into two or more parcels for sale or development.

Corn Products Refining Co. v. Commissioner

(Taxpayer) v. *(IRS)*

350 U.S. 46, 76 S.Ct. 20 (1955)

U.S. SUPREME COURT RULES THAT GAINS AND LOSSES FROM THE SALE OF FUTURES CONTRACTS USED TO ENSURE A READY SUPPLY OF RAW MATERIALS FOR A MANUFACTURER WERE ORDINARY, RATHER THAN CAPITAL INCOME/LOSS

■ **INSTANT FACTS** A manufacturer of corn products, which had bought corn future contracts to ensure a ready supply of raw materials and then later sold some of the contracts, appealed an IRS determination that the gains and losses constituted ordinary income.

■ **BLACK LETTER RULE** Gains and losses arising from the sale of future contracts bought to ensure a ready supply of raw materials for a manufacturer's everyday business operations are ordinary income and losses and not capital gains and losses.

■ **PROCEDURAL BASIS**

Appeal, following grant of certiorari by the U.S. Supreme Court, of a federal appeals court decision affirming a district court judgment upholding an IRS deficiency determination against a taxpayer.

■ **FACTS**

Corn Products Refining Co. ("Corn Products") (P) was a manufacturer of products made from grain corn. In 1934 and 1936, droughts had caused a major increase in the price of corn and Corn Products (P) found itself unable to buy corn at a price which would allow it to make a profit on its products. In 1937, to avoid this problem, Corn Products (P) established a system under which it would buy corn futures, contracts allowing it to buy corn at a specific time in the future at a specific price, at harvest time, when the price of corn appeared favorable. The company would take delivery on these contracts to meet the needs of its manufacturing plant, and would sell the remainder of the contracts in early summer, if no shortage of corn was imminent. In 1940, Corn Products (P) made a profit of $680,587.39 from the sale of corn futures. In 1942, it suffered a loss of $109,969.38 on the sale of the futures. Arguing that the futures trading was separate and apart from its manufacturing operations, Corn Products (P) contended that the futures it had sold were capital assets and that the gains and losses from the sales were therefore capital. The Commissioner ("IRS") (D), the Tax Court and a federal appeals court all found the futures transactions to be an integral part of Corn Products' (P) business, designed to assure a ready supply for future manufacturing and protect against price increases. Both the Tax Court and the federal appeals court upheld an IRS determination that the assets were non-capital. Corn Products (P) appealed to the U.S. Supreme Court, which granted certiorari.

■ **ISSUE**

Are gains and losses arising from the sale of future contracts bought to ensure a ready supply of raw materials for a manufacturer's everyday business operations, ordinary income and losses rather than capital gains and losses?

■ **DECISION AND RATIONALE**

(Clark, J.) Yes. We find nothing in the record to support Corn Products' (P) contention that its futures activity was separate and apart from its manufacturing operation. On the contrary, it appears the transactions were vitally important to the company's business as a form of insurance against increase in the price of corn. While admittedly, the corn futures do not come within the literal language of the exclusions set out in IRC § 1221 [Section of the Internal Revenue Code ("the Code") defining capital assets and specifically excluding certain listed items from capital asset treatment], that provision must not be applied so broadly as to defeat rather than further the purpose of Congress. Congress intended that profits and losses arising from the everyday operation of a business should be treated as ordinary income or loss rather than capital gain or loss. The preferential treatment provided by classification as a capital asset applies to transactions in property that are not the taxpayer's normal source of business income and was meant to relieve taxpayers from the burden of excessive gain on the conversion of capital investments and remove a deterrent to such transactions. Since this section is an exception from the normal tax requirements of the Code, the definition of "capital asset" must be narrowly applied and its exclusions interpreted broadly. This is necessary to effect the purpose of Congress. We thus treat the gain from the sale of the futures here as ordinary income. To hold otherwise, would permit those engaged in hedging transactions to transform ordinary income into capital gain at will. A hedger can either sell the corn future and buy corn in the spot market or take delivery of the contract itself. If the sale of the future created a capital transaction, while the delivery of the contract did not, a loophole in the statute would be created and the purpose of Congress frustrated. Affirmed.

Analysis:

While the property sold by Corn Products (P), the corn futures, did not fall literally within the meaning of stock in trade or inventory held for sale to customers under what is now IRC § 1221(1), the Court concludes that the futures were an integral part of Corn Products' everyday business, rather than a mere investment, and that Congress sought to treat profits from everyday business operations as ordinary income and not capital gain. The Court appeared to emphasize the taxpayer's motive for acquiring the property it eventually sold. Subsequent cases in the lower courts latched on to that reasoning and applied it broadly to sales of corporate stock that had been purchased for everyday business reasons, such as ensuring a steady supply of raw materials for manufacturing, rather than for a pure investment motive. Taxpayers who sold such stock at a loss were often successful in obtaining ordinary loss treatment, rather than the limited deductibility available through capital loss treatment, by arguing the *Corn Products* approach. Ultimately, in *Arkansas Best Corp. v. Commissioner*, the U.S. Supreme Court cut back the lower courts' interpretations of *Corn Products* by following the approach of several commentators and reading *Corn Products* to have involved an application of § 1221(1)'s inventory exception, rather than as having created a general exemption from capital asset status for assets acquired for a business purpose.

■ **CASE VOCABULARY**

FUTURES: Contracts for the purchase and delivery of a specified amount of a product at a specified date in the future for a specified price.

HEDGING: A method of dealing in commodity futures through which a business protects itself against price fluctuations at the time of delivery of a product which it sells or buys.

Arkansas Best Corp. v. Commissioner

(Taxpayer) v. *(IRS)*
485 U.S. 212, 108 S.Ct. 971 (1988)

COURT RETREATS FROM EARLIER RELIANCE ON TAXPAYER'S MOTIVE TO DETERMINE WHETHER PROPERTY ACQUIRED BY BUSINESS WAS CAPITAL ASSET

■ **INSTANT FACTS** Taxpayer acquired stock in a bank for business purposes and then claimed an ordinary loss when that stock was sold for less than it was purchased.

■ **BLACK LETTER RULE** Stock held by a business is a capital asset, regardless of whether it was purchased for business or investment purposes.

■ **PROCEDURAL BASIS**

ppeal from the Court of Appeals judgment reversing the Tax Court decision that the loss sustained by taxpayer was an ordinary loss.

■ **FACTS**

Arkansas Best (P) is a diversified holding company engaged in the business of buying, managing and selling stock. As part of its business activities, Arkansas Best (P) acquired stock in National Bank. From 1969 to 1974, the number of shares Arkansas Best (P) owned nearly tripled. The purchase of stock prior to 1972 arose out of National Bank's need for capital. In 1972, however, the bank was classified as a problem bank because of its loan portfolio problems, thereby requiring further infusion of capital. In 1975, Arkansas Best (P) sold virtually all of its stock in National Bank at a loss. Arkansas Best (P) reported the transaction as an ordinary loss. The IRS (D) disallowed the deduction, but the Tax Court reversed that decision in part. The Court of Appeals then reversed the Tax Court.

■ **ISSUE**

Is stock purchased by a business for business purposes a capital asset?

■ **DECISION AND RATIONALE**

(Marshall, J.) Yes. The IRS (D) determined that the gain or loss realized from the sale of stock is capital gain or loss. The Tax Court disagreed, however, concluding that under the rule established by *Corn Products* [property acquired and held for business purpose is not a capital asset] and its progeny the stock purchased by Arkansas Best (P) after 1972 was clearly purchased for business purposes rather than for mere investment and thus was not entitled to capital asset treatment. The Court of Appeals reversed, holding that all of the stock was entitled to capital asset treatment since stock clearly fell within the definition of a capital asset in § 1221. It was irrelevant, in the opinion of the Court of Appeals, for what purpose Arkansas Best (P) acquired the stock. § 1221 defined a capital asset as property held by a taxpayer whether or not connected with his trade or business, and then sets forth five classes of property that are not capital assets. These exceptions include property that is classified as inventory. Arkansas Best (P) argues that in *Corn Products* a literal interpretation of § 1221 [then § 117] was not required and that instead, assets purchased for business purposes should be treated as ordinary assets rather than capital ones. While this reading of *Corn Products* is supported by subsequent cases in the lower courts and academic literature, the statute itself refutes such an interpretation. Under Arkansas

Best's (P) reading, whether an asset is capital or not depends solely on the purpose for which it was acquired. This is in direct conflict, however, with the language in the statute that a capital asset is property held by a taxpayer whether or not connected with his trade or business. Again relying on *Corn Products*, Arkansas Best (P) argues that the list of exceptions is illustrative and not exhaustive. However, the statute reads that a capital asset is property held by a taxpayer but does not include certain classes of property. This clearly means that any property held by a taxpayer, so long as it does not fall within the classes of property listed in the exceptions, is a capital asset. This reading of the statute is supported by the legislative history, and without further instruction from Congress, the statute should not be interpreted as suggested by Arkansas Best (P), since such an interpretation renders meaningless the language in the statute that property held by a taxpayer whether or not in connection with a trade or business is a capital asset. Arkansas Best's (P) position is based solely on an expansive, and ultimately incorrect, expansive reading of *Corn Products*. While it is true that the *Corn Products* opinion states that the definition of capital asset is to be interpreted narrowly and its exceptions broadly, the opinion does not clarify whether the exceptions apply to the general definition or the specific exception for inventory. Since the corn futures at issue in *Corn Products* constituted part of the manufacturer's inventory program, even though they were not inventory per se. *Corn Products* is best read as holding that the inventory exception to the general definition of a capital asset is to be interpreted broadly. Arkansas Best (P) also argues that *Corn Products*, in placing reliance on whether an asset was purchased as an integral part of an everyday business, intended to create a general exemption from capital asset treatment for property acquired for business purposes. This reading misstates the relevance of the motivation behind purchase of the asset. The motivation behind the purchase of an asset is irrelevant for purposes of determining whether an asset is capital or not. However, the purpose behind the acquisition is relevant in determining whether the asset falls within a certain exception. This is especially true with the inventory exception at issue in *Corn Products*. The rule in *Corn Products* was not that the motivation of the taxpayer in purchasing the asset controls, but rather that "hedging transactions that are an integral part of a business' inventory-purchase program fall within the inventory exclusion of § 1221". As this case does not concern an inventory-purchase program, *Corn Products* is not applicable. Additionally, if the motive test were applied as Arkansas Best (P) suggests, the kind of abuse the court in *Corn Products* was afraid of would become even more practical. Thus, the proper rule is that the motivation in purchasing an asset has no relevance to whether or not it is a capital asset. As such, the loss at issue here, which arose from the sale of stock that is clearly within the definition of a capital asset, was a capital loss. Affirmed.

Analysis:

The Court here took great pains to demonstrate that the exceptions to the definition of a capital asset are limited to the specific statutory exceptions. This is interesting, especially in light of the language in the *Corn Products* opinion that specifically said the exceptions were not exhaustive. It is also interesting because the Court goes to great lengths to say that what was being interpreted broadly in *Corn Products* was the inventory exception, and not all of the exceptions. Does this make sense, given that the inventory exception was never mentioned in the *Corn Products* opinion? To get the result desired here, it was important to show that the property at issue in *Corn Products* fell within one of the specific exceptions. This case clearly put to rest the use of the business-motive test in determining whether property is a capital asset under § 1221.

■ **CASE VOCABULARY**

DIVERSIFIED HOLDING COMPANY: A company that operates solely as an owner and manager of stock in two or more companies.

LOAN PORTFOLIO: All of the interests in loans held by a lender.

Hort v. Commissioner

(Taxpayer) v. *(IRS)*

313 U.S. 28, 61 S.Ct. 757 (1941)

CANCELLATION OF LEASE DOES NOT CREATE LOSS FOR LANDLORD

■ **INSTANT FACTS** Taxpayer, a landlord, agreed to accept a sum certain in exchange for cancellation of a long-term lease and then claimed the foregone rent payments as a loss and the sum certain paid as a capital gain.

■ **BLACK LETTER RULE** Amounts accepted in exchange for cancellation of a lease constitute ordinary income to the landlord, from which the foregone rent payments cannot be offset as a loss.

■ FACTS

Mr. Hort (P) inherited property from his father on which a ten-story office building was located. Irving Trust leased the main floor of the building for a fifteen-year term, with yearly rent of $25,000. In 1933, just six years after entering the fifteen-year lease, Irving Trust found it unprofitable to maintain the branch in Mr. Hort's (P) building and negotiated with Mr. Hort (P) for the cancellation of the lease. Mr. Hort (P) agreed to the cancellation upon payment of $140,000. On his tax return for that year, Mr. Hort (P) did not include the $140,000 payment in his ordinary income and declared a loss in the amount of $21,494.75, which was equal to the amount of rent that he had lost due to cancellation of the lease, less the $140,000 payment. The IRS (D) determined that the $140,000 should have been included in Mr. Hort's (P) gross income and denied the loss he claimed entirely. The Board of Tax Appeals and the Circuit Court of Appeals affirmed the IRS' (D) determination.

■ ISSUE

May a taxpayer offset the amount of rental payments that will not be paid when a lease is cancelled?

■ DECISION AND RATIONALE

(Murphy, J.) No. Mr. Hort (P) argues that the amount he received in exchange for cancellation of the lease constituted capital rather than ordinary income. Mr. Hort (P) further argues that if the amount he received must be counted as ordinary income, the amount of rental payments that were "lost" offset the total amount of income. Contrary to his arguments, the entire amount received as compensation for cancellation of the lease must be included in ordinary income. Section 22(a) clearly states that gross income includes rental payments. Had the lease continued, all rental payments would have been included in ordinary income. It is also clear that had Mr. Hort (P) declined to cancel the lease and instead instituted a suit to recover the amount of rental payments that Irving Trust failed to pay, any amount recovered would have been included in ordinary income. The fact that Mr. Hort (P) decided to accept a lump sum payment in exchange for letting Irving Trust out of their lease does not change the character of the payment from rent. The fact that Mr. Hort (P) accepted an amount less than the total amount of rent due under the lease is irrelevant. Clearly, the payment received by Mr. Hort (P) constituted a substitute payment for the rent due under the lease. Additionally, the mere fact that the lease itself constituted "property" does not render the amount paid for cancellation of the lease a return of capital. Not all property is capital. In some cases, like this one, when a right to payment arises from ownership of property, those payments may constitute ordinary income. Regardless of how the payment received by Mr. Hort (P) is classified, there is no doubt that the payment was a substitute for rent. As such, Mr. Hort (P) must include the $140,000 payment as ordinary income. Furthermore, he is not entitled to deduct the foregone rental payments as a loss. To the extent he accepted less than the full amount of rent due under the lease, his gross income was reduced, thereby relieving Mr. Hort (P) of income tax liability for the foregone amount. Moreover, if the cancellation of the lease reduced the value of the property itself, then Mr. Hort (P) will be entitled to claim a loss if and when that loss is realized upon a sale of the property for less than its value with the lease. Affirmed.

Analysis:

Rental payments, although they arise from ownership of property that may be a capital asset, constitute ordinary income under the plain language of § 22(a). Thus, not all income from a capital asset is entitled to capital asset treatment. Notice, too, that the cancellation of the lease and loss of future rental payments does not equal a loss that is deductible by the landlord. In this case, the inability to deduct the amount of lost rental payments is insignificant in the long run, since Mr. Hort (P) received a lump sum payment of $140,000, which was substantially the amount of rent due under the lease. But keep in mind that the general rule is that cancellation of a lease does not entitle a landlord to declare a loss equal to the amount of rent that he loses. The rationale for this rule is that any payment a landlord agrees to accept in exchange for relinquishing his right to sue for breach of the lease and rent is actually a substitute for the rent the landlord could have collected. Looking at it this way, the rule makes perfect sense, since what the landlord is receiving is essentially rent, and rent is clearly considered ordinary income under § 22(a).

■ CASE VOCABULARY

DEVISE: A gift of specific property in a will.

Womack v. Commissioner

(Lottery Winner) v. *(IRS Commissioner)*

510 F.3d 1295 (11th Cir. 2007)

FUTURE LOTTERY–WINNINGS PAYMENTS ARE NOT CAPITAL ASSETS

■ **INSTANT FACTS** Womack (P) sold his rights to his future annual lottery-winnings payments and claimed that the sale proceeds were entitled to capital-assets treatment, but the tax court deemed the proceeds to be ordinary income; Womack (P) appealed.

■ **BLACK LETTER RULE** Under the substitute-for-ordinary-income doctrine, when a party receives a lump-sum payment essentially as a substitute for what otherwise would have been received, at a future time, as ordinary income, that lump sum payment is taxable as ordinary income as well.

■ **PROCEDURAL BASIS**

Appeal by taxpayer from a tax court decision against him.

■ **FACTS**

Womack (P) won the Florida state lottery. The prize was payable in twenty annual installments. Womack (P) took the first four payments and reported them as ordinary income. Then he sold the right to receive the remaining payments to a finance company. Womack (P) reported the amount received as proceeds from the sale of a long-term capital asset.

■ **ISSUE**

Are lottery rights capital assets?

■ **DECISION AND RATIONALE**

(Judge Undisclosed.) No. Under the substitute-for-ordinary-income doctrine, when a party receives a lump-sum payment essentially as a substitute for what otherwise would have been received, at a future time, as ordinary income, that lump sum payment is taxable as ordinary income as well. This doctrine applies to lottery rights. A lottery winner who does not sell his rights to future payments must report the winnings as ordinary income, whether the state pays him in a lump sum or in installments. When he sells the right to his winnings, he thus replaces future ordinary income. Congress did not intend for taxpayers to circumvent ordinary-income tax treatment by packaging ordinary-income payments and selling them to a third party. A capital asset is different. An asset like stock, for instance, has the potential to earn income in the future. Here, the taxpayer has already earned the income. Income need not be *accrued* to be *earned*. We therefore hold that lottery rights are not capital assets under the judicially recognized substitute-for-ordinary-income doctrine. Affirmed.

Analysis:

According to the tax court in *Womack*, no court has developed a bright-line rule defining which property rights are substitutes for ordinary income. The substitute-for-ordinary-income doctrine cannot, the court explained, be limited to a number of general factual categories. Instead, each situation must be evaluated according to its own specific facts to determine whether it falls within the doctrine. Following the general rule that a right to receive future ordinary income is not a capital asset, courts in the Second, Third, Ninth, Tenth, and Eleventh Circuits have uniformly upheld the IRS's position that a state lottery winner who, for a lump sum, sells or assigns his right to receive future installments of lottery winnings, recognizes ordinary income rather than a capital gain.

■ CASE VOCABULARY

ACCRUED INCOME: Money earned but not yet received.

CAPITAL ASSET: A long-term asset used in the operation of a business or used to produce goods or services, such as equipment, land, or an industrial plant; for income-tax purposes, any of most assets held by a taxpayer except those assets specifically excluded by the Internal Revenue Code. Excluded from the definition are, among other things, stock in trade, inventory, and property held by the taxpayer primarily for sale to customers in the ordinary course of trade or business.

ORDINARY INCOME: For individual income-tax purposes, income that is derived from sources such as wages, commissions, and interest (as opposed to income from capital gains).

McAllister v. Commissioner

(Taxpayer) v. *(IRS)*
157 F.2d 235 (2d Cir. 1946)

■ **INSTANT FACTS** A taxpayer appealed an IRS holding disallowing capital loss treatment for the sale of her life estate and requiring the amounts received from the sale to be treated as ordinary income.

■ **BLACK LETTER RULE** A life estate is a capital asset.

■ **FACTS**

McAllister (P) sold her life estate in a testamentary trust to the trust's remainderman for $55,000. Claiming that her basis in the life estate, computed from actuarial tables, was $63,790.20, McAllister (P) reported a capital loss from the sale of the life estate on her 1940 tax return of $8,790.20. The Commissioner of internal Revenue ("IRS") (D) disallowed the loss and treated the $55,000 McAllister (P) had received as ordinary income, reasoning that McAllister (P) had surrendered her rights to income payments from the trust and that the amount she received should therefore be treated as ordinary income. McAllister (P) appealed the IRS (D) decision to the U.S. Tax Court, which agreed with the IRS (D). McAllister (P) then appealed to the U.S. Court of Appeals for the Second Circuit.

■ **ISSUE**

Is a life estate a capital asset?

■ **DECISION AND RATIONALE**

(Clark, J.) Yes. In *Blair v. Commissioner* [U.S. Supreme Court case holding that the gift of a life estate represented the assignment of a property right in a trust, making the donee, rather than the donor taxable on income received from the trust], a life beneficiary of a trust assigned his children sums to be paid from the trust for the duration of his life estate. The U.S. Supreme Court held that the transfers were the assignment of a property right in the trust and that the children, rather than the parent were liable for the tax on the trust income. The reasoning of the *Blair* decision applies to this case. McAllister's (P) right to income for life from the trust estate was a right in the estate itself. Had she held a fee interest, the assignment of that interest would clearly have been regarded as the transfer of a capital asset. We see no reason why a different result should follow the transfer of the lesser, but still substantial, life interest. This case is distinguishable from that of *Hort v. Commissioner* [U.S. Supreme Court case holding that amounts accepted in exchange for the cancellation of a lease constituted ordinary income to the landlord]. In *Hort*, a landlord cancelled a lease having nine years left to run, in return for a lump sum payment. The Internal Revenue Code expressly taxed income derived from rent, and the lump-sum payment was viewed as a substitute for the rent as it fell due and taxed as ordinary income. The IRS (D) argues that McAllister (P) received an immediate payment here for "surrendering" her rights to future income payments from the trust. We find that this case is more like *Blair* and less like *Hort*, in that McAllister (P) transferred her entire interest in the property, as did the taxpayer in *Blair*, and did not sell the income from the trust for a few years only, as did the taxpayer in *Hort*. To accept the IRS (D) approach here, we would have to consider the *Blair* case as overruled, something the Supreme Court itself, has declined to do. Reversed.

■ **DISSENT**

(Frank, J.) I disagree with the majority's view that the *Blair* case is controlling. The fact that the donor of a life estate in that case was not taxable on trust income received by the donee, has nothing to do with the question in this case of whether the seller of a life estate should be viewed as having disposed of a capital asset. The capital gains provisions are an exception to the rules regarding what constitutes gross income, designed to give an incentive to dispose of capital investments. Courts have traditionally been cautious in interpreting clauses creating that exception, refusing to give capital treatment to transactions by which transferors have obtained advance payments of future income. The sale of a life estate is like the cancellation of the lease in *Hort*, with the consideration paid for such transfer being a substitute for future payments that would be taxable as ordinary income. It resembles the advance payment of dividends, interest, or salaries and should be taxed as ordinary income. I would affirm.

Analysis:

The court here concludes that the life estate is a capital asset and that McAllister (P) had a basis in the estate that could be used to report a loss from the sale. The majority views the fact the McAllister (P) transferred her entire interest in the life estate, as opposed to the use or benefits from the life estate for a short period of time, as controlling. The dissent, on the other hand, views the payment received for the life estate as a substitute for the income that would have been received in the future.

■ **CASE VOCABULARY**

DONEE: The recipient of a gift.

DONOR: One who gives a gift to another.

LIFE ESTATE: A property estate with a duration of ownership limited to the life of the person holding the estate.

REMAINDERMAN: One who becomes entitled to a property estate following the expiration of the tenant holding a life estate.

TESTAMENTARY TRUST: A trust that takes effect at the death of the person who establishes it, generally created within a will.

Commissioner v. P.G. Lake, Inc.

(*IRS*) v. (*Taxpayer*)

356 U.S. 260, 78 S.Ct. 691 (1958)

U.S. SUPREME COURT HOLDS THAT THE TRANSFER OF AN OIL PAYMENT RIGHT, CARVED OUT OF AN OIL LEASE, PRODUCED ORDINARY INCOME RATHER THAN CAPITAL GAIN

■ **INSTANT FACTS** The taxpayer accepted three years' worth of proceeds from the sale of oil and gas in exchange for cancellation of a debt.

■ **BLACK LETTER RULE** The assignment of a portion of a payment right to the proceeds of future sales of oil and gas from a working interest in an oil and gas lease, in return for the cancellation of a debt owed to the assignee, results in the assignor having realized ordinary income rather than capital gain.

■ **PROCEDURAL BASIS**

Appeal, following a grant of certiorari by the U.S. Supreme Court, of a federal appeals court decision affirming a U.S. Tax Court judgment overturning an IRS deficiency determination against a taxpayer.

■ **FACTS**

P.G. Lake, Inc. ("Lake") (P), was an oil and gas producer. It owned a seven-eighths working interest in two commercial oil and gas leases. In return for the cancellation of a $600,000 debt it owed to its corporate president, Lake (P) assigned the president its right to receive $600,000 out of the proceeds of future sales of oil from the leases. At the time of the assignment, the parties anticipated that the payout would take about three years, a period much shorter than the useful life of the interest Lake (P) owned in the leases. On its tax return for the year, Lake (P) reported the assignment as the sale of a capital asset, producing a long-term capital gain of $600,000. On audit, the Commissioner of Internal Revenue ("IRS") (D) ruled that the $600,000 was taxable as ordinary income and not as a capital gain. Lake (P) appealed to the U.S. Tax Court, which ruled in Lake's (P) favor and on appeal by the IRS (D), the U.S. Court of Appeals for the Fifth Circuit affirmed, concluding that the assigned right to an oil payment was an interest in land under Texas law and therefore constituted a capital asset. The IRS (D) then appealed to the U.S. Supreme Court, which granted certiorari.

■ **ISSUE**

Does the assignment of a portion of a payment right to the proceeds of future sales of oil and gas from a working interest in an oil and gas lease, in return for the cancellation of a debt owed to the assignee, result in the assignor having realized ordinary income rather than capital gain?

■ **DECISION AND RATIONALE**

(Douglas, J.) Yes. We do not see here a conversion of a capital investment. The lump sum payment seems to be essentially a substitute for what would otherwise be received at a future time as ordinary income. Only a fraction of the oil rights were transferred, the balance being retained. The substance of what was assigned was the right to receive future income. The substance of what was received was the present value of income which the recipient would otherwise obtain in the future. Thus, consideration was paid for the right to receive future income, not for an increase in the value of the income-producing property. Reversed.

Analysis:

As in *Hort v. Commissioner*, the Supreme Court here finds that a carved-out interest should be treated as an ordinary and not a capital asset. Had the life of Lake's (P) interest in the oil and gas leases been the same duration as the life of the assigned oil and gas payment, the Court would likely have concluded that Lake (P) had transferred a capital asset.

■ **CASE VOCABULARY**

ASSIGNMENT: The transfer of all or a part of an interest in or right to property.

WORKING INTEREST: The right to the mineral interest granted by an oil and gas lease. Under the lease, the lessee obtains the right to work the leased property to search for oil and gas which become the property of the lessee, if found.

Commissioner v. Brown

(IRS) v. (Taxpayer)

380 U.S. 563, 85 S.Ct. 1162 (1965)

U.S. SUPREME COURT INTERPRETS THE MEANING OF A "SALE" UNDER THE INTERNAL REVENUE CODE

■ **INSTANT FACTS** A group of taxpayers transferred their stock in a lumber company to a tax-exempt entity in return for a sum of money payable out of the future earnings of the lumber company which would be managed by the taxpayers under a leaseback arrangement.

■ **BLACK LETTER RULE** Property may be sold or exchanged within the meaning of the capital gains provisions of the Internal Revenue Code, even if the purchase price for the transferred property is payable out of the property's own future earnings.

■ **PROCEDURAL BASIS**

Appeal, following a grant of certiorari by the U.S. Supreme Court, of a federal appeals court decision affirming a U.S. Tax Court judgment overturning an IRS deficiency determination against a taxpayer.

■ **FACTS**

Clay Brown ("Brown") (P) and several members of his family owned all of the stock in a lumber company, Clay Brown & Company. They sold their stock to California Institute for Cancer Research ("the Institute"), a tax-exempt, charitable organization for $1,300,000, payable $5,000 down from the assets of the company and the balance within ten years out of the earnings of the company. The institute then leased the lumber company's assets back to an operating company managed and controlled by Brown (P). The operating company paid its profits to the Institute which would apply the profits to the payment of the $1,300,000 note held by Brown (P) and his relatives. On their tax returns, Brown (P) and his relatives reported the payments received from the Institute as gain from the sale of capital assets. On audit, the Commissioner of Internal Revenue ("IRS") (D) asserted that the payments were taxable as ordinary income and determined a deficiency, holding that the transaction was a sham and that Brown (P) and his relatives retained such an economic interest in and control over the lumber company property that the transaction could not be treated as a "sale" under the Internal Revenue Code's ("the Code") capital gain provisions. Brown (P) and his relatives appealed to the U.S. Tax Court, which found for the taxpayers, concluding that the price had been negotiated at arm's length between the parties, was a fair valuation for the lumber business, and that there had been a real change of economic benefit in the transaction. The U.S. Court of Appeals for the Ninth Circuit affirmed. The IRS (D) then appealed to the U.S. Supreme Court, which granted certiorari.

■ **ISSUE**

Can property be sold or exchanged within the meaning of the capital gains provisions of the Internal Revenue Code, even if the purchase price for the transferred property is payable out of the property's own future earnings?

■ **DECISION AND RATIONALE**

(White, J.) Yes. The IRS (D) argues that the transaction did not have the substance of a "sale" within the meaning of the capital gains provisions of the Code. They say that since the Institute invested nothing, assumed no independent liability for the purchase price, and promised only to pay over a percentage of the earnings of the company, the entire risk of the transaction remained on the sellers. This argument that there is no sale because there is no risk-shifting and there is no risk-shifting because the price to be paid is payable only from the income produced by the business sold, is not much different from saying that because the business earnings are usually taxable as ordinary income, they are subject to the same tax when paid over as the purchase price of the property. This is a rational argument, but it wrongly construes the meaning of the word "sale" and is contrary to the capital gains provisions of the Code. To require a sale for tax purposes to be to a financially responsible buyer who pays the purchase price from sources other than the earnings of the assets sold or to make a substantial down payment seems to us at odds with the commercial practice and common understanding of what constitutes a sale. The Code does not define the term "sale" and without legislative history indicating a contrary result, the common meaning of the term should control. In the transaction at issue here, the lumber company stock was transferred for a price payable on the installment basis from the earnings of the company. The Tax Court found the sale price was arrived at in an arm's length transaction, was the result of real negotiating, and was within a reasonable range in light of the corporation's earnings history and the value of the corporate assets. We think this transaction is a sale, and treating it as such is wholly consistent with the purposes of the Code to allow capital gains treatment for the realized enhanced value of a capital asset. The term "sale" is used many times within the Code and a wide variety of tax results hinge on whether a "sale" has occurred. To accept the IRS (D) definition of sale would have wide ramifications which we are not prepared to visit on taxpayers, absent congressional guidance in this area. Affirmed.

■ CONCURRENCE

(Harlan, J.) Yes. The Code gives the Institute a tax exemption which makes it capable of taking a greater after-tax return from a business than could a nontax-exempt individual or entity. Brown (P) and his relatives traded a residual interest in their lumber business for a faster payout, made possible by the Institute's exemption. Brown (P) and his relatives gave something up and received something substantially different in return. If words are to have meaning, there was a "sale or exchange." If such sales are considered a serious abuse, perhaps the remedy for the IRS (D) to pursue is not to deny the existence of a "sale or exchange," but to attack the Institute's exemption.

■ DISSENT

(Goldberg, J.) No. Brown (P) and his relatives essentially conveyed their interest in the lumber business to the Institute in return for 72 percent of the profits of the business and the right to recover the business assets if payments fell behind schedule. It might seem odd that the sellers would do this. Prior to the sale they had a right to 100 percent of the business income. After the sale, that right was reduced to only 72 percent and they would lose the business after ten years. The advantage they sought, however, was capital gain rather than ordinary income treatment for the share of the business profits they received. Moreover, because of its charitable exemption and the leaseback arrangement to Brown (P), the Institute believed that neither it nor Brown (P) would have to pay income tax on the earnings of the business. The sellers would receive, free of corporate taxation and subject to personal taxation at capital gains rates, 72 percent of the business earnings until they were paid $1,300,000. Without the sale, they would receive only 48 percent of the business earnings, the rest going to the IRS (D) in corporate taxes, and this 48 percent would be subject to personal taxation at ordinary income rates. In effect, the Institute sold Brown (P) and his relatives the use of its tax exemption, allowing them to collect $1,300,000 more quickly than they otherwise could and to pay tax on this amount at capital gains rates. In return, the Institute got a nominal amount of the profits while the $1,300,000 was being paid and kept the whole business once this debt was finished. In any realistic sense, the Institute used its tax exemption as part of an arrangement which allowed it to buy a business for nothing. I cannot believe that Congress intended this result. Brown (P) and his relatives retained a significant economic interest in the business and controlled its operations through the leaseback arrangement. I would hold on these facts that there was not a sufficient shift of economic risk or control of the business to warrant treating this transaction as a "sale" for tax purposes. I would reverse.

Analysis:

As the dissent explains, because the buyer was a tax-exempt entity and thus no corporate tax would have to be paid on the earnings of its business, the purchase price could be paid out of the earnings of the business much faster than if the buyer had been subject to corporate income tax. The Institute effectively acquired the business for nothing, by allowing Brown (P) and his relatives to take advantage of its tax exemption. The majority recognizes this fact, but concludes that it does not change the fact that the lumber company stock, a capital asset, was really sold. In his concurring opinion, Justice Harlan suggests that the right answer to this perceived tax abuse would be to attack the Institute's tax exemption, rather than trying to attack the existence of a sale under the Code. The majority suggests the answer to any abuse lies with Congress. In 1969, four years after the *Brown* decision. Congress went after this perceived abuse, adding § 514 to the Code. That section provides that a tax-exempt charity's unrelated business income from debt-financed property will be taxed to the charity at ordinary income rates.

■ CASE VOCABULARY

OPERATING COMPANY: A corporation organized to manage a business owned by another entity, generally in return for a management fee.

TAX–EXEMPT: Persons or property that are by law free from taxation.

Baker v. Commissioner

(Insurance Agent–Taxpayer) v. *(Internal Revenue Service)*

118 T.C. 452 (2002)

A RETURN OF ASSETS IS NOT A SALE WHEN THE RETURNEE DID NOT OWN THE ASSETS

■ **INSTANT FACTS** Baker (TP), a retired insurance agent, reported the termination payment he received from the insurance company, for which he had worked as an independent contractor, as a long-term capital gain.

■ **BLACK LETTER RULE** A termination payment made to an independent contractor-insurance agent, and that is conditioned on the return of assets of the business to the insurance company, is not a capital gain if the assets of the business belong to the insurance company.

■ **PROCEDURAL BASIS**

Petition for a redetermination of the IRS's decision to treat the termination payment paid to Baker (TP) as ordinary income.

■ **FACTS**

Baker (TP) was an insurance agent who sold policies exclusively for an insurance company with which he had entered into an independent contractor agreement. Among other things, the agreement provided that assets of his business, including any data relating to a policyholder he recorded on any paper, belonged to the insurance company. The agreement also required Baker (TP) to abide by a covenant not to compete for twelve months following the termination of the agreement. In addition, the agreement provided for a termination payment if Baker (TP) met certain years-of-service requirements and returned all property belonging to the insurance company within a specific number of days. Baker (TP) retired and terminated his relationship with the insurance company. Baker (TP) fully complied with provision in the agreement as to the property belonging to the insurance company and received a termination payment. Baker (TP) reported the amount of the payment on his federal income tax return as a long-term capital gain. The IRS determined that the termination payment was ordinary income and issued a notice of deficiency.

■ **ISSUE**

Is the termination payment that Baker (TP) received, pursuant to his independent-contractor agreement with the insurance company, a long-term capital gain?

■ **DECISION AND RATIONALE**

(Panauthos, J.) No. The termination payment that Baker (TP) received from the insurance company did not qualify as a long-term capital gain because compliance with termination provisions of the independent contractor agreement did not constitute the sale or exchange of a capital asset. All the assets that Baker (TP) returned to the insurance company upon terminating the agreement (i.e., a computer, books and records, customer lists, etc.) were, pursuant to the agreement, the property of the insurance company. Baker's (TP) argument that he sold the agency to the insurance company was not supported by the fact that the successor agent assumed his telephone number, or that the successor agent hired two of his former employees, or that he taught the successor agent about the agency and introduced him to policy holders, because there was no evidence than any of that was done in exchange for any portion of the termination payment that he received. Also, no portion of the termination payment could have been for the sale of good will because, to qualify as a sale of good will, a taxpayer must demonstrate that he sold the business, or a part of it, to which the good will attaches. Since Baker (TP) did not sell a business, he could not have sold goodwill. A portion of the termination payment could, however, be properly allocated to the covenant not to compete, because Baker (TP) would have forfeited the termination payment if he violated that covenant. The determination of the IRS is upheld.

Analysis:

The court in *Baker* determined that there could not have been a sale of assets to the insurance company because the independent contractor agreement established all the assets of the business as its property. Since the decision in *Baker* suggests that the independent contractor agreement controls whether the sale of assets occurs, it could be inferred that if the agreement had indicated that all the assets were the property of Baker (TP), returning those assets to the insurance company would constitute a sale. As a result, the termination payment that Baker (TP) received would qualify as a long-term capital gain, rather than ordinary income.

■ CASE VOCABULARY

INDEPENDENT CONTRACTOR: One who is hired to undertake a specific project but who is left free to do the assigned work and to choose the method for accomplishing it.

CAPITAL GAIN: The profit realized when a capital asset is sold or exchanged.

ORDINARY INCOME: For individual income tax purposes, income that is derived from sources such as wages, commissions, and interest (as opposed to income from capital gains).

ANNUITY: An obligation to pay a stated sum, usually monthly or annually, to a stated recipient.

COVENANT NOT TO COMPETE: A contractual provision, typically found in employment, partnership, or sale-of business agreements, in which one party agrees to refrain from conducting business similar to that of the other party.

Commissioner v. Ferrer

(*IRS*) v. (*Taxpayer*)

304 F.2d 125 (2d Cir.1962)

FEDERAL APPEALS COURT FINDS THEATRICAL PRODUCTION RIGHTS TO CONSTITUTE A CAPITAL ASSET

■ **INSTANT FACTS** A taxpayer sold the exclusive rights to the production of a play in return for a percentage of the profits from a film to be made based on the play.

■ **BLACK LETTER RULE** The release of an equitable property interest in the copyright of a play can constitute the sale or exchange of a capital asset within the meaning of the Internal Revenue Code.

■ **PROCEDURAL BASIS**

Appeal to the U.S. Court of Appeals for the Second Circuit of a U.S. Tax Court judgment overturning an IRS deficiency determination against a taxpayer.

■ **FACTS**

Jose Ferrer ("Ferrer") (P), a famous actor, entered into a contract with Pierre LaMure ("LaMure"), the author of a novel and play based on the life of the painter, Toulouse–Lautrec. The contract gave Ferrer (P) the right to produce the stage play, the right to prevent the sale of the film rights for the play for a period of time during which the play was to run, and the right to receive 40 percent of any proceeds from the sale of the film rights if the play was actually produced and the movie rights sold. Soon after Ferrer (P) signed the contract and before he had begun production of the play, John Huston ("Huston"), a famous movie director contacted Ferrer (P) and offered him a starring role in a film based on the novel and play. Ferrer (P) then entered into a contract with Huston under which he would receive a salary for acting in the film and a percentage of the film's profits. In 1953, Ferrer received his salary for the film, plus $178,751.46 as his percentage of the film's profits. He reported the salary as ordinary income, but treated the profit percentage as long-term capital gain. On audit, the Commissioner of Internal Revenue ("IRS") (D) determined a tax deficiency, asserting that the profit percentage should have been treated as ordinary income, because it represented compensation for personal services. Ferrer (P) appealed to the U.S. Tax Court, where Huston's attorney was permitted to testify that the profit percentage was intended to be Ferrer's (P) consideration for the cancellation of his original contract with LaMure. The Tax Court ruled in favor of Ferrer (P), holding that the profit percentage had been received in exchange for the assignment of the LaMure contract and that the contract constituted a capital asset. The IRS (D) then appealed to the U.S. Court of Appeals for the Second Circuit.

■ **ISSUE**

Can the release of an equitable property interest in the copyright of a play constitute the sale or exchange of a capital asset within the meaning of the Internal Revenue Code?

■ **DECISION AND RATIONALE**

(Friendly, J.) Yes. The Tax Court was not bound to accept the testimony by Huston's attorney as to the intent of the parties regarding payment. It could have lawfully found that the percentage compensation was in part added salary for Ferrer's (P) personal services and in part payment for the release. It found that the percentage payment was entirely for the release and we cannot say that it went beyond its power to do so. We must determine, however, whether what was sold by Ferrer (P) to Huston constituted a capital asset. When Huston displayed an interest in the film rights to the novel and play, Ferrer (P) possessed a bundle of rights. He had (1) a "lease" of the play; (2) a power incident to that lease, to prevent any sale of the film rights while he was producing the play; and, he was entitled to a 40 percent share of the proceeds of the film rights if he produced the play. In our view, he "sold or exchanged" all these rights, even though the parties set no separate price on them. While Huston had no interest in producing the play, Ferrer (P) did, unless a satisfactory substitute was provided. Thus Huston had to buy him out of that right, as well as to eliminate his temporary power to delay the sale of the film rights, and liquidate his option to obtain a share of their proceeds. Ferrer (P) held an equitable interest in the copyright of the play. This was similar to a lease of the play. We see no basis for holding that the payments he received for surrender of his lease of the play are excluded from capital gain treatment because the receipts from the play would have been ordinary income. Ferrer's (P) power to prevent the sale of the film rights until after production of the play also constituted an equitable interest in the copyright of the play. This right was analogous to a tenant giving up a right to prevent his landlord from leasing to another tenant in the same business, something we have previously held to be the sale or exchange of a capital asset. As to Ferrer's (P) sale of a right to 40 percent of the proceeds from any film, however, we take a different view. This right was comparable to the right of a tenant to receive from his landlord a percentage of what the landlord obtained from other tenants attracted to the building by the tenant's operations. Since such payments produce ordinary income if received during the term of the lease, the sale of the right to such payments also produces ordinary income. Thus, two of the rights Ferrer (P) sold were "capital assets" and one was not. In such instances, we must allocate the purchase price among the various parts of the transaction. We remand to the Tax Court to make that determination. Reversed and Remanded.

Analysis:

The IRS (D) argued here that the payment Ferrer (P) received for the film was really salary for his acting services and should have been treated as ordinary income. The court rejected that argument, concluding on the basis of the Tax Court's findings that the percentage of the profits Ferrer (P) received from Huston's film was meant to compensate him for the release of his rights from his contract with LaMure. The court held that two of the three rights at issue, the right to produce the play and the power to prevent the sale of the film rights while the play was being produced, were equitable interests in property and constituted capital assets. The court determined that the third right Ferrer (P) possessed, a right to share in any proceeds LaMure received from the sale of film rights to the play, was not a capital asset, because it was not a property interest that Ferrer (P) acquired from LaMure but was instead granted in anticipation of future income and should therefore be taxed as ordinary income.

■ CASE VOCABULARY

EQUITABLE INTEREST: Ownership rights in property that are protected in equity. A court will provide equitable relief, such as an injunction, to protect the rights of the property owner.

Miller v. Commissioner

(Taxpayer) v. *(IRS)*

299 F.2d 706 (2d Cir.1962)

FEDERAL APPEALS COURT HOLDS THAT FILM RIGHTS PAYMENT CONSTITUTES ORDINARY INCOME

■ **INSTANT FACTS** The wife of a deceased entertainer who had sold the exclusive right to her husband's story to a movie company appealed a U.S. Tax Court judgment that the sums received under the contract constituted ordinary income.

■ **BLACK LETTER RULE** Beneficiaries of the estate of a deceased entertainer do not receive a capitalizable "property interest" in the name, reputation, right of publicity, or public image of the deceased for purposes of the capital gains provisions of the Internal Revenue Code.

■ **PROCEDURAL BASIS**

Appeal to the U.S. Court of Appeals for the Second Circuit of a U.S. Tax Court judgment sustaining an IRS deficiency determination against a taxpayer.

■ **FACTS**

Helen D. Miller ("Mrs. Miller") (P) was the widow of band leader, Glenn Miller. She entered into a contract with Universal Pictures ("Universal") in connection with the production of a movie called "The Glenn Miller Story." Universal paid Mrs. Miller (P) $409,336.34 in consideration for her granting the studio the exclusive right to produce a movie based on Glenn Miller's life. Mrs. Miller (P) asserted that the payment should be considered gain from the sale or exchange of a capital asset. On audit, the IRS (D) sought to characterize the payment as ordinary income. Mrs. Miller (P) appealed to the U.S. Tax Court, which ruled in favor of the IRS (D). She then appealed to the U.S. Court of Appeals for the Second Circuit.

■ **ISSUE**

Do beneficiaries of the estate of a deceased entertainer receive a capitalizable "property interest" in the name, reputation, right of publicity, or public image of the deceased for purposes of the capital gains provisions of the Internal Revenue Code?

■ **DECISION AND RATIONALE**

(Kaufman, J.) No. The issue here is whether what Mrs. Miller (P) sold to Universal Pictures was "property" within the meaning of the capital gains provisions of the Internal Revenue Code ("the Code"). Since the Code does not define "property" as used in the capital gains provisions, we presume, in the absence of further evidence, that Congress had ordinary property concepts in mind as derived from state property law when it enacted the statutes at issue. Mrs. Miller (P) concedes that at the time of the "sale" there had been no authoritative decision that a decedent's successors had any "property right" to the public image of a deceased entertainer. Although having no case law to support her, Mrs. Miller (P) points out that Universal, a sophisticated corporation, paid her a lot of money and says that the reason Universal paid her this money must have been that there was a sale of a "property right." She is wrong. Many things can be sold which are not "property." One can sell his time and experience, for example, and no one would say that is "property." Here, what was sold appears to be the chance that a new theory of "property" might be advanced and be successful. Universal feared that it might, at some future time, be found to have infringed a property right. It got what it paid for: freedom from the danger that at a future date a defensible property right would be found to exist. But it did not pay for "property." We do not believe that for income tax computation purposes, beneficiaries of the estate of a deceased entertainer receive a capitalizable "property interest" in the name, reputation, right of publicity, or public image of the deceased. Mrs. Miller (P) owned no property and therefor the income she received from her contract with Universal is ordinary income. Affirmed.

Analysis:

The court here concludes that beneficiaries of the estate of a deceased entertainer do not receive a capitalizable "property interest" in the name, reputation, right of publicity, or public image of the deceased. Looking to state law as it existed at the time of the case, the court finds no support for considering such an interest "property" within the meaning of the capital gains provisions of the Code. More recently, some state courts have found a protected interest in the name, reputation, or interest of entertainers. Some commentators have questioned the court's approach here, noting that Mrs. Miller (P) was really not selling her personal services to Universal and probably did not deserve ordinary income treatment. Nevertheless, in the absence of a clear understanding that what was sold constituted "property," the decision was sound from a statutory interpretation standpoint.

■ **CASE VOCABULARY**

BENEFICIARY: A person benefitting under a will from the transfer of rights or property.

DECEDENT: A person who has died.

Gregory v. Helvering

(*Taxpayer*) v. (*IRS*)

293 U.S. 465, 55 S.Ct. 266 (1935)

SUPREME COURT DISREGARDS A CORPORATE REORGANIZATION LACKING A BUSINESS PUR-POSE OTHER THAN TAX AVOIDANCE

■ **INSTANT FACTS** A taxpayer transferred stock from a corporation she owned to a newly formed corporation and then dissolved the new corporation to receive the stock.

■ **BLACK LETTER RULE** Although meeting the literal requirements for a tax-free corporate reorganization, a proposed reorganization will not be recognized as tax-exempt if it lacks a business purpose other than tax avoidance.

■ **PROCEDURAL BASIS**

Appeal, following a grant of certiorari by the U.S. Supreme Court, of a decision of the U.S. Court of Appeals for the Second Circuit reversing a U.S. Board of Tax Appeals decision overturning an IRS deficiency determination against a taxpayer.

■ **FACTS**

Mrs. Gregory (P) owned all of the stock of United Mortgage Corporation ("United"), which held 1000 shares of Monitor Securities Corporation ("Monitor"). Had she caused United to give her a dividend of the 1000 Monitor shares, she would have had ordinary income on the transaction. In an attempt to avoid this result, Mrs. Gregory (P) sought to effect a corporate reorganization under a statutory predecessor to IRC § 368(a)(1)(D) [provision of the Internal Revenue Code making tax-free the transfer by a corporation of all or a part of its assets to another corporation if immediately after the transfer, the transferor corporation or one or more of its shareholders, controls the transferee corporation]. She created a new corporation, Averill Corporation ("Averill"), and then transferred to it the 1000 shares of Monitor stock. In return, Mrs. Gregory received all of Averill's stock. She then dissolved and liquidated Averill by distributing its assets, the Monitor shares, to herself. All of these steps occurred over the course of a few days. Mrs. Gregory (P) then sold the Monitor shares and reported the gain on the shares as a capital gain. On audit, the Commissioner of Internal Revenue, Helvering ("the IRS") (D), held that the attempted reorganization should be disregarded and that Mrs. Gregory (P) was liable for a tax as if United had paid her a dividend in the amount realized from the sale of the Monitor shares. Mrs. Gregory (P) appealed to the U.S. Board of Tax Appeals, which ruled in her favor. That decision was reversed by the U.S. Court of Appeals for the Second Circuit, on appeal by the IRS (D). The U.S. Supreme Court then accepted Mrs. Gregory's petition for certiorari.

■ **ISSUE**

Although meeting the literal requirements for a tax-free corporate reorganization, will a proposed reorganization be recognized as tax-exempt if it lacks a business purpose other than tax avoidance?

■ **DECISION AND RATIONALE**

(Sutherland, J.) No. It is admitted that every element required to effect a corporate reorganization through a transfer of assets under the statute occurred in this instance. Nevertheless, this asset transfer was a mere device which put on the form of a corporate reorganization as a disguise to try to conceal its real character. The object of the transfer here was not to reorganize a business, but to transfer some stock to Mrs. Gregory (P). It had no other purpose. When that limited function had been exercised, the corporation was immediately put to death. It was an elaborate and devious form of conveyance pretending to be a corporate reorganization. This was not contemplated by Congress in enacting the reorganization provisions. To hold otherwise would exalt form over reality and deprive the statute of all serious purpose. Affirmed.

Analysis:

Under the reorganization provisions at issue in this case, a corporation could transfer all or part of its property to another corporation, tax-free, if the first corporation or its shareholders were in control of the second corporation immediately after the transfer. In addition, the shareholders of the first corporation would recognize no gain if stock of the second corporation was distributed to them as part of the reorganization. Mrs. Gregory's (P) transactions met the literal requirements to achieve the tax-free treatment provided by the statute, but the evidence showed she had only engaged in the transactions in order to try to convert ordinary income into capital gain. Had she simply caused United to dividend to her the Monitor shares, she would have been taxed at ordinary income rates on the dividend. Entering into the attempted reorganization, Mrs. Gregory (P) thought she could end up with the Monitor shares with no dividend, by liquidating Averil, the new corporation. When she then sold the shares, she thought the sale would produce capital gain. The Supreme Court rules here, however, that even though all of the literal requirements for a tax-free corporate reorganization were met in this instance, since the purpose of the transactions at issue was solely to assist Mrs. Gregory (P) in avoiding ordinary income treatment from receipt of a dividend, the reorganization had to be disregarded.

■ **CASE VOCABULARY**

CORPORATE REORGANIZATION: A transaction or series of transactions whereby a corporation exchanges its stock or assets for the stock or assets of another corporation. If certain requirements are met under the Internal Revenue Code, such transactions may qualify as tax-free to the corporations and their shareholders.

DIVIDEND: A taxable distribution to the shareholders of a corporation.

Williams v. McGowan

(Taxpayer) v. *(IRS Representative)*
152 F.2d 570 (2d Cir.1945)

IRC § 1221 CHARACTERIZES CERTAIN PROPERTY AS CAPITAL ASSETS AND OTHER PROPERTY AS ORDINARY ASSETS

■ **INSTANT FACTS** A taxpayer sued the IRS to recover taxes which he felt should not have been paid.

■ **BLACK LETTER RULE** When a going business is sold, it should be comminuted into fragments that are matched against the definition in § 117(a)(1) to determine whether gains or losses realized upon sale are to be characterized as capital or ordinary.

■ **PROCEDURAL BASIS**

Certification to the United States Court of Appeals for the Second Circuit of an appeal of a judgment dismissing the complaint in an action by a taxpayer to recover income taxes paid for the year 1940.

■ **FACTS**

Both Williams (P) and Reynolds were engaged in the hardware business for many years. On January 20, 1926, they entered into a partnership in which Williams (P) was entitled to 2/3 of the profits and Reynolds entitled to 1/3. They agreed that on February 1, 1925, the capital invested in the business had been $118,082.05, of which $29,029.03 was credited to Reynolds. They also agreed that at the end of every business year, Reynolds would pay Williams (P) interest upon the amount of the difference between his share of the capital and 1/3 of the total as shown by the inventory. The business was carried on through the fiscal year ending on January 31, 1940, and ended upon Reynolds' death on July 18th of that same year. At that point, Williams (P) settled with Reynolds' executrix under an agreement by which he would pay her $12,187.90 and would thereby assume all liability of the business. Later that year, Williams (P) sold the business in its entirety for $63,926.28 to the Corning Building Company. This amount was made up of cash of about $8,100, receivables of about $7,000, fixtures of about $800, and a merchandise inventory of about $49,000, less approximately $1,000 for bills payable. To this was added about $6,000 credited to Williams (P) for profits between the beginning of the fiscal year and the ultimate sale. Thus, the total was approximately $70,000. Upon this sale, Williams (P) suffered a loss upon his original 2/3 of the business, but he made a small gain upon the 1/3 which he bought from Reynolds' estate; and in his income tax return he entered both as items of ordinary income, not as transactions in capital assets. The commissioner disallowed such a characterization and recomputed the tax. Williams (P) paid the difference and then sued to recover it.

■ **ISSUE**

When a business is sold as a going concern, should it be treated as a single piece of property for tax purposes?

■ **DECISION AND RATIONALE**

(Hand, J.) No. It has been held that a partner's interest in a going firm is regarded as a capital asset for tax purposes. As this is true, it is likely also true that a dead partner's interest is the same. But we need

---

not decide for sure. When Williams (P) bought out Reynolds' interest, he became the sole owner of the business, and the situation for tax purposes was no other than if Reynolds had never been a partner at all, except that to the extent of one-third of the "amount realized" on Williams' sale to the Corning Company, his basis was different. We have to decide only whether upon the sale of a going business it is to be comminuted into its fragments, and these are to be separately matched against the definition in IRC § 117(a)(1) [which characterizes assets as capital or ordinary], or whether the whole business is to be treated as if it were a single piece of property. Even though we might agree that under the influence of the Uniform Partnership Act a partner's interest in the firm should be treated as indivisible, and for that reason a capital asset within § 117(a)(1), we should be wary about extending further so exotic a jural concept. Be that as it may, in this instance the section itself furnishes the answer. It starts in the broadest way by declaring that all property is capital assets, and then makes three exceptions. The first is "stock in trade . . . or other property of a kind which would properly be included in the inventory;" next comes "property held . . . primarily for sale to customers;" and finally, property "used in the trade or business of a character which is subject to . . . allowance for depreciation." In the face of this language, although it may be true that a "stock in trade" taken by itself should be treated as a "universitas facti," by no possibility can a whole business be so treated; and the same is true as to any property within the other exceptions. Congress plainly did mean to comminute the elements of a business; plainly it did not regard the whole as "capital assets." As has already appeared, Williams (P) transferred to the Corning Company "cash," "receivables," "fixtures" and a "merchandise inventory." "Fixtures" are not capital assets because they are subject to a depreciation allowance; the inventory is expressly excluded. There can be no gain or loss in the transfer of cash; and, although Williams (P) does appear to have made a gain of $1,072.71 upon the "receivables," the point has not been argued that they are not subject to a depreciation allowance. That we leave open for decision by the district court, if the parties cannot agree. The gain or loss upon every other item should be computed as an item in ordinary income. Reversed.

■ DISSENT

(Frank, J.) I do not agree that we should ignore what the parties to the sale, Williams (P) and the Corning Company, actually did. They did not arrange for a transfer to the buyer, as if in separate bundles, of the several ingredients of the business. They contracted for the sale of the entire business as a going concern. To carve up the transaction into distinct sales of cash, receivables, fixtures, etc., is to do violence to the realities. I do not think congress intended any such artificial result.

Analysis:

Williams is an instructive case because it applies the definition of a capital asset to the sale of a business to determine which parts of the sale result in capital gains and losses and which result in ordinary gains and losses—it demonstrates how IRC § 1221 works in a real-world situation. It also makes it clear that a business sold as a going concern is not to be treated as one piece of property for tax purposes, but it should be broken up into smaller fragments (though the case does not make clear how, exactly, and to what extent this should be done). (Other courts have disagreed on this point, siding with the dissent.) It is useful to note the procedural history of this case. The IRS did not go after Williams (P) for the taxes, but he paid them and then sought to recover what he felt was the excess. In that way, Williams (P) was able to seek his money and resolve the dispute with the IRS, without subjecting himself to any criminal liability for avoiding taxes.

■ CASE VOCABULARY

COMMINUTE: To break up into smaller sections.

UNIVERSITAS FACTI: A group of similar items that are treated as a whole (e.g., a group of basketball players is treated as a team).

Merchants National Bank v. Commissioner

(Taxpayer) v. *(IRS)*
199 F.2d 657 (5th Cir.1952)

FEDERAL APPEALS COURT CORRELATES CHARACTER OF GAIN RECEIVED IN A TRANSACTION WITH POSITION TAXPAYER TOOK IN A PRIOR, RELATED TRANSACTION

■ **INSTANT FACTS** A taxpayer bank that had charged off notes it held as worthless and deducted their value as ordinary income in a prior tax year appealed an IRS ruling that amounts received from the sale of those notes in a subsequent tax year should be treated as ordinary income rather than capital gain.

■ **BLACK LETTER RULE** When a deduction for income tax purposes is taken and allowed for debts deemed worthless, a recovery on the debts in a later year constitutes taxable income for that year, to the extent that a tax benefit was received from the prior year deduction.

■ **PROCEDURAL BASIS**

Appeal to the U.S. Court of Appeals for the Fifth Circuit of a U.S. Tax Court decision sustaining an IRS deficiency determination against a taxpayer.

■ **FACTS**

Merchants National Bank ("Bank") (P) held notes of Alabama Naval Stores Co. ("Stores") with a balance of $49,025, which, at the direction of national bank examiners, Bank (P) charged off as worthless in 1941 and 1943. Bank (P) still held the notes, but after the charge-off, held them at a zero basis. Bank (P) took ordinary loss deductions on its 1941 and 1943 tax returns for the charge-offs. In 1944, Bank (P) sold the notes to a third party, for $18,460.58, which it reported on its 1944 tax return as a long-term capital gain. On audit, the Commissioner of Internal Revenue ("IRS") (D) held that the sale proceeds should be treated as ordinary income. Bank (P) appealed to the U.S. Tax Court, which sustained the IRS (D). Bank (P) then appealed to the U.S. Court of Appeals for the Fifth Circuit.

■ **ISSUE**

When a deduction for income tax purposes is taken for debts deemed worthless, will a recovery on the debts in a later year constitute taxable income for that year to the extent that a tax benefit was received from the prior year's deduction?

■ **DECISION AND RATIONALE**

(Strum, J.) Yes. To permit Bank (P) to reduce its ordinary income by the amount of the loss and gain maximum tax advantage on that basis and then permit it to treat the amount later recovered on the notes as a capital gain, taxed at much lower rates than ordinary income, would afford it a tax advantage on the transaction not contemplated by the income tax laws. The rule is well settled that when a deduction for income tax purposes is taken and allowed for debts deemed worthless, a recovery on the debts in a later year constitutes taxable income for that year, to the extent that a tax benefit was received from the prior year deduction. Here, when Bank (P) charged off the bad debt, it deducted that amount from its ordinary income, escaping taxation on that part of its income in 1941 and 1943. The amount subsequently recovered on the notes restores the same amount originally deducted from ordinary income and must be taxed as ordinary income, not capital gain. When the notes were charged off, Bank (P) recovered its loss by deducting it from its current income. When it made that deduction, the notes were no longer capital assets for income tax purposes. It does not matter that the bank sold the notes to a third party instead of collecting the amount owed from the maker of the notes. Affirmed.

Analysis:

The court here sensibly requires the taxpayer to report its income and losses consistently in different tax years. In 1941 and 1943, the Bank (P) charged off the notes as worthless for accounting purposes and deducted their value as ordinary losses in those years. It still held onto the notes, however, but reduced the tax basis of the notes to zero. When it eventually sold the notes in 1944, the Bank (P) realized a gain in that any amount received over the zero basis would be a gain. The Bank (P) sought to characterize that gain as capital. The IRS (D) and the court held, however, that the amount received from the sale of the notes was ordinary income, because the notes were no longer capital assets once the Bank (P) had recovered its investment through its prior year deductions.

■ CASE VOCABULARY

CHARGE–OFF: To treat as a loss an amount originally recorded as an asset for accounting purposes.

MAKER: One who signs a note to borrow money, assuming the obligation to repay the amount borrowed, usually with interest.

NOTE: A negotiable instrument containing the written promise of a signer to pay a sum of money on demand or at a stated time.

Arrowsmith v. Commissioner

(Taxpayer) v. *(IRS)*

344 U.S. 6, 73 S.Ct. 71 (1952)

U.S. SUPREME COURT CORRELATES CHARACTER OF LOSS WITH TAX BENEFIT TAXPAYER RECEIVED IN A PRIOR, RELATED TRANSACTION

■ **INSTANT FACTS** A former shareholder of a liquidated corporation was personally required to pay a judgment issued against his old corporation in a tax year subsequent to the liquidation. He appealed an IRS holding that the payment in the subsequent year was a capital loss rather than an ordinary loss.

■ **BLACK LETTER RULE** A transaction that is related to a transaction in a prior tax year must take its character as ordinary or capital on the basis of the tax benefit claimed by the taxpayer in the earlier year.

■ **PROCEDURAL BASIS**

Appeal, following a grant of certiorari by the U.S. Supreme Court, of a decision of the U.S. Court of Appeals for the Second Circuit, reversing a U.S. Tax Court decision overturning an IRS deficiency determination against a taxpayer.

■ **FACTS**

Arrowsmith (P) was the co-owner of a corporation. He and the other shareholder decided to liquidate and divide the corporation's assets. They reported their gain on the liquidation of the corporation as capital gain for the 1940 tax year. In 1944, as transferees of the corporation's assets, Arrowsmith (P) and the other shareholder were required to pay a judgment that had been rendered against their old corporation. They each then reported their payment of the judgment as an ordinary business loss in 1944, the year of payment, deducting it in full from their ordinary income for the year. On audit, the Commissioner of Internal Revenue ("IRS") (D) held that the payment of the judgment should have been treated as a capital loss because the payment of the corporate debt was related to the corporation's prior liquidation and took its character from the liquidation. Arrowsmith (P) and the other shareholder appealed to the U.S. Tax Court, which found in their favor. The IRS (D) then appealed to the U.S. Court of Appeals for the Second Circuit, which reversed the Tax Court. Arrowsmith (P) and the other shareholder then appealed to the U.S. Supreme Court, which granted certiorari.

■ **ISSUE**

Must a transaction that is related to a transaction in a prior year take its character as ordinary or capital on the basis of the tax benefit claimed by the taxpayer in the earlier year?

■ **DECISION AND RATIONALE**

(Black, J.) Yes. Arrowsmith (P) was required to pay the judgment because of the liability imposed on him as a transferee of the liquidated assets of the corporation. Arrowsmith (P) does not deny that, had this judgment been paid after the liquidation, but during the same tax year as the liquidation, the losses would properly have been treated as capital. Arrowsmith (P) argues, however, that this payment, which would have been a capital transaction in that year, was transformed into an ordinary business transaction in the subsequent year in which it actually occurred because of the rule that each taxable year is a separate unit for tax accounting purposes. This principle, however, is not breached by considering all of the liquidation transaction events in order to classify the nature of the post-liquidation loss for tax purposes. This is not an attempt to reopen and readjust the prior year tax returns. A transaction that is related to a transaction in a prior tax year must take its character as ordinary or capital on the basis of the tax benefit claimed by the taxpayer in the earlier year. The losses at issue here fall within the definition of "capital losses." Affirmed.

■ DISSENT

(Douglas, J.) These losses should be treated as ordinary and not capital. There were no capital transactions in the year in which the losses were suffered. Those transactions occurred and were accounted for in earlier years under the established principle that each year is a separate unit for tax accounting purposes. We should force each year to stand on its own footing, whoever may gain or lose from it in a particular case. I would reverse.

■ DISSENT

(Jackson, J.) Looking at the equities here, it is hard to decide who should win. If we take the taxpayer's position, he might be seen as obtaining a windfall in that he gets to deduct the judgment amount against his ordinary income which might be taxed as high as 87 percent, while if the liability had been assessed against the corporation before liquidation, it would have reduced the taxpayer's capital gain, which was taxable at only 25 percent. On the other hand, adoption of the IRS (D) approach may penalize the taxpayer because there are limitations on the deductibility of capital losses against ordinary income and because if the corporation had discharged the liability, it would probably have been able to deduct that payment, while, here, the stockholders cannot deduct such liability. Suppose that subsequent to liquidation, it is found that a corporation has undisclosed claims (as opposed to liabilities) which can be prosecuted for the benefit of the stockholders. The logic of the majority's decision here, if followed, would result in a lesser return to the government than if the recoveries were considered ordinary income. Would it be so clear to the majority that this is a capital loss, if the shoe were on the other foot? Where the statute is unclear, I would defer to the judgment of the Tax Court, which is more competent and steady in creating a systematic body of tax law than is this Court. I would reverse.

Analysis:

Like the Fifth Circuit in *Merchants National Bank v. Commissioner*, the Supreme Court here requires a transaction that is related to a transaction in a prior year to take its character on the basis of the tax benefit claimed by the taxpayer in the earlier year. This is known as the tax benefit rule. The dissent by Justice Douglas suggests that the majority approach somehow violates the annual accounting principle that each tax year is separate. The majority rightly points out that the annual tax accounting principle is not violated; no prior tax year is opened up for readjustment. The Court is merely looking to the treatment obtained in the prior year to classify how the present year's payment should be characterized.

■ CASE VOCABULARY

LIQUIDATION: The distribution of the net assets of a corporation to its shareholders in return for their stock, followed by the dissolution of the corporation. Amounts received by the shareholders in a liquidation are generally treated as arising from the sale or exchange of their stock, a capital asset.